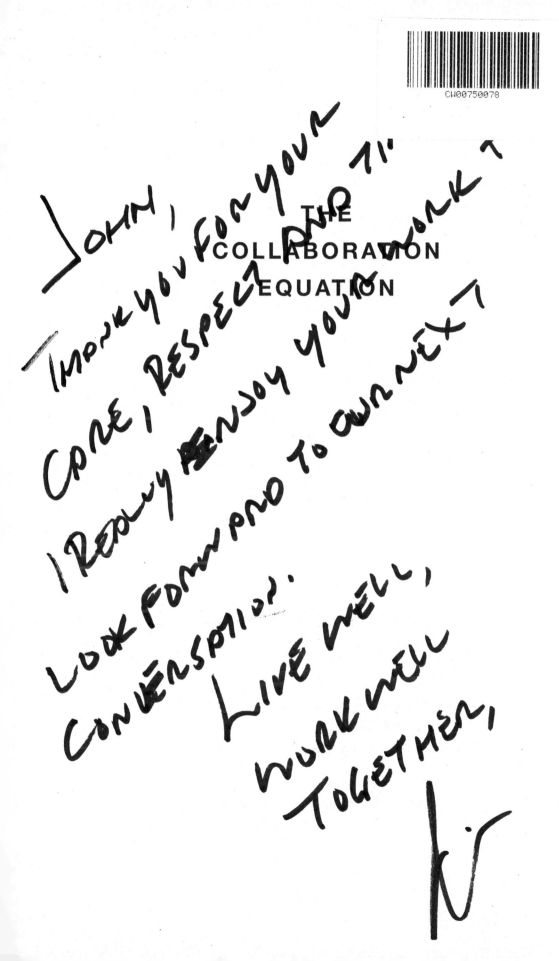

John,

Thank you for your time and core, respect.

I really enjoy your work.

I really enjoy your work. Look forward to our next conversation.

Live well, work well, together,

THE COLLABORATION EQUATION

The Collaboration Equation
Strong Professionals | Strong Teams | Strong Delivery

First Modus Cooperandi Press
Edition September 2022

ISBN: 978-0-9890812-8-3

Editor: Tom Ehrenfeld
Cover Design and Layout: Olivier Darbonville
Copy Editor: Brian Frastaci
Source of Constant Support: Tonianne DeMaria

For bulk copies, educational discounts, interviews, or
other inquiries, write: sales@moduscooperandi.com.

The Collaboration Equation

Strong Professionals,
Strong Teams,
Strong Delivery

Jim Benson

Creator and Co-Author of *Personal Kanban*
Winner of the Shingo Research Award

Contents

People I am Grateful For..XI

Foreword ....**XV**
Preface: The Collaboration Equation **1**
Corey's Basement, Grand Island, Nebraska, 1980..1
Giving Professionals the Tools They Need 2
    Never Let a Good Emergency Go to Waste...3
Being a Collaborative Professional 4
    Working Better as Professionals...5
Building a Better World..8
Performance, Collaboration, Professionalism 9
    Aggressive Diplomacy...9
    We Work Together or We Don't Work 12
The Boldness of the Collaboration Equation..13

Chapter One: Acting with Confidence **17**
The Confidence of Information..18
There is an "I" in Team After All...21
The Natural Fear of Change 22
The Collaboration Equation 24
Kevin's Confidence Had a Practical Architecture.......................................25
    Kevin's Structure..26
The Principles of Professional Collaboration 29
You Don't Know Anything about Collaboration...31
Five Principles of Collaboration..32
    Principle One: Pay Attention (Situational Awareness)............................33
    Principle Two: Give a Damn (Relationships) 33
    Principle Three: Improvement is Your Job (Responsibility)....................33
    Principle Four: Information Drives Action (Communications) 33
    Principle Five: Trust but Visualize (Respect)..33
The Collaboration Equation 34

Chapter Two: Individuals Becoming Teams **37**

Impossible Requests Collaboratively Solved 37

Two Collaborative Craniums Are Better than One Harried Head 40

    Building Healthy Expectations 43

    The Impacts of Pairing.. 44

All Things Thrive in The Right Environment.. 46

    The Case of the Underwater Hospital.. 48

Solving Problems in a Right Environment 50

Grace under Pressure Can Be Designed 53

Actions as Collaborative Metrics.. 54

    The Components of a Collaborative Right Environment..................... 56

    Current State: Your Teams Don't Know Who or Why They Are............ 58

Individuals in Teams...Creating Value.. 60

Chapter Three: Professionals Build Professional Systems **63**

The Tale of the Unsupported Support Team 63

Are You Failing By Design?... 66

    Individuals *In Teams* Create Value 68

    Success Is More than Metrics 70

    Work is Processed, Not Tackled.. 71

    Building TLC's Collaboration 72

Professionals Discover Healthy Teams 73

    What TLC's Team Did... 73

    Collaborative Teams Exceed Expectations.................................... 76

Agency, Information Flow, and Abuse 78

    Common Worst Practices for Agency.. 79

    The Systematic Structure of Siloed Sub-Humanity......................... 85

    The Final Residue of Worst Practices.. 87

Choose Agency... 87

Towards a Collaborative Architecture.. 88

    Balancing Structure and Agency 89

Creating Value through Teams of Individuals.. 90

Chapter Four: Collaborating in the Real World............................**93**

Seeing the Prison That Is Our Silo 93

    Bottleneck 101.. 95

    Using Bottlenecks and Visualization to Help the Database Group 97

    Collaboratively Exploiting and Relieving the Bottleneck.................... 99

Why This Is Incredibly Rare 102

Visualization Ensures Professional Action 103
Triggering Action 103
Using Feedback and PDSA to Solve Bottlenecks **105**
Feedback Is not Comments 107
The System of Professional Feedback 108
How PDSA Impacts Decision Making 109
The Planning Loop 112
The Work and Discovery Loop 116
A System That Processes Complexity 119
Quality and Completion Loop 123
The Collaboration Equation of Bottlenecks and Learning **125**
Creative Collaboration Creates Expectations **126**

Chapter Five: Building a Practical Right Environment **129**
The Modus Right Environment Exercise **130**
The Problems We Need to Solve 131
The Promise: Breaking Out of Cycle 132
Focusing on Root Causes 133
The How: The Right Environment Exercise **134**
The Flow of a Right Environment Exercise 135
Why This Structure? Culture Is a System 137
Stage Zero: Recognizing Value **139**
REE Stage Zero: Always Capture Value 142
Stage One: The VSM—the Foundation of Your Collaborative Architecture ...**144**
REE Stage One: How to Value Stream Map 146
Value Stream Map Prepping: What You Need to Know 148
Value Stream Map Prepping: Using Color to Tell the Whole Story 150
REE Stage One: How to Value Stream Map: The Power in Collaboration.....152
Coaches' Corner: VSM Implementation Guidance.....................................154
Stages Two and Three: The Charter and the Communicaitons Agreement ...**156**
How to Affinity Map 157
A Modus Cooperandi One Sheet 158
The Charter Exercise: Seeing and Acting on Your Culture 160
The Communication Agreement 162
Stage Four: The Roadmap: Making Culture Actionable **164**
REE Stage Four: The Roadmap 166
REE Stage Four: The Implementation Plan...168
REE Implementation Guidance 170
The Endgame after the REE **171**
The Collaboration Equation of the Right Environment **173**

Chapter Six: See Your Work..**175**

We Learn with Stories.. 176

    Context Visualized: Seven Elements of Visual Management...........177

Your Obeya is YOUR Obeya.. 179

    Creating Intentional Visualizations in Your Obeya....................179

    Owned Commitment Boards...182

    Evolving Commitment Boards 184

    Time and Progress Boards..186

    Availability and Action Boards 188

    Pull Planning Boards and Exercise 190

    Blocker Boards..192

    Kaizen Boards 194

The Collaboration Equation of the Obeya.................................. 196

Chapter Seven: Finding Your Way.....................................**199**

We Are Spirits in the Material World 200

    This Is the Way: Building Collaboration into the Culture................201

    Three Ways from This Book...202

The Social Obeya and the Working Session 203

    Perform Rather than Inform—Let's Get to Work 203

Routine Working Sessions 204

    Routine Working Session 1: Huddles...................................204

    Routine Working Session 2: Lean Coffee...............................209

    A Modus One Sheet...211

Focused Working Sessions 212

    Focused Working Session 1: The Doominator 213

    Focused Working Session 2: The I Am Angry Exercise................218

    Focused Working Session 3: Conflixt Mapping........................220

Alignment/Strategic Working Sessions..................................... 221

    Alignment Working Session 1: Value Stream Mapping................222

    Alignment Working Session 2: Pull Planning 225

Restorative Working Sessions 228

    Restorative Working Session 1: Retrospectives.......................228

    Restorative Working Session 2: Kaizen Events 229

    Restorative Working Session 3: Offsites and Right Environment Events............230

Just Plain Old Working Sessions 231

    Pairing...231

    Mobbing 231

The Collaboration Equation of Working Sessions.........................232

Chapter Eight: Leadership is an Action **235**

Let's Get One Thing Straight... 235

A Pull Model of Collaborative Leadership 236

Start with the Principles, not the Principals 238

Share the Load/Distribute the Responsibility 240

The Leadership of the Change Agent................................... 242

    Migrating from Accountability to Responsibility................243

Humble Hubris 246

The Expectations of Collaborative Leadership................... 251

    The Battle of Brittle 251

    Designing the Structure 252

Giving the Collaborative System Form and Substance 255

    The Four Horsemen of the Leadpocolypse 257

    Design Charettes..261

Pull Leadership Requires Pull Planning 263

    A Quick Tale of an Evolving Environment........................264

    Building a Real Big Board 267

    Conversational Kanban..269

    How Sharing the Big Picture Builds Distributed Leadership....270

    Finding Lost Opportunities through Collaborative Leadership 272

    Building a Collaborative and Flexible Plan........................274

    Endgame: A Structure for Collaborative Planning and Leadership....275

    Collaborative Goal Setting..276

    The Big Wall...277

    Pull Planning 278

    Team Planning 280

    Nested Roadmaps..282

    The Full-On Obeya: The Product and the Focus of a Professional Team.............285

Coda: Leadership Is a Verb 288

Chapter Nine: The Enduring Collaboration...**291**

Change Is Necessary, Change Is Frustrating 293

The Audacity of Practicality 296

The Modality of Hope 297

    Just Build It 299

HF OP TYs..**302**

Modus Press: Exporing the Future of Work **304**

Modus Offerings: How to Go Deeper **306**

Index..**309**

People I am Grateful For

Thanking for this book is obvious. Everyone mentioned in every story has been a crucial part of my personal journey. So much to learn, so much to build, so much to talk about.

Beyond this, there are some standouts....

Nancy White is a pivot sprinkler of potential, an uninterrupted press pot of patience, and a particularly poignant yet imperturbable professional who recommended Toni and me for key projects (like the World Bank story in this book) that seemed small at the time but were game-changing collaborations.

John Shook, who has always been interested in how things work. People, systems, flow. John brought Toni and me into the Lean Enterprise Institute as faculty and introduced me to Turner Construction. This book would not be nearly as cohesive without the experiences I had with the Turner and LEI teams.

Josh Howell and I were partners working together the first year of my time with Turner. We had long, creative conversations designing interactions and direction for the teams we were helping. That was a wonderful collaboration.

Jim Barrett is the Chief Innovation Officer at Turner and was responsible for bringing the LEI team in and me with them. He's Turner's perennial square peg that just seems to always find the right way to nudge the company's evolution.

Charlie Whitney, who made me feel like part of the Turner family, listened intently, called bullshit multiple times, continued to listen after calling bullshit, taught me plenty, and annoyingly changed his dietary restrictions halfway through working together.

Charlie Murphy, who made every word of the Leadership section possible, while not being mentioned in it at all. It was you that had the wisdom of governance that allowed Kevin, Amanda, Savanna, Chris, Paul, Whitney, Tom, and everyone else in the business unit find ways to act with confidence.

Matt Moran, who gleefully threw me into the middle of a violent corporate mosh pit and laughed from the balcony as I transformed them into line dancers.

Tomasz Stachowiak, who was always looking for how he fit in to a collaborative world, fascinated by it, wanting it, and always Tom, which sometimes meant sentences like, "You all collaborate right now!" With "all" being replaced with something not quite repeatable in print. Tom was a model leader to work with, always asking questions, always processing, always ready to try new things. I'm proud to call you a friend; my wife is ridiculously protective of you.

Christian J. Kristensen....it seems like half this book is about you, and you still want to be in the acknowledgements?! In the book I talk about humble hubris. Your humble hubris is the only way Coney could have ever been successful. Building the most right of Right Environments to collaboratively manage the most perilous of projects, that is some skillful choreography.

Tonianne DeMaria, who gave me so much space to write, re-write, re-re-rewrite, and lament about this book. Letting it derail other plans or even necessities. And then came in at the last second to provide the insight and care I have come to rely so heavily on. Modus Institute is humming because of you.

Collaborate:

(co - together)

(labor - work)

(ate - action)

Foreword

The environment of construction is fast paced, dynamic, aggressive, and often involves dangerous work. Pressures to work faster, to be more productive, to work harder are ever present. These factors, at times, blind us from the consideration of the human beings responsible for making it all happen.

We first met Jim in 2016 as we were taking the first steps in a long journey to drive this concept of the "Right Environment". He wanted us to think about its implementation with no Key Performance Indicators, no metrics or case studies. "Trust me," he said. It became obvious that this concept was something that Jim had long intuited, but like us had not taken the time to name or define. Jim went from being a curious bystander to an active participant and partner in this process over the course of the next several years.

We soon understood that this seemingly "soft" concept would be the foundation of our transformation. As Jim mentions throughout his journey, there is a practical architecture in how an organization can rebuild itself. Here is the trick we discovered: don't talk about fight club. It is less important to label the thing. It is more important to set expectations and have leaders model the behaviors of the Right Environment. It's the Senior Vice President observing concrete trade workers struggle through an arduous and dangerous task and asking his leadership to "make the hard work easier" for them. It is a General Manager dedicating an hour every week, almost without fail, for line leader engagement. They are not equals in the organizational hierarchy. However, for one hour every week they exhibit the tenets of a respectful partnership. The Right Environment respects leadership but allows vulnerability, safety, and <u>everyone</u> to have a voice in the discussion without fear of judgement or repercussion. Collaboration no longer serves as a buzzword. It serves as practiced culture, structurally supported by the following pillars: teamwork, transparency, accountability, and mental self-awareness. This is the polar opposite of the results obtained by directors and dictators. This new culture allows vulnerability of its stakeholders, which reveals truth that leads to sound sustainable solutions.

To learn, you must endeavor to understand the systems we expose humanity to for the sake of production. To grow, you must endeavor to understand the humans we are responsible for. Keep it simple. Do not make it distracting. Allow organic moments of conflict and problem solving and watch sporadic moments of genius become more prevalent. You may not be able to measure the Right Environment, but it is necessary.

Take the literature you bear in your hands as an adventurous technical and mental guide, demonstrating how the power of collaboration shifts your work from a torture device to a productive system that encourages respect for the human beings that operate in its space. With his anecdotal first-hand experience, Jim will guide you through the fundamentals of collaboration and how to use it correctly.

Savanna Sampson | Kevin Chase | Charlie Whitney
Turner Construction
New York City
August 2022

Preface: The Collaboration Equation

INDIVIDUALS WORK TOGETHER TO CREATE VALUE.

COREY'S BASEMENT, GRAND ISLAND, NEBRASKA, 1980

Like all process geeks, I started out as an ~~employee of Toyota~~ angry punk rocker in Grand Island, Nebraska. In the late 1970s and early 1980s, my bandmates and I had to learn the music business and how to *be a business*.

We had to learn to play instruments, scream without losing our voices, work audio and recording gear, make tapes, produce albums, ship to foreign countries, build a distribution chain, book venues, promote, build a community, get reviewers to notice us, and come up with messaging. We learned quality production, marketing, and building a brand. We did this in a place where there were significantly few punk rockers[1] and no internet.

Punk always said it was DIY (Do It Yourself), but you never met a successful lonely punk.

It was really DIT—Do It Together.

---

1 The Dead Kennedys' Jello Biafra once said, "There's no Punk Rock in Afghanistan, Iran...Nebraska." He was off by a few people, but we were a significant few, as those who remember The Drumstick in Lincoln will tell you.

We punks are now all old enough to have written several books. Go read them all. Patti Smith, Vivien Goldman, Bob Mould, there's more than a few. All of them talk about the "I" and the "we". They all talk about themselves as individuals building something *with their teams*, their bands. Every last one of them talks about the business, the network, the practical and necessary collaborations that made them who they were then and who they are today.

In the end, DIY sounded punk, but DIT got the job done.

GIVING PROFESSIONALS THE TOOLS THEY NEED

Human beings naturally specialize (work alone) in order to collaborate (work together) and vice versa. Your breakfast involved hundreds of specialized people working together to create the value of your eggs and toast. We rely on collaboration for everything we do.

I have been collaborating with people intentionally since I was a kid. Writing screenplays, books, music, starting companies, or even just playing. Through my winding careers in music, urban planning, transportation engineering, software, writing, business ownership, and in more than a dozen years helping companies and teams worldwide find better ways of working, I've seen my share of well-formed and poorly run endeavors.

Without fail, every well-run endeavor involves collaboration. Every real collaboration is a system; when people remember the experience, they remember knowing what to do. In this way, collaboration brings its own psychological safety. Collaborators fearlessly sharing leadership as they learn more and get closer to completion. Every real collaboration has the guts to work for real success.

Bold collaboration, regardless of complexity, size of team, distribution, or any other excuses people create to excuse their failures to work together, involves people making real commitments to learning, improvement, completion, quality, and making work exciting.

Scale is not an issue. Complexity is not an issue. I've built freeways and subways and cities with teams of over 1,000 people, and I wrote *Personal Kanban* in a one-to-one collaboration with Tonianne DeMaria and everything in between. Collaboration scales, solves complexity, and aligns the team. Our fear and excuses that keep us from working together need to be dispelled.

The question is, *are we committed to being real professionals?*

Never Let a Good Emergency Go to Waste

We are beginning to realize the value of having other people around, learning from them, and building together.

Before 2020, it was inconceivable that people could work from home at the rate that the global Covid pandemic forced upon us. This globally scaled experiment led to changes in hiring, project management, team identity, individual decision-making, and clarity that had been needed but unexplored for decades. Collaboration became a primary need of our work. We had to be more explicit about what we wanted, what we could provide, and how we spent time together.

As professionals, we started demanding more clarity (to know the why) of our work. We began to schedule more time together (video calls meant scheduling, as impromptu meetings were no longer as easy as leaning back in your chair and shouting, "*Hey, you gotta minute?*"), as tools like Slack and Zoom made it easier to have short five- or ten-minute collaborations, make a shared decision, and resume work.

While the workplace has returned to "normal", the lessons learned from the Covid years will stick with us. Collaborative, intentional, work saves time, results in better product, and reduces stress.

BEING A COLLABORATIVE PROFESSIONAL

Regardless of whether you are in manufacturing, law enforcement, software development, cookie science, or space exploration: human beings *do their work in collaborative systems*.

"System" sounds scary, and it often is. We let fetid, frustrating, and flawed ways of working develop over time while we ignore them. They become bloated bureaucracies with no one to care for them.

Our system is how we work. The system generates the work, gives people boundaries of action, defines latitude to improve (or not), supplies the tools with which to work, provides payment for their expertise, and most importantly gives them the ability to solve problems. If we don't pay attention and build these systems to serve our needs, the system *will not serve our needs*.

Let's look at what we're talking about here:

Collaboration is the act of two or more people working in concert to achieve a goal.

Professionalism is the understanding by these people that their goal has value and with every act they learn more about their goal and how to achieve it in a better way.

Professional Satisfaction is being able to collaborate in a way that satisfies one's personal needs.

A System is an agreed set of values, interactions, and processes that allow individuals to come together in teams and act in concert to provide value.

If your system does not allow for professionalism or collaboration, you will get neither. Professionalism and collaboration are inextricably linked. Without them, we get:

Anti-Collaboration, which is any system that works at cross purposes to collaboration, professionalism, and/or the creation of value.

Put all these together, and you quickly see flaws in how we work, and possibilities in how we'd rather work. We see where collaboration can increase professional satisfaction and result in better work that we enjoy.

A system doesn't have to be big, expensive, or invite a lot of change. When Tonianne DeMaria and I wrote *Personal Kanban*,[2] we were focused on getting people clarity around their work, their collaborations, and their paths to completion. The *Personal Kanban* "system" worked whether you were doing something alone, as a pair, as a team, or part of a huge organization. It simply asked people to visualize their work and limit their work in progress. People are made aware of their work: who it is for, when it needs to be done, what is stopping it from being completed, and most important *how to do it better next time (continuous improvement)*.

Working Better as Professionals

In the early 1990s, I was lucky enough to join David Evans and Associates, a consulting engineering company based in Portland. David Evans and Associates[3] had barely 100 people. It was stable, known for its quality, and extremely humane. It was a successful environment made up of collaborative professionals. When I left, we were a respected top-50 consulting firm.

At DEA, we had a motto penned by Dave Evans himself.

We take outstanding professionals and give them the tools they need to do an outstanding job.

For a young professional like me, the respect in that statement was powerful. The fact that DEA acted on it so well was astounding. Before tech companies claimed they invented humane benefits like limitless va-

---

2 Benson, J., & Barry, T. D. (2011). Personal Kanban: Mapping Work, Navigating Life. Seattle, WA: Modus Cooperandi Press.

3 Deainc.com

cation and sick leave or working from anywhere we wanted, we had them. We could put in crazy hours or give ourselves some slack, and always had anyone's ear. We even became an Employee-Owned Company in the late '90s to make that commitment self-governed.

DEA's practical commitment to professionalism meant they would give you what you felt you needed. You would deliver on the exchange, of course, *because you are a professional*. You would do an outstanding job. David Evans and Associates was a relationship.

The consulting engineering world is interesting because you almost always form interdisciplinary teams to solve client needs. At DEA, we'd routinely team *with other companies*[4] (the competition) when seeking work. The margins were thin; no one could dominate the market. There were companies that would have winning streaks, but the public procurement process (in ethical states, anyway) meant work was distributed. Steady and healthy competition was always possible because of the historically collaborative system of team contracting.

We would team on huge projects like light rail systems or freeways. Collaborations involved hundreds of people globally back when email was still unknown. And we succeeded, brilliantly and profitably.

> DEA UNDERSTOOD THAT EACH PROFESSIONAL IN THE COMPANY WAS AN INVESTMENT AND THAT EVERY TEAM WAS A PORTFOLIO OF VALUE.

DEA understood that each professional in the company was an investment and that **every team was a portfolio of value**. DEA also understood that professionals are responsible, directed, human beings. If Claudia needed time to run a professional organization, or Mark needed to spend time with his kids, or William needed some

---

4 Most companies I work with outside civil engineering can't even team on projects inside their own company.

time hiking to clear his mind...they were professionals. They were adults. They could do that.

As I said, we all returned this favor. Leaving DEA was a difficult decision for me and for the others that joined and left. DEA invested in us, and we did our best to invest in DEA and each other. We were always improving ourselves as professionals: teaching other new things, recommending books, or just talking.

This created an air of psychological safety in the company. Psychological safety is often confused with the ability to openly mention that something is wrong, but it is deeper than that.

Psychological safety[5,6] is a condition under which any team member can freely operate as a professional in general, and it never comes from working in isolation. It cannot exist without a collaborative and professional system.

David Evans and Associates intentionally built a collaborative, professional company, and by extension a *successful* company. They did this by creating a culture of collaborative professionalism. DEA made sure that we recognized our role in maintaining our culture as part of our daily work. Since we had control over our professional actions *and* could succeed only by working well with our colleagues, we frequently had conversations about culture, process, ethics, and action.

Since we had transparency into company operations and its finances, coupled with the trust of upper management, we didn't have to worry about internal politics (yes, it was there but much less pronounced or stressful than other anti-collaborative companies I experienced). Instead, we could focus on providing quality product to our customers.

---

5 Kahn, W. A. (n.d.). *Holding Fast: The Struggle to Create Resilient Caregiving Organizations.* Brunner-Routledge.

6 Edmondson, A. C. (2019). *The fearless organization: Creating psychological safety in the workplace for learning, innovation, and growth.*

That was always the game at DEA. *Can we figure out a way to do this better, give the client more, and learn something new while we do it?*

> *"Society is the product of relationship, of yours and mine together. If we change in our relationship, society changes."*
>
> — KRISHNAMURTI

BUILDING A BETTER WORLD

One of my ethical personal heroes is W. Edwards Deming, a punk rocker in his own right. Deming made a career of pointing out the logical fallacies in daily management. He saw how poorly business treats people and how frustrated they become with the underperformance that results. Deming worked and taught into his 90s. On the day of his death, his calendar was filled with appearances he would not make. He started each class saying, "We are here to build a better world."

We still need Deming's guidance. Our need for collaboration is acute. Business today spends much of its time and energy paying for outmoded anti-collaborative management schemes that thwart collaboration and stifle growth.

Anti-collaborative systems are unfortunately accepted as business "best" practices. To build a better world, we are going to have to come to terms with how these are actually "worst" practices that increase overhead, decrease participation, and destroy value.

This book takes lessons from around the world and very different contexts where real professionals created their own resilient, collaborative teams to create value. Each chapter provides at least one flexible tool for your toolkit. Each chapter has at least one story showing these ideas at work in the real world. Every chapter will give you something to think about and something to act on.

These lessons will not be cut and paste. This isn't a new Jack Welch to mindlessly mimic. Business and work require thought and attention. This isn't a cookbook; it's a book about technique. That means many of the stories are counterintuitive and the tools oblique. Just like life.

In the end, you will know the basics of building sustainable collaboration. You will have tools to see dysfunction, to align teams around improvement, and to build visual and cultural systems of collaboration and improvement. You will take demotivated co-workers and gain impassioned professionals.

PERFORMANCE, COLLABORATION, PROFESSIONALISM

Every high-performing team I have worked with enjoyed high collaboration. It's the grease on the gears, the charge for the battery, the wind at the back of any successful outcome. At DEA, collaboration was bolstered by the respect the company had for us. They showed their respect by greatly raising our clarity. We knew the finances of the company, we knew every project the company was involved in, we helped projects we were not part of when they had crunches. We were not perfect, but that wasn't the goal. The goal was to be responsible professionals.

Perfect doesn't exist; professionalism does.

Collaboration rested on us having the information we needed and the authority to act on that information. Professionalism required us to get other people the information they needed, know when they needed it, and when, even if we had authority, we should work with others.

Aggressive Diplomacy

It sounds like collaboration is all silk and roses, an idyllic alternate reality where work is beautiful and nothing hurts. Well, that's not the case. Collaboration can and should be rocky from time to time. Creative tension is necessary.

Before I worked at DEA, I worked at Metro, the regional government for Portland, Oregon. My boss was the late visionary urban designer, John Fregonese. He and I didn't always see eye-to-eye. One day, he and I got into a heated argument about a parking study I was in charge of. I don't remember the specifics, but we were very loud in a city and office that doesn't do loud.[7]

After we were done yelling at each other, I stormed out of his office to my cubicle and steamed.

I could hear Frego in his office angrily moving paper. If you could slam paper, he was doing it.

Then, our shop steward appears in my cubicle and says conspiratorially, "Do you wanna file a grievance?"

I said, "What?"

He replied, "Frego just can't yell at you like that, it makes a hostile environment. You need to file a grievance."

I was still worked up and said loudly, "John wasn't yelling at me, I was yelling at him! John's an adult and so am I. We just had a <bleep>ing argument! A hostile work environment is when you can't have a <bleep>ing argument! We respect each other, we think different things, we can yell at each other and that's okay! It's creative tension! I'm not doing any <bleep>ing grievance."

He looked at me like I was from Mars. "He's management, you're rank-and-file. This is a labor issue." Typical anti-collaborative, divisive thinking.

I said, "No." With a long, pointed set of Os.

The shop steward left, and, in the distance, I could hear Frego laughing, or unsuccessfully trying not to laugh. An hour later, he brought me a mocha and we figured out a middle ground. Creative tension broken, problem solved.

---

7 You've heard of "Minnesota nice"? Well, Oregon's version is "Portland Passive-Aggressive". But neither of us were from Portland...

The parking study was my project. I felt comfortable at Metro. We had a great team. Even though John and I yelled, I knew that was part of our professional process. John and I were more hot-blooded than anyone else in the building, but we all got along. We were safe. I was able to voice my opinion, he his, and in the end we worked things out.

Obviously, I'm **not** suggesting that yelling creates a great working environment. What I am suggesting is that I had other bosses in my career who were anti-collaborative and my voice would never have been heard at all. They were "strong decision makers" who were so scared of failure, they could not abide conflict. Thin-skinned and lacking self-assurance, they would go into a defensive mode that would involve retribution for professionalism they saw as insubordination.

I wouldn't have fought them like I did John that day. My ideas would have died on the vine.

Anti-collaborative bosses would have given me a suboptimal solution. I would not have the freedom to speak up, I would go do it, it would fail, I would be blamed and likely made an example of. You know it because you've been there, too.

In the two rare times that John and I yelled at each other, it was always between him and me. Mary, Stewart, David, Karen, the rest of that team...I would never yell at (or with) them.

When John brought me that mocha and we figured out how to move forward, we did the work together, we learned together—we *collaborated*. We produced the work after our creative tension. I wish he were still around to read this.

In the end, the Region 2040 plan we all wrote together is something I consider to be a high point in my career. It was a beautiful, collaborative, thoughtful document written by people who truly cared about a great American city/region.

We Work Together or We Don't Work

Collaboration isn't just working together at a table. It's working together as a team...different roles, different focuses, but all working towards a common goal. It's knowing where and when to lend your skills to improving the culture, the product, or the process.

> **WITHOUT COLLABORATION, WE BECOME SILOS OF ONE.**

Without collaboration, we become silos of one. Prisons of lazy management. Each person toiling away, making their own numbers, not informing others of important facts, increasingly fighting no-win territory battles with our colleagues, and creating **a corporate system laden with the overhead of politics and territory**.

Funny thing about territory, it needs to be defended. When some person or some group in a company obtains territory, they need to spend time and resources protecting it. This siloing behavior creates overhead and extremely short-sighted decision making. Your vision isn't what is possible (bravery); it's looking for threats (fear).

Historically, we are much more likely to choose defending over tending...because **the choices and threats in fighting are clearer**. It's hard to be a good steward of your land: there's serious work and study involved. It's much easier to shoot anything that seems like a trespasser.

> **SILOS ARE THE NUMBER ONE INDICATOR OF ANTI-COLLABORATIVE PRACTICES.**

Silos are the number one indicator of anti-collaborative practices. They slow productive conversations, stifle decision making, crush growth, and create rampant zero-sum games. But we can break that vicious cycle of Engineering versus Marketing versus HR versus etc. We can build low-overhead systems of collaboration that run on good decisions made by informed professionals at the right time.

THE BOLDNESS OF THE COLLABORATION EQUATION

The collaboration equation is: **Individuals in Teams Create Value**.[8]

This book provides a bold choice. We can continue to be inefficient, ineffective piles of pain, shooting at whatever encroaches the boundaries of our petty fiefdoms. Or we can be professionals and work together.[9]

We can recognize that we've hired and are spending considerable money on an army of brains that has judgement, perspective, and potential. We can act on this realization by creating simple systems that allow these professionals to thrive, create value, and grow in worth to themselves, their teams, the company, the customer, and society as a whole.

Too many times, we walk into companies and meet people who require weeks of conversations just to describe how their working systems are hurting them. Many, if not most, of these people will say, "That's just the way it is around here," willfully sacrificing their professionalism to a historically unproductive, unrewarding environment. They begin to think that *there can't possibly be anything better*.[10]

The working styles of personal insult, embarrassment over delivering shoddy product, political infighting, good decisions rescinded, bad decisions imposed, blame, are all costly, all unnecessary, and all status quo and taught as best practices over time.

In this book, we will discover together how to build collaborative teams and undo this cycle of productivity-killing abuse. We'll look at real case studies lived by real people that Tonianne DeMaria and I have worked with

---

8 We can argue about whether this is Individuals + Teams = Value or Individuals ^ Teams = Value or Value = Individuals (Teams) on social media now.

9 This was, originally, or we can grow up and work together. No one liked that but me. I still like it, so punk rocker Jim is putting it in this footnote. Work structure has historically been driven by scared managers who couldn't take the time to really leverage the resources they were paying for. Asking for people to magically get quality work done without ever taking the time to satisfy the professional prerequisites of quality. We can do better.

10 This is called Learned Helplessness and will be discussed in-detail in the rest of the book.

over the years. We'll see how *they constructed their collaboration*. We will look at how they managed and benefited from their humane systems. We will look at how these people changed their interactions and behaviors. And we will discuss the psychology of work.

To get through all that, we'll be discussing how they built collaborative systems *unique to their work*. How they centered their improvements around a shared, defined, and acted-upon *Right Environment*. This is nothing more and nothing less than an explicit culture that expects professional, collaborative behaviors and benefits from everyone on the team. We discuss the role of leadership and how it is not centered on management, but is a trait exhibited by all professionals. This will show that when we have a complete, collaborative, and intentional professional team, we will, by default, have agency, psychological safety, and the ability to solve difficult problems.

That's a pretty full plate.

Collaboration requires attention and work. Books like this tend to be used as quick-start guides to fixing other human beings or trying to make problems disappear. They promise false certainty by making difficult problems seem easily solved.

While I know people will try to force this book into that mold, I'm hoping that most readers will realize that **individuals work in teams to create value**...and those individuals are human beings.

You cannot have collaboration without individual human beings. You cannot have a band with different talents. You cannot have a team without professionals looking to support each other.

Collaboration has its challenges. We will always be dealing with humans, disagreements, and a natural resistance to change. Creating that change is hard work and often frustrating. This is life. Either we care enough to do the work, or we don't.

But I have to tell you. Every time I've seen management write off a team or a division of people, those same people gleefully and professional-ly create better working conditions for themselves when given the chance. That doesn't mean lazy conditions: it means they remove the impediments others have placed between them and their team and providing value. Every written-off team in an anti-collaborative environment has always... **always**...exceeded expectations when they create their own outstanding environment.

We can do better. We can make a better world.

Acting with Confidence

COLLABORATION CREATES PROFESSIONALS.

In 2016, Kevin Chase was a procurement agent at Turner Construction in New York City. He wasn't the "I need some pencils" type of procurement agent. His life was significantly higher stakes.

Kevin was responsible for finding every plumber, every electrician, every piece of tile, every nut and bolt for billion-dollar projects at Turner. He was responsible for finding, interviewing, selecting, and negotiating with every contractor that would work on the building. Kevin was a very busy man.

> **AGENCY:** THE ABILITY OF ANY PROFESSIONAL TO ACT WITH **CONFIDENCE WITHOUT FEAR** OF REPRISAL, BLAME, OR SECOND-GUESSING.

Agents have a very short window of time (months) to procure thousands of workers and objects. If this sounds difficult, it's actually worse. Construction projects are a sea of constant change: constantly being redesigned or altered, the agent is always buying for a moving target. That made Kevin a moving target, every decision costing money and time with a high likelihood of being wrong.

We were working together on a fairly typical project for New York City: around a billion dollars, aggressive timeline, and many stakeholders. There were maybe 30 of these projects going on simultaneously in the office at the time. Kevin sat with dozens of other procurement agents, each swimming against their own strong currents.

THE CONFIDENCE OF INFORMATION

It's early evening, and Kevin is showing his *Obeya* to dozens of Turner's global HR leaders.

An Obeya *is* a room with charts, graphs, and tools that visualizes and broadcasts work being done in real time. It holds the information necessary to quickly see what work is being done, what problems are being solved, and what different collaborators are doing to make the project a success.

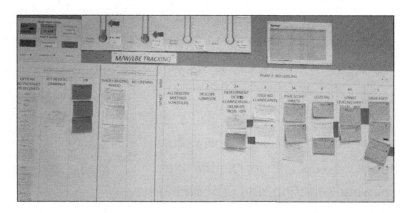

He is showing the HR leadership how he tracks his work, keeps an eye on objects "in peril", and manages daily workflow. Kevin is talking to them about how he measures success, handles hand-offs, and *sees* problems before they start. The visualizations in his Obeya keep him in contact with management and stakeholders and guide him in his daily work.

One of the HR people pushes deeper, asking him, "Hey Kevin, does this impact your work–life balance?" The other HR people laugh, "what an HR thing to say."

Kevin takes the question in stride, but also sees the bigger picture, the *humane picture*.

"I work in construction," he says with a wry smile, "nothing is going to impact my work-life balance. But what my Obeya does is let everyone up the chain of command here know in real-time the state of everything I'm doing. They know when something is in peril. When something requires attention from Frank (head of Procurement), Rick (the Project Manager), Charlie W. (Rick's Boss), or Charlie M. (everyone's boss), they know immediately.

*"More importantly, they know when I'm stuck with something or if I'm okay just working the blockage on my own. So, everyone is informed, and can lend a hand immediately...and **that lets me act with confidence.** They trust me and they've got my back.*

"And that impacts my quality of life. So, work-life balance, no. Quality of life, absolutely."

Act...with...confidence.

Let that sit for a minute. Think about *not* being able to act with confidence and how common that is at work. We humans are unfortunately skilled at leading people to be *unconfident*. We build the systems that starve professionals of information, making them question themselves and their decisions. We build structures that force competent and thoughtful people to wait passively or hopefully for direction, which often never comes.

> AN **OBEYA**, IS A SINGLE PLACE WHERE ALL INFORMATION THAT DRIVES A PROJECT, ITS DECISIONS, AND ITS PROGRESS LIVES. IT IS A LOCUS FOR EFFECTIVE COLLABORATIVE MANAGEMENT.

Most professionals are left hanging. Never receiving help or feedback and therefore never able to improve or act with confidence.

The more we don't receive that help or feedback, the more we take it for granted that receiving information isn't part of being a professional at all. We internalize that need for information and buy in to the anti-collaborative notion that being a professional means you always *figure it out your-*

self. We then spread this management malpractice, putting other people in likely-to-fail situations and blaming them when they fail to "go the extra (and unnecessary) mile".

Learned Helplessness is the tendency not to act at all because you increasingly expect the system to thwart you and then penalize you for even trying. Logically, it is safer to not act (to give up your agency). It is easy to blame the victim and tell people to go that extra mile, but learned helplessness isn't simply giving up. Learned helplessness is the result of realistically assessing no-win situations and realizing that action will yield no or negative results. In an anti-collaborative environment, acting with confidence is dangerous, which means that professionalism is dangerous.

Kevin was able to act with confidence because Turner was invested in his success. They were more interested in results than control. The visualizations in his Obeya enabled effective collaboration between different team members at different ranks...*without meetings*. The information was there when they needed it. When action was required, the boards in the Obeya alerted the right people at the right time. Turner had helped him build an environment that respected his professionalism, realized that his work was complex, and provided everyone at all levels with appropriate triggers for the right action at the right time.

The fact that this was a visual system is important. Kevin was *showing* the HR people how *seeing* the work and *sharing* it with others in the company removed stress and allowed him to act as a professional. Everyone in that room was seeing all the elements of the Obeya, gathering an idea of the entire system, and interpreting that information broadly. They were able to take in much deeper context about the work and the relationships.

This visual system gave Kevin ***agency***: Kevin could make decisions and act on them quickly because the lifeline to people with greater authority was clear and immediate. He neither had to worry about accountability or blame, because there was a collaborative system that made those things irrelevant. The system trusted him and had his back. He could be responsible and focused.

Kevin was spending over $800 million in a few months. There are many opportunities to make a decision that would put the company at risk. This collaboration freed him from worrying about every decision, because they were all visual and broadcast in real time. Anyone could step in and ask for deeper information about a particular item and, if necessary, give advice or help. Most of the work, though, was routine and didn't require constant costly scrutiny. The Obeya provided a system of collaboration that increased the certainty of his actions (agency) in a professional environment (psychological safety) where multiple people knew what was going on all the time (quality, leadership, peer review).

> **Kevin, the professional, was a vital part of a greater team that was creating value.**

THERE IS AN "I" IN TEAM AFTER ALL

At the time of Kevin's HR meeting, Kevin is an individual, responsible for specific work. He has a small, growing team of procurement agents, but the definition of "team" stops there. His little silo of cordoned-off work, getting instructions or control from a management stack, and giving finished product to the construction engineers. Their definition of team quickly changes when the Obeya arrives.

The Obeya provided visual information that was crucial for, but unavailable to, the "stakeholders". A stakeholder is someone who should be a team member that you were previously too busy to talk to. Here they'd include management, engineers, and estimators.

The management stack went from governance and oversight to *team members*. The engineers that would build the project began to meet in Kevin's Obeya as *team members*. The estimators that worked on the numbers before Kevin started purchasing, who previously lost track of work when it passed on to procurement, became more involved.

Team **became the people needing to help to get the work done, not just Kevin's group in purchasing.**

And in the middle of all that new collaborative team, we find the individual. Kevin Chase. Kevin was an I.

The Collaboration Equation is **individuals in teams create value—professionals coming together to accomplish good work.** It's about *teams of individuals.*

For any healthy collaboration to exist, individuals, teams, and value must be planned for, improved, and celebrated by the people doing the work. The individual is the foundation of the team. Their talents, their drive, their perspective combine in a team to solve problems, learn, and get work done.

I've observed throughout my life, whether in music, construction, software development, urban design, manufacturing...in everything we do as humans we do it faster, with higher quality, and with greater satisfaction when we do it with others. We do better work together.

> ISOLATION AND DIVISION ARE NEVER A RECIPE FOR SUCCESS.

Isolation and division are never a recipe for success.

I have also, unfortunately, watched smart, creative people languish in jobs where their bosses, incentivized to focus on productivity over professionalism, tell them they "are not paid to think". This is and can only be a system of enforced mediocrity, and we have tolerated it for too long.

You can help change that.

You are an individual in a team.

THE NATURAL FEAR OF CHANGE

The failure to effectively collaborate has obvious penalties. Underinformed people work without understanding. Divisions between silos or teams put professionals in frequent conflict. Under-planned or overprescribed work inevitably leads to shoddy product released at the wrong time. Lack of coordination with other teams leads to additional work, re-work, and waste. Anti-collaborative systems thrive on generating over-head and delay.

You've seen it. You know it. You live it.

We all know we need to work with other people. Without them, we'd have no restaurants, hospitals, or games. We *know* that without other peo-ple we'd rapidly perish. Even small interruptions in the global supply chain show how much we rely on each other. We *expect* that other people are there for us.

So, we individuals need collaboration, but we also *fear it*. It is threat-ening. Collaboration feels wild, untamed, unpredictable. We feel we *must* work with other people, but we don't know what they might do. We are al-ready overloaded, we are frustrated, we don't have time to find out. Those other people feel like risk; they feel like *change*.

Human beings naturally fear change, and it seems like there is an un-limited supply. We struggle with fears of risk, being undermined, derailed, or used. We build systems (social media, gossip, poorly planned work, etc.) that provide so much fear that we lose the ability to act. We become para-lyzed waiting to see what will happen, to learn what is safe.

This **fearful behavior** becomes the norm. The more we don't act, the more we feel that it is natural for people to not act. We feel it is normal not to collaborate. Simply put, anti-collaborative systems have created a belief that people are by nature anti-collaborative.[11] Fear itself is a system.

We then internalize that fear, assuming that everyone works better alone, and creating unreasonable anti-collaborative expectations of our-selves. We don't want to be the ones who fail, so we hoard work, not want-ing others to see it until it is perfect. We take on too much work for fear

---

11 This is beyond simply being "jaded": this is building a vicious cycle of assuming the worst and then acti-vely working to make sure the worst happens by not actively working to make sure it doesn't.

of being seen as lazy or combative. We begin to fear our own failure with others watching. We don't want to be judged.

Our roles then become murky. We end up doing what other people ask, but their requests are vague, arbitrary, or unreasonable. We lose track of who we are or why we are there. We cannot act with confidence.

When collaboration comes along, we don't trust it because we don't know *how to act*. We ask, "*what is my role*" in this collaborative effort? We look for reassurance that we will do our part and others will do theirs. This is entirely because we've lived for so long in anti-collaborative systems that guarantee individual failure and provide little thought for individual success. This fear then makes us over-plan, prematurely define success, limit learning, and virtually assure failure.

We can solve this by recognizing one simple truth: **Individuals work in teams to create value**. When we only focus on cost, deadlines, or mindless productivity and not the people or the teams doing the work, we will always be ignoring how the work actually gets done.

Kevin broke that pattern by building a system that greatly enhanced his ability to act with other people, providing rapid feedback, giving him confidence that his actions were valid, his learning shared, and his opportunities for success realistic. This collaboration allowed him to succeed.

THE COLLABORATION EQUATION

We are all trying to collaborate every day. We are engaging in labor together. (Co—together) (Labor—work) (ate—action). We as individuals are gathering with others to get something done. We bring our hands, minds, and hearts together to complete work.

We have the *ability* to collaborate, and we do so every minute of every day. We work together to build families, nicer yards, products, services, art, education...whatever human beings can dream up. We start new companies (to be in the company of others). Everything we can do...*we do*.

When Kevin said that he could act with confidence, the HR people didn't know what to do. They knew the words were powerful, but there wasn't a set pattern to say, "Oh, this means <buzzword>." The recognition that communication of state by the Obeya led to Kevin receiving more respect because it was clear he was delivering on his responsibilities was immediate. It was an exciting and uncomfortable moment that showed how great the delta was between common work processes and a humane work environment.

Teams made of professionals can act with confidence. An organization that knows it has people they can trust because the organization has their backs. Customers who know that if they do business with you, they can have faith that everyone will be taken care of.

KEVIN'S CONFIDENCE HAD A PRACTICAL ARCHITECTURE

No game is played without rules; no collaboration is successful without victory conditions. Action is easier if we can easily see the most successful path between where we are (current state) and where we want to go (future state). We also need to see what is going to make our journey difficult and what we need to learn to get past the difficulty.

HR wanted a quick fix. They wanted something that would make everyone's pain immediately disappear. They wanted Kevin to say the Obeya immediately took away all his troubles. This might be what you want to hear, as well, but that's not how professionalism works.

Kevin told them the truth. The Obeya *gave him the information and support to confidently address his work, easy or difficult*. It didn't solve the problems for him; it gave him an environment to solve problems effectively. The Obeya enabled true collaboration.

He was now an individual in a team that could confidently create value.

To achieve this, Kevin's Obeya room needed a practical and specific collaborative architecture. It required structure, an architecture, and a language. It gave Kevin what he needed to be a confident professional.

The items on the walls of this Obeya room detailed the active process of procurement, complete with known pitfalls. It showed how work was supposed to happen, where improvements were underway, and the current work in process (the work that was currently being done). This meant everyone could see what work required what action and by whom from moment to moment.

This is collaboration: The actions of professionals coming together to lend their individual talents to completing an endeavor. They don't have to work together, side by side, all the time. They simply need to know when to act with confidence. When they find that confidence, they also find it comes part and parcel with a culture...a Right Environment that is enabling professionalism.

Kevin's Structure

Collaboration requires structure. Information and actions need to be clear. Any Obeya uses this structure to make routine and exceptional information quickly and predictably available so everyone, not just Kevin, can act with confidence. The project's Obeya was in a small conference room, with information delegated to three walls.

Wall One—Workflow and Improvements: Had the original planning (a value stream map[12]) created for the project that showed the then-current state for

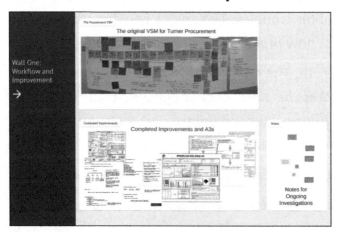

12 We will discuss value stream mapping in chapters 4,5,6, and 7. For now, it is an exercise that helps a team understand their culture, workflow, and improvement needs.

how work flowed, where collaborations happened, and where problems often arose. There was also a long list of improvements that the Turner procurement team had come up with to remove some of those problems. This wall also kept track of those improvements. Lastly there was a Notes and Direction section where we kept track of changes to the process, the work being done currently, and decisions that were made that would drive change.

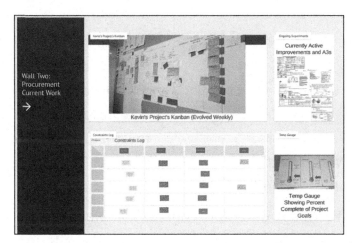

Wall Two—Managing Work in Progress and Collaboration: Had a large Personal Kanban that tracked procurement work as it happened. Each procurement package became a ticket, information about each package was written on a ticket, the ticket was flagged if it became stuck or was otherwise "in peril", the severity of the problem was also shown by color, and work flowed from left to right...from not yet started through each stage to complete. This wall also held the status of ongoing experiments by others in procurement on A3s (a collaborative problem-solving format we will cover later) and a constraints log which showed where there were current impediments to completing work.

Wall Three—Huddles, Expectations, and Quickly Evolving Conversations: There were boards to help facilitate daily or weekly huddles with the procurement team, the engineering team, and management. In one place, he had all the information needed to get work done and inform others about their responsibilities.

The room provided information to the entire procurement team, Kevin's project team, the engineering team, the estimating team, the customer, and management. Everyone could see the board and knew in real

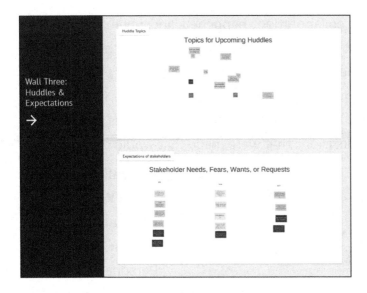

Wall Three: Huddles & Expectations →

time how they could help Kevin, where he might need help but not know it, or when they needed to step back and just let the man work.

When Kevin made a decision or took an action, this was captured on the board. If no one came to him and said, "Whoa! Wait!", he knew everything was fine and he could...say it with me...*act with confidence*.

The architecture of the Obeya gave Kevin operational and cognitive freedom by cutting out unnecessary meetings to ask permission to act, to update actions, to review issues, etc. The board captured all of this essential information visually. In so doing, it eliminated hours of meetings while increasing every person's ability to act. Every time Kevin's ability to act increased, his professional respect also increased. The impediments that kept others seeing his professionalism were removed.

The project Obeya provided a single place where status, forecasts, frustrations, and victories were all visible, apparent, and actionable.

The Obeya was a hub of information that spawned collaboration, cost-savings, time-savings, increased quality, and professional satisfaction.

A test of these benefits came when Kevin started onboarding new procurement agents. Ordinarily, Kevin would give new agents simple tasks and would devote a significant amount of time answering questions about status, actions, different actors in the system, etc. In other words, he'd be verbally telling new staff, "Here is everything you need to know."

With the Obeya, new agents came on board, looked at the room, *sat and worked in the room*. The walls gave instant context and clarity, so they asked far fewer questions, helped in more places more quickly, and added to Kevin's productivity rather than reduced it. When other staff entered the Obeya and asked a question, new staffers were far more likely to have an answer, and less likely to defer to Kevin. They were able to be individual professionals acting and not waiting.

The ability of the Obeya room to make tacit knowledge explicit was invaluable.

This played out with the engineering team and others as well. Information that previously needed to be slowly said in a long boring meeting was now imparted instantly, in a picture (which we are more likely to remember), leaving the meetings to focus on "*what do we do*" as opposed to "*what do we know?*" This instant information and ability to act let every individual in the room worry less about themselves and more about helping create value.

THE PRINCIPLES OF PROFESSIONAL COLLABORATION

"A bad system will beat a good person every time."

— W. EDWARDS DEMING

We all want to experience an environment in which people can act with confidence. This is culture activated. It is culture that is operationalized. It is a culture that is defined by those doing the work. It is both practical and humane.

We need work to be more humane before we can be more professional. My years of building large projects with Lean and continuous improvement have taught me to look at the system and not the people—to seek systemic changes that enable success before ascribing failure to (blaming) a particular person.

Yet *the people are the system*. They are the actors, the components, the victims, the beneficiaries, the architects, and the prisoners. They are the individuals in the team that creates value.

The humans and the systems are symbiotic.

System Blindness: Our once-helpful rhetoric to look only at the mechanics of the system before looking at its humanity led us down paths of mindless hyper-productivity and worker fungibility. We focused on rituals and standard work. We focused on set, rote processes that removed individuals from the role of decision making and alienated professionals from their work.

Today, we regularly build and maintain anti-collaborative cultural systems without realizing it. Our Lean and Agile rhetoric works against its original intent. We are anxious to blindly *follow* the patterns, not *thoughtfully deploy* them to solve problems or make things better.

Almost every company on earth is organized, managed, and run via arbitrary collections of interactions and reactions that have gathered over time, like so many barnacles on the bottom of a boat. Every corporate culture is one of emergent neglect and negative reaction.

Rather than carefully cultivating culture like an intentional Japanese garden, most companies operate with processes resembling the giant Pacific Ocean garbage patch. Solid, dangerous, entrenched, toxic, and with such mass and gravitas that no one could even begin to know where to start with the cleanup.

This is not sustainable. We can and we must do better. We must build humane, collaborative cultures focused on professionalism. We must make work interesting.

YOU DON'T KNOW ANYTHING ABOUT COLLABORATION

"If you can't describe what you are doing as a process,
you don't know what you're doing."

— W. EDWARDS DEMING

Our culture is the agreements we've made, tacit or explicit, for how we collaborate. A healthy culture allows professional work to get done. To make sure that we own, maintain, and ultimately benefit from our corporate and team cultures, we need to take responsibility for them. We need to understand that our culture, our process, and our product are part of the same flow of need, information, and action.

To build on the Deming quote above, if we can't describe what we are doing as a process, and our culture and process are symbiotic, we also likely can't describe our culture.

If we can't describe our culture, which most teams can't...**we simply don't know who we are or what we are doing**. If we don't know who we are or why we are at work, how do we expect to act with confidence? Our culture is intrinsically linked with the work we've agreed to do, have in flight, and is in peril. You cannot effectively visualize your culture without seeing your work.

In business today, acting with confidence languishes as no one defines, cares for, or extends their culture. Under the crushing weight of value-negative tasks like status meetings, alignment meetings, searching for information, redefining our product, or disciplining each other, overhead consistently accrues. Everyone is inexorably bogged down, looking at the weight of the value they are asked to provide and "pushing back", rather than finding ways to comfortably do more work they are proud of.

Every team we have worked with begins in this fetid bog, because people think culture just magically happens or that it comes from someone's prescription or buzzword list. We can, we should, we must, we are professionally required to fix this, but we lack the tools and examples to create our own collaborations. We need a set of simple principles to make sure that we are building a Right Environment that defines, rewards, and improves upon our professional behavior in our context.

FIVE PRINCIPLES OF COLLABORATION

Whether you are a leader like Kevin's bosses and bosses' bosses or you are a leader like Kevin, a "rank and file" worker who was taking Turner Construction into entirely new ways of working, you are making decisions every day. You are building or denying collaborative opportunities. You are improving the way everyone works, or you are destroying with entropy.

At a minimum, a humane collaborative system requires that we as individuals, we as teams, and the systems that we build have situational awareness, improve our work, inform our colleagues, visualize action, and give a damn. These five principles, detailed below, are minimum criteria for entry into a collaborative system.

They are not THE five principles. They are five principles. Your teams will *always* have more. You will have principles unique to your Right Environment. At Turner Construction, for example, physical safety is always going to be at the top of their humane management principles. When you are done reading about these, ask yourself, *what would I add to this list?*

And, in the future, anytime anyone gives you a prescriptive list about anything at all...ask the same question. *What would I add?* This is the basic notion of collaboration. You have good ideas, they have good ideas, we mix them together to arrive at the best ideas.

In a collaborative culture, one size does not fit all.

PRINCIPLE ONE **Pay Attention (Situational Awareness)**

Paying attention to the needs of the customer, the team, leadership, the company, the market, and each other creates an expectation to always inform and be informed.

PRINCIPLE TWO **Give a Damn (Relationships)**

Caring about the quality of the culture, the product, and relationships with the customer, the team, leadership, the company, the market, and each other creates an expectation to be able to voice opinion, raise issues, and provide professional feedback in a professional manner.

PRINCIPLE THREE **Improvement is Your Job (Responsibility)**

Professionalism is based on continuous improvement—the constant leveling up of our capabilities, our processes, our relationships, quality, and predictability in delivery.

PRINCIPLE FOUR **Information Drives Action (Communications)**

Informed professionals act on information: they expect to provide information to others and to receive it when they need it. Remove barriers to the flow of information such that decisions are made in the light of good information.

PRINCIPLE FIVE **Trust but Visualize (Respect)**

Seeing and sharing work and capacity visually increases speed, quality, and collaboration. Professionals can see patterns in the flow of work, improve based on evolving information, and can be protected from overload. Seeing and sharing the results of learning provide the entire team with the value of individual professionals' experience, allowing faster growth and adoption of better methods.

THE COLLABORATION EQUATION

Individuals in Teams Create Value

Collaboration is people coming together to achieve something. **Individuals** forming a team with a goal that someone values. There are no teams that don't learn along the way, and it's incredibly rare that we do something only for ourselves or no one at all. For the most part, someone wants or needs something, and we try to meet that need.

Professionals Need Impact. Human beings want to make a difference. We want to have impact and know that our effort resulted in someone, somewhere ending their day better than they started it. There are many books out there about building teams, but a scant few of them include the people on the teams. Your team is a group of people who can either work with each other or in spite of each other. We have a choice. You have a choice.

Individual Needs Are Team Needs: The individual professionals engaged in your endeavor all bring perspective, judgement, and acumen. These gifts strengthen the team if they are a natural part of the system. These gifts quickly become liabilities if they are ignored, shunned, or attacked. No individual starts out disgruntled: *inhumane process creates disgruntlement*. One can only realize oneself as a professional in relationship to others: teammates, customers, management, etc.

The Visual Is Action: The individuals working on your project require information to act with confidence. They can either fight to find that information, or they can have one predictable place to go to obtain it, interpret it, and act on it. The Obeya is that hub.

The Individual Focus Must Be the Team Focus: A team is group of individuals that have a focus.

If the team is over-focused, it is a silo. If the team is under-focused, it lacks direction. If a team's focus is provided from the outside, they are order takers. If the team's focus is entirely inward, they are craftspeople. If a team's focus is a collaboration between the professionals on the team, the goals of the company, and the needs of the customer, then they are professionals.

The Next Step: In order for a group of individuals to form a coherent and highly performing team, they need to understand and agree on how they collaborate. They need to understand how they are informed, how they interact, how they help each other, how their work flows, and how they improve and what they have improved.

They need to be serious about being a professional team.

Individuals Becoming Teams

THE PRACTICAL BRIDGE BETWEEN ME AND WE

IMPOSSIBLE REQUESTS COLLABORATIVELY SOLVED

Work is life, and life often presents us with challenges. Projects come along with demands that seem unreasonable. They have deadlines, budgets, or other restrictions that make it difficult to see the path to victory. Collaboration is the key to seeing past our fears and finding success.

In 2009, Tonianne and I had a project with the World Bank. By design, it lasted a total of five days. We were there to facilitate the writing of the REDD+ manual, a document that would be responsible for distributing carbon credit dollars to local landowners worldwide who engaged in various forms of sustainable practices.

The stated problem: We have 12 scientists, economists, and analysts from 11 countries, and they have never met each other. Each is a subject matter expert in their respective areas. They have five days to write this highly technical document. Can you make that happen?

We said, "Well, that sounds impossible...we'd love to!"

On Monday morning, we convened at the World Bank offices in Washington, DC. The document was 12 chapters long, and each subject matter expert was responsible for a chapter that corresponded to their expertise.

They, and everyone else, saw themselves as **12 silos**, focused on individual products (the chapters).

They sat down, took out their laptops, and got ready to write.

We walked around the table and closed every other laptop.

They looked alarmed and confused. *"How can we write on closed laptops?"*

We asked them to **pair-write**. "You are chapter eight and you are chapter three? Now you two are chapters eight *and* three." The assignments were arbitrary, based on who was sitting next to whom. They were unhappy with this system, but they were already resigned to failure (because they *knew* they didn't have enough time). Frankly, they accepted our structure because they *knew* it would fail. They could then blame this crazy pairing system, so they went with it. It gave them an out.

Tonianne and I set up a board at the front of the room. Every twenty minutes, we'd ask the group three questions:

▸ On a scale of 1 to 10, how far are you on your outline?

▸ On a scale of 1 to 10, how far are you on your text?

▸ Do you have questions for any of the other researchers in the room?

And we'd write the results on a big piece of paper at the front of the room.

They thought it was highly weird. They were right. I mean, if you are in a hurry, why would you do something that would slow down the writing of individual chapters? We need productivity! We need fast typing with the fingers!

If it took five days to write this document alone, wouldn't it take 10 days writing it together?

They started to write, silently or quietly conversing. The room was polite, orderly.

Twenty minutes later, we interrupted them and asked the questions, marking their answers down on a flip chart. Then again, again, again. An hour, two, three, four, passed, and we were filling the flip chart with data. "I am a three on my outline." Next hour, "I am a seven on my outline." Next hour, "I am a nine on my outline and a one on my text." Next hour…"We are a six on our outline."

As they looked closely at their work, as they questioned it regularly, they gathered real data and understanding which *helped them guide their work and understand how much effort success would take.*

Each time we interrupted them, they would ask each other questions.

The next day, the room was a little noisier; **they became less likely to wait to ask questions** of each other. In Google Docs, they were now sharing their sections of the document with the other pairs. Questions went from inquiry to requests for input directly in their sections. No interpretation! Direct collaboration. By the third day, I stopped interrupting them; it was a productive cacophony.

The pairs, the reluctant collaborators, naturally became a mob of excited collaborators.

Creative tension. Productivity. Laughter. Completion, *effectiveness.* Shared work, shared direction, shared success.

Remember, the stated problem was: *We have 12 scientists, economists, and analysts from 11 countries, and they have never met each other. They have five days to write this document. Can you make that happen?*

They were afraid of the time. The five days to write a document seemed impossible. But we asked ourselves, "What really makes this hard?" The answer was clear: the natural tendency to over-produce was the important constraint, not the time.

The team needed a system that would create a shared focus on complete and concise text written effectively. The collaboration required a structure, a set of rules focused on a quality product delivered in a timely fashion that fully utilized the individual professional capabilities of the team. They realized they weren't there to type quickly; they were there to process siloed information into a collaborative product.

TWO COLLABORATIVE CRANIUMS ARE BETTER THAN ONE HARRIED HEAD

"Excite" is a word we should discuss. When you expose objects to heat or chemicals, atoms or molecules get excited, they change, they transform. People are no different. When we create things together, we see the completion of the task, but are also exposed to the heat and chemistry of other people's creativity and perspective. They do exciting and unexpected things.

In 1969, Herbie Hancock was sitting in a dark room in New York City recording with Miles Davis. The tracks they were recording were all improvisations on themes. There was a very loose, general structure, but everyone was just creating together, listening to each other, feeling the flow of the product, and helping.

At one point, as Herbie tells it, he made a mistake. He played the "wrong" notes at the "wrong" time. He lifted up his hands, frustrated, expecting everyone else to stop playing and for them to try it again. Instead, Miles replayed Herbie's piano "mistake" on the trumpet, and played it again, and again, and transformed it into quality product.

When Herbie put his hands back on the keyboard, he was *excited*. Not only was the product going forward, the collaboration with Miles, the tangible, real, practical collaboration with Miles, exposed the young Herbie to a perspective that strongly influenced his career.[13]

---

13 See Herbie Hancock's class on Masterclass (www.masterclass.com) for his specific telling.

Two kinds of excitement when we are working together are relevant here.

Processing Excitement is when people working together form a connection that not only increases productivity, but changes the quality of the product—this results in professional satisfaction.

Potential Excitement is when the end product achieves more, is enjoyed more, or solves a novel problem—this results in personal and professional growth.

What would happen if we took people who truly felt they never needed to collaborate and gave them a structure to define, refine, and deliver their work together?

In his 1997 work *Extreme Programming Explained*, author and practical visionary Kent Beck introduced the concept of *Pairing*.[14] Kent realized that if something was difficult, or filled with unknowns, or someone needed to upskill, or if we were just interested in increasing quality, it helped to *pair* with another person. In working together, *we could simultaneously do and check the work*. We could discuss when we were stuck; we could question decisions as they were being made.

In the modern workplace, we make so many decisions so quickly they feel like they are obvious and natural. Then, when something goes wrong, someone else says something like, "*Why the hell did you do that?*" We generally have *an excuse*, but not an answer. That frustrates both us and the asker, and trust erodes.

The fact is, *we don't know* why or even remember that we made the decision. It just felt logical at the time, and we likely didn't think much of it. Our daily job is to solve problems, make decisions, and make professional judgements. The problem is we are often slightly or not-so-slightly wrong.

---

14 Beck, K., & Andres, C. (2004). *Extreme Programming Explained: Embrace Change. Sydney: Addison Wesley.*

We are hindered by solo work and our illusion that it is worthwhile.[15] Psychologist Paul Nutt's work[16] shows that *individuals* make suboptimal solutions 70% of the time. Your mileage will vary, but not by much.

The solution is simple: more perspective. Your judgement may be sound, but your perspective is limited (it's only you). Including even one more voice in making a decision greatly improves the quality of that decision by deploying more personal, technical, operational, organizational, and other perspectives.

While working, simply having someone else sitting with us when a decision like that flows from our fingers has massive impacts. They look at the product as it is being created and say, "Hold up, what does that mean?" In the moment, before any product has actually been released, you can edit, alter, augment, change, fold, spindle, or mutilate your original decision with the benefit of the perspective of another person.

Kent wrote that we wanted to "change when the cost of change is low." Micro-edits during the creation of something is the cheapest change you can invest in and will have the most immediate returns. The REDD+ team wrote their entire document by consistent micro-edits.

The cost of change runs deeper than simply monetary or time penalties. There is our emotional and personal investment in the status quo, which has a decidedly ugly impact on improvement. Entrenchment is costly.

If I create something alone and consider it done in my head, I imbue that product with a bit of my ego. The product becomes part of me, and fu-

---

15 **Tom Ehrenfeld 22 Aug:** Imprecise sentence, implies that all solo work is not worthwhile. Can you tweak?
Jim Benson 22 Aug: There is no solo work.

— This exchange between me and my editor looks pedantic, even to me, but we need to recognize that solo work is almost always an illusion. We may complete a task alone, but it is for a customer, it is for a human being, whose life will be changed by our product. It's usually done with suppliers, with instructors, with history. All our work is a collaboration; we have a self-centered pathology that tells us otherwise.

16 Nutt, P. C. (2002). *Why Decisions Fail: Avoiding the Blunders and Traps That Lead to Debacles.* San Francisco, CA: Berrett-Koehler Publishers.

ture edits or changes feel like a personal attack. It's like, "*I made this thing, I think it is good, if you think otherwise you are attacking my professionalism and capabilities, I will and must defend it/myself.*" If you and I are pairing, and you make a small adjustment, my ego remains intact because *we* are doing this *together* and the change is simply part of us working together; it happens in context during creation before entrenchment sets in.

Pairing (as a collaboration) is a wonderfully effective practice that reduces production time, increases quality, and diffuses politics and unhealthy ownership. Pairing is also *a behavior*, not natural at first, but quickly becomes comfortable in a collaborative system that spurs us to pair at appropriate times. If pairing is expected and logical, it becomes second-nature.

Building Healthy Expectations

Left to their own devices, any social scientist, myself included, would sit behind their laptops, writing to impress themselves. They would assume they knew everything about their discipline and all the others. They would have written until they personally felt their section was *complete*.

"Complete" is a whole lot of typing.

When we work solo, we don't always optimize for a quality product. We optimize for anti-collaborative stressors like meeting a deadline (rushing), while assuming we know what people need (solutioning) or doing the "best" job we could possibly do (over-solving/perfectionism). In a solo setting, our team would have never finished because they had no collaboration, no interaction, and no "customer" to set expectations. They had no **beneficial constraints**.

A beneficial constraint is the edges of the pavement on the roadway. They keep us moving in the right direction, while still allowing us a choice of vehicles and destinations. Collaboration with your team and customers provide beneficial constraints that allow value to be defined, experimented with, partially satisfied, learned from, and reconfigured to provide the most value in the most creative way with the least effort.

With the REDD+ team, we paired people together to make them immediately write for an audience. Their pairing partner became a real-time customer (a beneficial constraint), consuming new content as it became available. The fact that the person they were pairing with was also a subject matter expert in another discipline meant that they discussed *and extended* the content even at the outline level. Their unique perspectives refined, enhanced, and extended each chapter. Their presence triggered the authors to solve problems in real time and work quickly and accurately.

The Impacts of Pairing

Each pair, and the team as a whole, engaged in collaborative behaviors spurred on by pairing and mobbing. The definitions of value, expectations of each other, definition of end product, and shared learning led to immediate professional satisfaction by the individuals on the team. What was previously a stressful individual effort became a joyous moment of creativity and growth.

Collaboratively Defining Value:

The team's success relied on a shared definition of value, which shifted from the individual's definition of

Productivity: *What is the most detail I can provide?*

To a collaborative team definition of

Effectiveness: *What does the customer need to understand*?

Value was now defined by their interactions, questions, and professionalism, not simply by producing "more."

Expectations of Behavior:

The team found this effectiveness through a simple system that encouraged professional behavior. By interrupting the work every 20 minutes and asking if they had questions for each other, the system created a collaborative flow that expected them to process together as a team and make the most of the expertise around the table. Because that *expectation existed*, they started coming up with questions and paying attention to their progress relative to each other. The team was not siloed; it was self-aware.

Quality-and Delivery-Focused:

Isolation would have had no expectations. If we just let them write individually, they would never ask questions, *even if they had them*. The table would have been silent, reserved. *No one would want to interrupt anyone else.* They would write on their own until they were personally satisfied with their section. A level of satisfaction that, for some, would never be achieved.

Then we'd blend the sections together and learn how none of them fit. The sections would have 12 voices and would slightly or significantly contradict each other. The group would not have written the document; 12 individuals would have written 12 disjointed essays.

Learning Driving Improvement:

At the end of our week pairing/mobbing together, we'd written over 80% of a coordinated, organized, and clear document. A few weeks later, it was complete and ready for use. The team left the weeklong session strangely energized, coordinating their flights to see if they could continue to work together in the airport. What should have been a slog of manic solo typing resulted in not only a quality product, but a great experience for the authors. As professionals, they grew and learned.

> **COLLABORATION WINS GAMES. TRUST BUILDS SHORTCUTS TO QUALITY. TEAMS SUCCEED.**

Collaboration wins games. Trust builds shortcuts to quality. Teams succeed.

ALL THINGS THRIVE IN THE RIGHT ENVIRONMENT

At David Evans and Associates, we specifically created and maintained a workplace where professionals could pay attention and give a damn. In the preface, we talked about this in detail, but ultimately, our culture actively (not tacitly) placed expectations on us and gave us the information, agency, and respect we needed to act with confidence. We teamed internally, chose what projects we wanted to work on, and were directly involved in the strategy and quality delivery of the company.

With the discussion of pairing, we saw how individuals can easily build cultures of two and eventually more people. They built systems that understood the work by understanding each other. As they did that, they built a larger professional collaborative culture designed to achieve group success...a completed REDD+ Report. They did this easily with a focused team of 12.

If (1) individuals in (2) teams create (3) value, our systems need to attend to the success of all three. They cannot happen only happen in isolation; we must scale the experience in the World Bank conference room to larger teams that last longer. We need to build systems that allow all our professionals to be professionally satisfied and never lose sight of improving and delivering value to the customer.

Teams must be able to quickly define who they are as individual professionals *and* a professional team. They must define the product and the mechanisms they employ to create that product. They need to know this as a group, not operate on assumptions.

Turner Construction knows how costly assumptions can be. To make sure their job site cultures are clear and professional, they created some-thing called **The Right Environment**, which answers and acts on the fol-lowing questions: *What are the needs of the professionals as individuals? What do they need as a team? How can they lend the most to the team and grow professionally? How does the team see their product, their cus-tomers, and their schedules or demands? What do they need to achieve professional satisfaction in culture, workflow, and product?*

In the case of the World Bank team, we built a quick system, in one day, which achieved results by providing the Right Environment for that team, in that place, at that time. The team members were constantly informed by each other, had expectations of specific behaviors (ask questions, write to-gether, converse), and formed immediate respect because all team mem-bers could demonstrate their worth. And this was a team of introverts, ex-troverts, and a hodgepodge of cultures.

Scaling up significantly, a Turner capital project in New York City can range from 100 million to billions of dollars. Each project is better fund-ed than most businesses on earth. It is seriously difficult work with tight deadlines and real pressure to perform. Even missing a deadline by a week can cost millions of dollars.

Every Turner project has a job site, and every job site has an office, usu-ally in a construction trailer. Historically, trailers and job sites have been run in anti-collaborative ways. Yelling, berating, turf wars, posturing, and incredibly rigid power dynamics.

But not too many years ago, Turner decided there was a relation-ship between quality build, site safety, and something amorphous that their CEO Peter Davoren called "The Right Environment." Over my years working with Turner, I watched The Right Environment morph from a joke to a buzzword to a platitude to a fully functional prerequisite to a successful job.

It was a beautiful thing to watch.

The Case of the Underwater Hospital

Out of all the Turner job sites I worked with, there is one story that expresses the depth of the Right Environment, revealing why it is the bedrock of any collaborative culture regardless of industry or size, and how its resilience can be expressed.

In 2012, Hurricane Sandy left Brooklyn's Coney Island Hospital a devastated wreck. Just a six-minute drive from the Atlantic Ocean, this level-one trauma center suffered the combined blow of flooding and wind causing electrical and mechanical failures and forcing two-thirds of its patients to require evacuation. Think floating hospital beds.

Like many hospital campuses, Coney Island was made up of buildings pieced together over the course of a century. While considered clinically innovative, the campus was nevertheless an architectural eyesore. It was a hodgepodge of aging buildings relying on one antiquated basement equipment room.

Basements don't generally do well in floods.

When the basement flooded (as in completely submerged), the hospital lost power, water, internet connectivity, everything. This 1,000-year storm had caught everyone off guard. Patients were still in the hospital, now totally dark. Streets were under feet of water; vehicles had no way of reaching them. It was an ugly scene.

FEMA, NYC Health and Hospitals, and other agencies pooled money together to fund a new Coney Island Hospital, one that could withstand the next "1,000-year storm", which is estimated to hit in the next five years or so. Turner and McKissack Construction created a joint venture to oversee construction. The architects at NBBJ designed the historic structure. LERA's structural engineers made sure the engineering would hold against future disasters.

From the very beginning, this project was different.

- There was a **flat budget** for the project—there would be no additional funding for change orders.
- There were **multiple stakeholders**—FEMA, NYC Health and Hospitals, Coney Island Hospital itself, and more.
- There were **design mandates**—the hospital would be able to withstand a now-frequent "1,000-year" storm.

Everyone involved in this project needed to be thoughtful. The designers, the engineers, the general contractor, the trades, the stakeholders... all were tasked to build an unprecedented building with lots of unknowns and innovations for essentially a fixed fee. Innovation at a guaranteed rate.

Before the project was even fully awarded, before there was even a trailer, Turner called stakeholders together to start planning the project, understanding the complexity, and building a collaborative partnership throughout the greater team. They knew that the number-one cause of overhead was lack of alignment and information hoarding.

From the start, the greater team openly discussed what they needed in order to be successful professionals, holding a Right Environment exercise. For this group, there could be no mistakes, and no avoidable surprises. Team behavior was important. They set up visual controls for themselves and for the teams. Their entire trailer (which is the size of a small building) would become an Obeya. This would be a team of 100 Kevins.

When the team moved to the trailer, the experience was even more profound. Senior leadership for the project, Chris Kristiansen and Paul Dorsi, set out to make sure that the team was always informing each other, always collaborative, always collegial.

Real-time information helps everyone involved (Turner, trades, everyone) plan their day, do their work, react to sudden change, and discover areas of improvement. The Coney team's daily huddles are...*fun*. They have a dog. They watch out for each other.

SOLVING PROBLEMS IN A RIGHT ENVIRONMENT

In construction, especially in a large hospital project, there are "got-chas"—emergent problems you don't see coming. Projects are logistically, operationally, and financially complex. There is always stress, yet in the Coney trailer there are always people laughing and working together. The Right Environment creates resilience by making difficult problems routinely solvable.

Turner as a company is filled with problem solvers. This is important, but problems cost money the project didn't have; this team needed to be problem anticipators so well informed they saw the problem very early and had an expectation it would be solved immediately and then designed out of future work.

There are three quick mini-stories that stand out about the Coney Team, each describing a different problem that was solved so quickly and professionally that some didn't even notice it was there at all. The Right Environment and the Obeya combine to create clarity of action, information, and purpose for the team, making stressful problem solving just another day at the office.

> ▸ **Problem solving beats blame pinning:** Coney Island Hospital is literally blocks from the ocean, and that means a high water table. During the placement of pilings for the foundation, one corner of the area ended up being much wetter than anticipated. Often a discovery of this magnitude leads to blame trails, lawsuits, and lengthy pain. With their Right Environment, focused on professionalism rather than blame, there was psychological safety. The professional, who in this case was not a Turner person, quickly noted that it was their individual oversight, and everyone went into redesign mode. The team as a whole (engineering, design, trades, and GC) had a quick workshop and came up with a solution, and within a week the problem was history. *The emphasis was always on solving the prob-*

lem, not on blame. Mistakes happen, that particular person was an excellent professional, it simply needed to be fixed. It was clear from the beginning that the Coney project's Right Environment was focused on rapid problem solving. Forcing blame didn't fit here. (This was a truly heroic moment).

▸ **Respect works its way outside:** There has always been tension between general contractors and tradespeople. This is "normal" tension between management and labor that has stemmed from our 20th-century anti-collaborative industrial history. The Coney Island project's internal Right Environment and Obeya were interesting enough that tradespeople were coming in the trailer more often. The trailer was an informative, constructive, and professional place where work could get done. The trades were asking questions and sharing information more. This win could have ended there, but the Coney Island team noticed that there wasn't a similar place for tradespeople to go to talk to each other—*the trades didn't have an Obeya of their own.* By this time, there were several floors (just concrete and steel) in place. The Turner team built out a room with a kitchen, lockers, tables, and an Obeya providing schedules, examples, and details for future construction. The trades now had a defensible space to hold morning meetings, solve problems, and put their stuff. It can get bone-chillingly cold and heat-stroke hot on a New York construction site; this room had air con, heat, and coffee. It was clean, it was humane. *It was the Right Environment expressed as a sign of respect for other professionals.*

▸ **Right Environments rapidly adjust collaboratively:** The Coney Island Hospital project was ahead of schedule, people were happy to come to work, things felt great. Then Covid-19 led to a shutdown of all construction in New York. If there is an industry that is hands-on, it's construction. All projects reacted differently, but Coney's response included two elements, the value of which cannot be understated.

- **Responsive (Function):** The team immediately began work on plans to open the project back up. Who would be "essential workers"? What would an incomplete staff look like on a very busy project? Would we have access to fabricators? What trades can operate with social distancing? Will we have a reliable supply chain? What happens to our existing deadlines? What information can we process from home? Are the trades going to have office staff still active? The Coney Island team had a cogent response back to their head office in a few days. *This was almost entirely possible because the project's Right Environment had clarity and was managed collaboratively.* Their Covid response became a template for other projects around the world.

- **Zoom and Flex (Culture):** Every team in Turner starts the day with "stretch and flex", a series of simple calisthenics to begin the day. Most projects treat this as either a necessary evil, or a chore. Coney's took the form of five-minute micro-parties, complete with music, attitude, and, oddly, *focus*. People take it more seriously because it is not a chore. To say that the Coney Island job site was inconveniently located for most of the staff to commute to would be an understatement. Yet, before Covid, most people showed up early *to make sure they didn't miss stretch and flex*. After they were all working from home, they continued it via Zoom—now involving some family members (and likely amusing others). *Their Right Environment fostered and maintained a culture was not only that important to them, expressing it was part of their professionalism.*

These three stories are just a few examples of the resilience and acumen of the Coney Island team. The value expressed in these stories isn't for any one actor. It's not furthering one person's career, though many careers thrived through this project. When problems arose, the team was not getting things organized or panicking about where information was stored or wondering who would be responsible for what...their culture and their processes were already clear. This was just another problem to solve.

The value here was expressed in constructing a challenging, quality building that would save lives in times of crisis. The value from this Right Environment helped the team, its leadership, the owners, the stakeholders, the design team, the tradespeople, Turner as a corporation, the hospital staff, and the people of New York City and Brooklyn in particular.

Collaboration is possible when professionals have communications, relationships, and respect *built into their system*. Not platitudes or posters. But someone must have the guts to build it operationally. We can no longer abide lazy, unprofessional, anti-collaborative behavior.

GRACE UNDER PRESSURE CAN BE DESIGNED

Chris Kristensen, the Coney Construction Executive (the CEO of the project), likes to share the following story. When we first started working together, when the project was still in the planning stages, I asked him, "What if I told you that you could have a totally collaborative project where everyone worked together, had the information they needed, and solved problems quickly?"

"That would be great." he said.

"Okay," I said, "How are you going to do it?"

A year later, there was a day in the trailer where Chris and I were supposed to speak with the project's Chief Superintendent about various improvements in which the team was engaged. But there was a problem that day which involved getting information to a stakeholder, an unreasonable and antagonistic stakeholder. The information was extremely hard to locate, and the stakeholder was on site, lurking and waiting...*impatiently*.

The team was running around us, gathering data, processing it. I didn't want to be in the way, so I kept trying to leave.

Chris kept saying with this zen-like face, "It's okay, just sit, we can wait." And we did. We just sat there...for hours.

They got the information out, the stakeholder was satisfied, and we met as a group. We talked about what just happened, came up with some possible improvements to make sure it didn't happen again, and I left.

When I came back a few weeks later, they'd developed a fully-fledged solution that was better than we'd discussed and had already launched most of it. They improved on the improvement. In fact, they'd already incorporated their solution into a system used throughout Turner and had held training sessions on other job sites. Millions of dollars in value created from a momentary inconvenience.

He always told that story about our beginning like I was being unreasonable, but here he was showing me, just through observation, that they had arrived. There would be improvement after this experience, the experience was painful but collaborative, and, even though there was some grumbling, no one made the stakeholder feel unwelcome or foolish or like a bother.

They were professionals, learning in real time. And they were sharing their learning.

ACTIONS AS COLLABORATIVE METRICS

It's important to note what Chris was *not* doing. Construction is an old business in an old industry built on strong silos, explicit power distance, and...*yelling*. On projects of the past, it would not be at all unexpected for the Construction Executive or the Project Executive to yell at the stakeholder then come back to yell at the staff and call up to yell at the architects for good measure. Everyone loves to yell at architects.

Chris just zenned out and watched his well-behaved, professional machine competently collaborate through an emotionally charged situation.

He was there, he wasn't interfering, he trusted his team and reveled in their grace under pressure.

This wasn't because of Chris (the construction executive), it wasn't because of Paul (the project executive), though they certainly could have ruined it. This situation was solvable and survivable because they built the Right Environment *with their team*. A collaborative system of agency, respect, and professionalism. An evolving collaborative *design*.[17]

And that collaborative system, after the upsetting event concluded, immediately set to work figuring out how to make that bad experience never happen again. Elvis, Kahli, Nicole, Ayo, Sebastian, and the rest of the immediate team just walked into the conference room and went to work, solving a hole in the way they worked and ensuring that frustration would never happen again.

Yes, they could have and did gripe about the stakeholder, but they understood that people would always be unreasonable; this wasn't about the stakeholder—the failing was in their inability to gracefully and immediately deal with the request for information. Their professionalism drove them to stop future events like that before they started; this is called **error proofing**.

Error proofing like this saves time and money for the project in the future, sure, but the real savings come from future reduction of *professional annoyance*. The professionals and the team were stressed and annoyed by this interruption, which cost not just time, but also energy. The day left them exhausted, and tomorrow still held all the work they needed to do today. Error proofing by finding the root cause of a problem and eliminating it allowed these professionals to have even greater job satisfaction in the future.

---

17 The design of the Right Environment allowed Chris to show true leadership by not interfering and allowing the real leadership of the moment to be expressed by the superintendents and team members in the trailer. The chapter on Leadership goes deeper into this, but leadership is a verb that can be expressed at any time by any collaborative team member. If your team members do not express leadership when necessary, you have little to no leadership at all.

To be clear, this collaborative problem solving/error proofing meant that the next time a stakeholder asked for information, they would receive it immediately. The team would be free of stress and extra work, and the customer would be happier. They didn't just solve the immediate problem; they found the root cause and made sure that problem would never happen again.

The system they implemented also allowed them to get that information anytime, anywhere. This meant that they could now take tablets onto the construction site and, with a few quick actions, have all the detailed drawings of the work they were discussing, doing, or reviewing. An improvement designed to solve that annoying situation revealed an innovation opportunity.

This team had the agency, the professionalism, and the structure to fix the problem and fix it in a way other teams could replicate. They didn't just solve the problem for them; they solved it for everyone. One unreasonable customer led to an innovation for all of Turner, simply because they had a collaborative Right Environment.

That is performance through collaboration. That is acting with confidence. That is learning together.

And it is the epitome of professionalism.

The Components of a Collaborative Right Environment

Collaboration builds professional resilient systems to replace our brittle siloed systems.

Regardless of scale, complexity, or funding, human beings work together in teams to create value.

At the start of our relationship, I had given Chris a lot of Lean Sensei–like vague direction. "See the work." "Always offer help first." "Trust your feelings, Luke." "There is no spoon." "Walk on that rice paper." That sort of thing.

One day, he pulled me aside. "Look, I want to do this stuff. But I am a construction engineer. You," he said, poking my arm, "you used to be an urban planner; you were a *design engineer*. I am a *construction engineer*. I take plans and make them real. You...you make plans. You give me plans; even if they are horrible, I will build something out of them."

It was probably the most self-aware thing anyone has ever said to me.

I left with marching orders. I needed to provide a flexible starter system that would take the Right Environment Chris and Paul were already creating and help *make it resilient*. I needed to design their basic structure; they would take care of the rest.

What do we mean by resilient?

We see here two meanings and a lot of synonyms. Combined, they give us some insight into what a resilient system might include. We can see a resilient system can withstand and recover quickly from difficult conditions (**Strength**). And that a resilient system retains its shape after abuse (**Character)**.

We have seen both types of resilience in the collaborative systems and dedication to solving problems at Coney Island. We saw how the Right Environment and collaborative ideals gave Kevin Chase a foundation from which to act with confidence.

We see that coherence in the system, ownership of professionalism, and learning all combine to create a resilient Right Environment that the *team members understand* and can therefore maintain. We see systems that engage people professionally, leaving them energized at the end of the day and not tired and spent.

Current State: Your Teams Don't Know Who or Why They Are

Identity is at the core of strength and character. You need definition. Who you are, why you are there, what role you play, what roles you can play, who you are there with, what their capabilities are, what is understood, what could change, etc. This sounds...obvious.

Unfortunately, most teams I have met have no explicit definition. They have no identity. They haven't talked about what they want, need, or aspire to. They don't know how they help or hinder each other's work. They don't know what is going on moment to moment or day to day. They can—and do—go weeks without talking to each other.

If a team is clueless about these basic elements of being a team, they cannot be a team, they cannot be collaborative, and they certainly can't have a Right Environment. They haven't put the basic effort into being able to work together. **Their culture is one of ignorance.**

You cannot communicate with each other if you don't know why you are there, what your team is capable of doing, and how your work flows. This basic cultural ignorance makes relationships anemic, hides real team and customer needs, and removes any hope of agency. Simply put: *You lack the information you need to act with confidence*.

This leaves you waiting for some arbitrary person to trigger you to action. If you are waiting for a "leader" to tell you what to do, one thing should be clear: *you don't know what to do.* Waiting isn't a strategy, it's certainly not a system, and if you are honest with yourself, you'll find no shortage of ways your current working environment is this catastrophically underdefined.

> ## WAITING ISN'T A STRATEGY, IT'S CERTAINLY NOT A SYSTEM.

You are a clueless person in an undefined team attempting to create poorly understood value.

This is curable. Identity gives grounding so that action and collaboration are possible. *A team* must do the basic work of defining who and what they are so they can realize when they have changed, are being tested, or are under attack. The team requires information and expectations to defend itself and seize opportunities. This allows the team to react elegantly to change or the unexpected.

A Metric for Identity: If teams react to the unexpected with anger or even rage, that is an indication they don't have the agency to solve the problem or control their work. They are likely in an anti-collaborative system, and perhaps one of their own, inattentive design. **Watch for the team's mood**; there are likely clear indications that the issues are not the crisis you are experiencing, but the information and agency starvation of your brittle (not resilient) team.

If the Coney team was brittle, they would have suffered through the stakeholder request, complained bitterly for weeks into the future, and then suffered through the same problem again in the future. The project itself also showed resilience by not tolerating mediocrity.

Implementing Culture: There is a prominent belief that culture is vague or a "soft skill". Culture is not vague; in fact, we can define it, maintain it, and care for it.

> **BENSON'S LAW OF UNDERVALUED CONSEQUENCES:** TODAY'S MEDIOCRITY IS TOMORROW'S CATASTROPHE.

In all the teams we've discussed so far, people at various levels of leadership were able to act in beneficial ways during daily work, at times of intense work and stress, because they had defined their own Right Environment built on these very real, very measurable, very actionable collaborative pillars.

INDIVIDUALS IN TEAMS...CREATING VALUE

Individuals in teams create value.

We just discussed the middle of the sentence: "In teams".

Forming a Collaborative Culture: The individuals in this chapter formed a strong team with a right environment that supported their professionalism. They wanted to collaborate and work effectively. They didn't just decide "we are a team," nor did they let proximity create the illusion of a team; they made conscious decisions to work together. Their systems were intentional.

Collaboration and Improvement Go Hand in Hand: We talked about grace under pressure and how that wasn't just because the people were individually amazing. This desired state happened because they *designed* their culture, their systems of work, and the way these supported everyone on the team to have agency, make good decisions, and exhibit leadership.

Collaboration Increases Value: We can achieve tasks that were once considered impossible. We can respond well to minor or major changes, raise future fully trained and experienced managers from today's young hires, and get the right work done at the right time. This is an investment, and like any investment we are giving something now (time and attention) to achieve future rewards (faster work, higher quality, less waste, more enjoyable work, etc.).

The Next Step: We need to invest in our collaborations up front, and for many of us "up front" was a long time ago. Our teams exist; we not only have a current culture, we have baggage. In chapter three, we will discuss the individuals in their teams relearning, rediscovering, and redefining how they create value.

Professionals Build Professional Systems

THE TALE OF THE UNSUPPORTED SUPPORT TEAM

In rural West Virginia sits The Library Corporation (TLC), a 50ish-year-old mid-sized software company with a global clientele. From their campus, they help manage a large percentage of the world's libraries. Their call center of around 24 people found themselves mired in a huge backlog of work. Their ticketing system contained over 2,000 aging, festering requests for help.

This depressing backlog of work maliciously greeted them every morning.

They were on a Sisyphean mission of completing 250 tickets a day and receiving 250 tickets a day. Working hard, barely keeping up, and not seeing progress was soul-crushing. Tickets left dangling at day's end would likely fall into the backlog, never to be completed.

Their monstrous backlog ominously loomed over them, destroying morale and inviting feelings of failure that were accentuated by constant conversation throughout the company. Everyone knew how "terrible" the support team was.

Nuisance overhead, historically, is the number-one business response to any challenge. In a world where so few people are trained in problem solving, no cultures consider problems to be part of work, and people are so focused on and terrified by productivity over effectiveness, the immediate response to a problem is rampant and comedic dysfunction. In short, it's an organized panic, a wet frightened kitten in business causal.

The terrible backlog caused many meetings to be held, with management *demanding* that ticket count be reduced. More meetings looked into why it was there. Still more meetings tried valiantly and loudly to figure out which members of the support department "weren't carrying their weight". And yet more meetings happened to figure out if these lazy lima beans needed more training. And of course, there were emergency one-on-ones to review performance.

Obviously, the problem was lazy workers. Obviously, *they* were the problem and we were going to have as many meetings as it took...but...wait...

Surely, these individuals needed *an incentive*!

To this end, management applied a "friendly competition" approach to the problem. They gave an award to those who could clear the most tickets each day. Management believed that if they incentivized the people in customer support, *these people would work extra hard and do even more tickets*.

They'd give 110%. They'd go the distance. They'd be an army of Rambos.

Following this anti-collaborative logic, if we gave extra incentive to an egg carton it could carry more than a dozen eggs or that if we paid a baseball player more money he would hit more home runs or that if we gave pregnant women a bonus they'd have babies faster or if we paid a CEO more money they would magically create a better company.

This is a simple logical fallacy we all engage in regularly.

This logic assumes that individuals magically create value without teams or a system in which to work.

Unfortunately, all systems have designed operations, capacities, and bottlenecks that do not respond to bribes or gifts. The anti-collaborative system inefficiently and ineffectively processes the work; the individual professionals get the blame.

"A bad system will beat a good person every time," the quote goes.[18]

There is a widely accepted myth that competition will always spur people to do better. People will raise their individual performance and that will raise everyone's game. We think this because it is both romantic and lets us all off the hook when problems arise. Someone must not have played hard enough, but it wasn't me. This **lazy management malpractice** is pervasive.

An individual might win our little internal competition, but the team, the product, quality, and the customer will suffer. Everyone becomes a silo of one.

Mindless competition creates an anti-collaborative system called a "Zero Sum Game" (ZSG). A Zero Sum Game creates one winner (+1) and one loser (−1), effectively making the net value to the company zero (0). Yes, someone one wins the prize every day, but...

In the case of our Support team, there would be one winner (+1) and twenty-three losers (−23).

---

18 This quote is attributed to W. Edwards Deming, but noted Deming scholars Jamie Flinchbaugh and Mark Graban have other opinions.

There is another quote that is wrongly attributed to Deming: "A bad system will beat a good person every single time." I've researched this one an abnormally large amount of time, and it is not something Deming ever said. He probably believed it, but never said it, at least not like that.—Mark

"Twitter has helped increase the sloppiness about quotes. I see people leave off attributions, intentionally or not taking credit themselves." —Jamie

I've used that short version, maybe incorrectly, the other day.

The longer version of the quote (which I am also struggling to find a primary reference on) is this:

"If you pit a good performer against a bad system, the system will win almost every time. We spend too much time fixing people who are not broken and not enough time fixing organizational systems that are broken. Only leadership has the power and responsibility to change the systems."—Mark

Do. The. Math.[19]

For the client in West Virginia, both the goal (processing tickets) and the morale of the team suffered under this ZSG. Rather than increasing production, Zero Sum Games often *greatly limit* the value that can be produced. The limitation comes from **a collaborative bottleneck**. Narrowly defining success (a single metric like closing tickets) narrowly defines the ways professionals can achieve success.

In an anti-collaborative system, people naturally optimize their behavior to achieve what limited success they can. It is what the system demands. In the example of faster-baby production, one could horribly imagine premature, but viable, c-sections at six months. ***Perverse incentives***—incentives designed for a good purpose that inadvertently, but predictably, reward or foster bad behavior—are rampant in anti-collaborative systems. And they are status quo in every company on earth.

ARE YOU FAILING BY DESIGN?

For our West Virginia support team, their incentive game would only allow one daily winner, and that "win" would not be satisfying. The winner may have achieved the goal, but often just happened to clear more tickets. There was no healthy or professional system of ticket clearing.

Wins were therefore arbitrary. Arbitrary wins create systems of doubt and distrust...you *want* to win, but don't know how. The behavior generated by the system is therefore equally arbitrary and dysfunctional. Good for Las Vegas, but not good for your team.

This pointless award did have an impact, though. It was extremely destructive to the operations and culture of the team and therefore hurt the company as a whole. Every day, someone would win, everyone else would

---

19 Annually, this would be about 200 winners and 4,600 losers. That's a whole lot of losing, but who's counting?

grumble about how they "cherry-picked easy tickets" or "didn't really carry their weight."[20]

> ## BENSON'S LAW OF LIMITED THINKING
> ### FETISHIZING INDIVIDUAL METRICS MANUFACTURES UNPROFESSIONAL BEHAVIOR.

The artificial and thoughtless metric of "number of tickets" was a **productivity metric**. It measured the rate of completion but did not care for quality of customer satisfaction. Professional support people care for customers; they do not answer as many tickets as possible. This created stress by alienating the professionals from the achievement of a goal (care for customers and reduce the backlog) to the unwilling participation in a mindless game (process the most tickets quickly).

The insidious part of this is there was coherent but false logic in creating the game; *it felt intentional*. A lot of people processing the most tickets in a day sounds like it would reduce the backlog, doesn't it?

Yet it didn't. It made the backlog worse. *Why?*

Awards before goals is a lousy strategy for achievement. The number of tickets in the backlog would never be reduced because the support staff was now being forced to individually focus on winning an award (anti-collaborative) and not actually serving customers, developing better ways to solve problems, or even simply maintaining the ticketing system (collaborative).

The root cause to be addressed was the structure of collaborative work,

---

20 Worse yet, it is pretty clear that even if everyone sat on their hands all day long and someone just marked one ticket "completed", they would win. Simple variation meant that everyday an arbitrary person won the award. If someone focused on winning the award, they did so at the expense of the customers or colleagues.

not character of the professionals. The only people at fault here were the people looking to find fault in the people.

Individuals *In Teams* Create Value

The "ticket processing game" made sense intuitively because support was assumed to be a collection of (lazy) individual efforts and not a team process. They all sat at their own desks, on their own phone calls, talking to people directly. They *looked* like they had their own, individual work. If you visited their workspace, it would appear that these were all single processors.

Management saw this apparent collection of *individual* efforts and wanted to increase the number of tickets being processed by individuals through *individual* incentives. Again, there is logic to this. It is flawed and easily dismissed logic, but logic nonetheless. And it was no one's job to question the logic or offer alternatives.

> **BENSON'S LAW OF CONSTRAINED INCENTIVES**
> INDIVIDUAL INCENTIVES WILL NEVER
> IMPROVE SYSTEM CAPACITY.

The ticket backlog was never the problem; it was a symptom.

It quickly became apparent that these 24 individuals were processing as just that—24 individuals. Each person isolated at their desks, processing tickets as they came in, first-in first-out. The reception of a call by any support person was completely arbitrary. You answer it—you do it.

If all people in the group were equally trained, equally knowledgeable of all the company's staggering 35 products, equally rested, equally caffeinated, and equally able to troubleshoot problems, this may have worked.

But the West Virginia team unfortunately worked in reality. They were not clones.

Their systems were complex, there were different levels of seniority, there were calls and callers that required special attention, and business-to-business support is relationship- or deep expertise–based. Some calls would always go to Damon, some would always go to Cody. Some users had direct numbers to reach their favorite TLC'er, and those calls might never even have a ticket.

Due to this, recorded call efficiency was less than management wanted. While the customers themselves reported that they were *extremely happy* with the service they received, the backlog remained.

Why? Because the competition actually *created more tickets*, which kept the team from making steady progress on the backlog. The game created new anti-collaborative and counter-productive behaviors.

Here is how it works:

You call in and get a Support person. That person is super-friendly, empathetic, and awesome. They get you to describe your issue. They dig into their records to see if that issue has come up before. It hasn't. So, they call up the program you are using and see if they can replicate it. They can't.

Then they want to confer with a colleague who is an expert on your system, but she's on a call and it looks nasty. They ask if they can call you back. An hour later, they get their team member, and they both call you, but you are in a meeting, so you get the voicemail and call them back an hour later, but they're on another call, then the cycle repeats with longer and longer gaps between attempts.

Every support center is run like this. Management treats support like a nuisance, when the entire department is employed solely because the rest of the company is providing substandard or confusing experiences for the customer. Management wants the problem of customers needing help to go away, but rather than fix they product, they abuse the support staff.

Meanwhile, the professionals in the call center are trying desperately to help their customer, but if there's any collaboration needed the "competitive ticket clearing" system is driving people to clear tickets quickly. Quickly—not thoughtfully. In this regime, they aren't going to call you back right away because they are frantically trying to answer other easier calls.

In-process tickets mount, requiring frequent attempts by the support staff to contact the customer instead of finishing up front. This churn is time consuming in terms of calls, staff coordination, and cognitive load (the support staff needs to remember each ticket and what happened until it is done).

Success Is More than Metrics

This dynamic made their customer approval ratings fall from incredibly high (a customer score of 95) to just slightly less than incredibly high (a score of 89).[21] Their bosses became even angrier. *Why weren't these individuals succeeding—are they **afraid of a little competition?**[22]*

The irony was customer approval ratings for the Library Corporation were incredibly impressive. The customers loved their Support people. At TLC user conferences, customers would seek out their favorite support people, bring them gifts, and buy them food. They were rock stars.

The irony is they were successful *despite* the reward system.

But no one inside The Library Corporation, not even them, could see their success. They were incentivized to fail and then blamed that failure on themselves. **They quickly grew to identify with the manufactured**

---

21 For context: The Net Promoter Score uses a scale of –100 to 100, and an above 80 NPS score is considered excellent, world-class. TLC? They had an 89—9 points beyond world class.

22 Don't gloss over this italicized bit, a huge management anti-pattern is blaming professionals for your stupid decisions.

failure. This created turnover for a company located in the middle of a forest surrounded by fields attached to a town of 1,100 people. They could not afford turnover.

> ## BENSON'S LAW OF SELF-DIRECTION
> ### TEAM IDENTITY, POSITIVE OR NEGATIVE, IS ALWAYS INTERNALIZED AND AMPLIFIED.

Internally, customer opinion of the service (success) was not nearly as important to everyone as the 2,000 tickets looming over everyone's heads (minor annoyance). The act of "**Personalization**" is blaming individuals or groups for a systemic failure, and it was killing TLC.

Work is Processed, Not Tackled

The solution was as simple as it was unintuitive. The 2,000-ticket issue was indeed problematic, but it was merely a symptom in an overall systemic breakdown in collaboration. Over-focusing on the individual's *number* of tickets created myriad subsequent problems. **It turned a single systemic challenge into the personal failing of each of the 24 support team members.**

These team members, driven by a numbers target with a misapplied personalized goal, became fixated on the (their) *number*, internalized the problem (it's my fault), and began to pay less attention to customer satisfaction, internal training, or a humane, professional working environment.

Call targets for sales, support, or other customer-facing work always fail because the person answering the phone can't control flow, severity, or attention. This systemic problem wasn't solved by a single person rushing out to tackle a single problem. It required the entire team to process the problem and collaborate on the solution.

Building TLC's Collaboration

To create a professional support system, it was important to meet customer needs and provide a professional working environment that fostered learning and improvement. But first, we needed to identify an achievable shared goal.

The Goal: Create a system that continues to provide world-class service and reduces tickets in the backlog *through healthy operations*.

> PERSONALIZATION –
> THE MISATTRIBUTION
> OF A SYSTEMIC
> PROBLEM TO
> AN INDIVIDUAL
> PROFESSIONAL.

Note that this goal isn't *reduce ticket backlog*. This goal isn't responding to a single metric. This goal directly confronts issues that complicate success. This goal recognizes the needs and interactions of our desired future state require *a collaborative professional system*.

This goal is simultaneously aspirational and achievable. It inspires and provides a target.

There are multiple variables (service and ticket reduction) and a beneficial constraint (healthy operations).

With this goal as a guide, the group can begin to form a professional, collaborative team. The first obstacle this team faced was to change their unhealthy focus on a single toxic metric (ticket reduction) to something more healthy. Their existing operations already proved that the system that created the backlog wouldn't reduce it.

Blame and games in a broken system did not achieve results.

They needed to **create real working teams**.

PROFESSIONALS DISCOVER HEALTHY TEAMS

Even with a Right Environment, we need to have a system of work. Yes, the Support team now had a clear goal that was aspirational and achievable, but goals are just platitudes until they have *structure*.

The TLC Support team couldn't afford this to be another agile retrospective or Lean Kaizen Event where everyone came together, got to vent, agreed on improvements, only to return to the crushing workload and broken system that wouldn't allow improvement to take place.

They needed to create a real culture of continuous improvement and lose the culture of continuously talking about improvement or complaining about the way things are.

Collaborative measures were required to achieve practical and repeatable results. These professionals needed a collaborative, coherent, visual system in which to work with confidence. Their desire for a healthy team required a real, healthy system *of their own design*.

What TLC's Team Did

A healthy system must support the needs of the individuals in the team so they can come together and create legitimate value. Since most industries are sorely hurting in the continuous improvement realm, this can't come from industry standards which are, at best, institutionalized mediocrity. The support team needed to come together and build something that would help their unique professionals with their large number of products help customers worldwide who were all power users. They needed to do better than industry standard (and so do you).

Build coherent teams. First, there needed to be *actual* teams. No longer would a room of alienated individuals suffice. After mapping their value stream[23] (the individual steps they take to create value) and understanding

---

23 Value stream mapping is covered in chapter five.

their needs, our 24 West Virginian individuals *organized themselves* into three teams of eight members.[24]

Create clear, flexible, and professional roles. To ensure that work had a flow beyond "answer phone, talk fast, hang up," the support group made sure each of these teams had two new roles:

▸ a "**Smooth Operator**" who did call triage and handled tickets taking five minutes or less and

▸ a "**Ticket Slayer**" that took calls from 5 to 15 minutes.

Everyone else on a team was a team member who did everything else.

Humane Provisioning: The new roles were high-demand, high-stress positions, so people on the team cycled in and out of those roles during the day. The rest of the team took time-consuming, more involved calls.

Conspicuous Onboarding: New team members would pair with experienced staff. Over the course of several months, they would transition from observing calls to assisting with them, to leading them, then to being on their own. With the Ticket Slayer and Smooth Operator roles, they were able to see and appreciate both the complexity of the work Support did as a whole and the collaborative nature of the individual positions.

Upskilling/Cross-skilling: There was special attention paid to calls that required expertise that could be taught to other team members. At those times (which were common), two staff members would pair so the veteran could teach their colleagues.

Daily Huddles: Each morning, the teams would huddle, discuss the call volumes from the day before, select who would assume Ticket Slayer and Smooth Operator roles and when, discuss any improvements they'd undertaken along with their results, and spent some time with each other mentally and operationally preparing for the day.

---

24 Do not lose sight of the fact that this team built their own way of working. While we helped guide the team, their organization was their own. They needed to own their own processes in order to improve them in the future.

The Deming Meeting: After the huddle, the teams would send a representative to their "Deming Meeting,"[25] a separate huddle with the director of support where they would talk about the improvements that were happening in each team and throughout the company as a whole. Between the actual support work, the huddles, and the Deming Meeting, the Support team had built a complete continuous improvement loop with ample feedback and opportunities to share and extend what they learned.

The Obeya: They built an entry-level always-on Obeya with Personal Kanbans, decision-making boards, and ongoing Deming Meeting experiments. For statistical real-time information, 80-inch screens showed everyone in Support crucial statistics and the status of work being done. Here we see a portion of that Obeya from the early days which shows the then-current 805 tickets in the backlog, 153 tickets on today's Board, 42 open backlog tickets, 44 closed backlog tickets, and 6 of emergency status. The three new teams (Blue, Green, and Red) have individual stats for work underway today. Of course, their Obeya evolved over time.

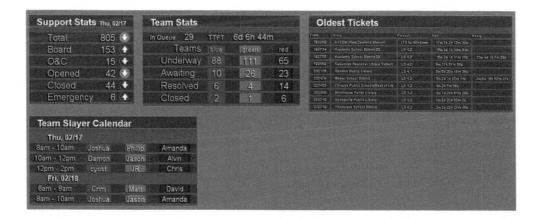

---

25 The TLC teams called it a Deming Meeting after W. Edwards Deming, seen as the progenitor of the continuous improvement movement.

Built to Suit Their Needs: The system helped a team in West Virginia working with libraries around the world satisfy their support needs with 35 products and a vast array of individual problems. This system trained and upskilled effectively in a situation where people were working hard and constantly. These professionals were hungry for focus of both work and improvement to thrive, and they built their culture and their processes to suit.

Collaborative Teams Exceed Expectations

With this new collaborative system in place, work flowed with shocking speed. This team, which was quick to point out they had no formal process training, had, on their own, re-invented a Lean work cell, simply because they needed one. Work cells are made up of small numbers of professionals with known but flexible role definition. This structure creates a stable environment to process expected and unexpected work—meaning, people know what to do, who they are doing it with, and how to get it done together.

The newly effective system immediately increased capacity and professional satisfaction. They were now able to not simply react to the backlog in a panic state, but as professionals solving a real problem. They were able to experience agency. And reap its rewards.

The team needed to address their root causes, not treat the symptoms. Just like with the REDD+ team, they had an apparent problem (which showed pain and triggered action), but now they needed to investigate a real solution.

They asked themselves, *"What is the apparent problem we are trying to solve?"*

The apparent problem was, *"There is an unacceptable backlog that needs to be reduced."*

This led Customer Support, now operating as a group of professional problem solvers, to ask an important question: *"Why is the backlog so high?"* In other words, they stepped past the symptom and started to look for the root causes of why the backlog was so high.

This is good, professional, classic problem-solving behavior. So, why is it remarkable here?

Their focus on creating a collaborative way of working *encouraged that behavior*. Rather than building a system that made them panic, they built one that gave them space to solve problems professionally. This is the nature of agency. Like culture, we treat it like something innate, that just arises from people spontaneously. Yet it is actually something that occurs naturally in an environment that supports its growth.

Even with their very young collaborative system, the team, previously written off by themselves and their management, was able to calm their own overload. This allowed them to focus on the needs of the professionals in their group and the needs of the customers. That focus, in turn, allowed them to rapidly create systems to increase team workflow, decrease pressure on the individuals, and open everyone up to focus on value.

They still used all the industry-standard metrics of support like call duration, time to first touch, and wait times, but they used them as professionals to improve their own system, not as targets to stress over with no ability to actually impact. Their numbers improved because it was inherent in the collaborative system to improve.

With their new-found Right Environment, the team became very excited about reducing the backlog. The old management demand, *"You bad support people reduce that damn backlog you created,"* now became a self-directed, *"Okay, we have a huge backlog we, as professionals, hate. Why is it there in the first place?"*

Agency (respect) allowed them to ask this new, very interesting question (communication) that has a lot of potential answers. Every answer leads the team simultaneously to a reduction of the backlog (flow) and learning about how to make sure that root cause does not happen again (PDSA).

No games, no coercion, just professionals getting their work done collaboratively.

AGENCY, INFORMATION FLOW, AND ABUSE

The team's heroic increase in throughput was in no way caused by reforming the individuals in the group. There was no incentive program that caused the decrease in ticket backlog. Compensation remained static throughout the transition. But the individuals on the team certainly did perform better individually and as a group.

These people solved their problems because they were professionals who now were in charge of, and could act on, their professionalism.

This is agency.

In this case, just a little shared understanding that the team could control their own environment gave already dedicated professionals the ability to create what they needed: better communication with each other and their customers, real-time actionable information that led to better on-the-job training and problem solving, respect for their work, intelligent and flexible workflow, and a cycle of continuous improvement that was nearly effortless.

This wasn't empowerment; it was allowing natural collaboration to happen. Collaboration didn't raise people's performance; it simply removed the impediments to their natural level of performance. This was done in a humane way that worked better than incentives, personal improvement plans, or annual reviews ever could.

Common Worst Practices for Agency

Cooperation begins where competition leaves off.

— FRANKLIN D. ROOSEVELT

In the world of coaching and relationships, there are good practices we would like to follow and worst practices we would like to avoid. It is helpful from time to time to look at what not to do, because our cognitive biases love to trick us into thinking we are doing the right thing when we are, in reality, hurting people.

Management at TLC was trying to help when they set up the incentive program. Annual reviews are an honest attempt at helping people improve. Micromanagers are honestly trying to help workflow and teams succeed. In each of these cases, in very rare instances they can work, but by and large these pervasive worst practices crush agency and rob professionals of the ability to help their teams and their companies.

The fact is, we don't work alone. We process information, value, and meaning into products and services with our team. However, teams can be stunted or even abusive if we don't recognize that it's the individual perspectives and drive of the professionals that makes the team run well.

Agency, transparency, and psychological safety are symbiotic. When a team has a high degree of agency (being able to act with confidence), they must have psychological safety (the ability to act without fear). Teams cannot act with confidence without information and direction (transparency). This may seem like a slight distinction, but we find often that the solutions to confidence hinderances are different than fear generators.

Let's look at a few extremely common worst practices that destroy professionalism and greatly limit the value we create. Please note that there isn't an MBA program in the world that doesn't teach people specifically and pointedly to do these anti-collaborative worst practices.

ANTI-COLLABORATIVE WORST PRACTICE 1:
Infantilization - Tell them what to do

The Action:

Individuals are told what, when, and how to do their work. Ordered around like children, highly paid professionals are infantilized into waiting for the adults to tell them what to do. Once set, a direction cannot be altered. There is a distinct chain of command.

The Reaction:

Professionals cannot act without permission, which creates an explicit system that requires them to expect that they *must* be told when and how to work. The professionals in this system stall out, working slowly to fit and serve the micromanagement bottleneck.

Management sees these highly paid people stall, work only to satisfy deadlines, and stop innovating. Management, who built this management system in the first place, then becomes frustrated. "Why do I have to tell you people everything?" they exclaim in staff meetings.

The Residue:

Management doubles down on telling the professionals how to work. They come to the erroneous conclusion that the professionals are the problem, and they send the professionals to agency and psychological safety training, while doubling down on micromanagement. Telling people what to do becomes a new way to *withhold* information. Management becomes more anti-collaborative, reducing the flow of communication in hopes that less distraction and more direction will help the professionals focus. The system allows no agency, is psychologically combative, and rewards the ill behavior of micromanagement.

ANTI-COLLABORATIVE WORST PRACTICE 2:
Asphyxiation - Withhold crucial information regularly

The Action:

Everyone makes better decisions when they are informed, and yet organizations regularly withhold information or simply have no means of disseminating it. Information asphyxiation happens when:

▸ crucial information becomes someone's property,

▸ a solo task is being completed without conversation or feedback,

▸ information is held by a specific manager until a meeting happens,

▸ information is withheld because someone is afraid to speak about it,

▸ information feels inconvenient and letting others know will create more work.

Information becomes centralized at specific departments or roles and is held there until an anti-collaborative individual makes a decision, disseminates it, weaponizes it, or, worse yet, ignores it. Please note that some of this asphyxiation is due to malevolence, some to the system, and some due to fear.

The Reaction:

No one is searching for the crucial information because they are used to waiting for it or never receiving it. Information-deprived decisions are made without the benefit of information the company already has, and the strength of those decisions suffers. Wrong decisions are common. Good decisions die of asphyxiation.

Professionals find themselves throwing incomplete work away, redoing completed work, or getting into trouble because they make decisions based on the meager information they have and are unaware of the information the company was hiding from them.

The Residue:

These underinformed decisions rarely go well and cause the people who make them to hesitate with future choices. This is a form of **Learned Helplessness**, where the professionals learn to act slowly because they can never be sure if the information they have is complete or up to date. When you starve professionals of information, their decisions become anemic and start to die out.

ANTI-COLLABORATIVE WORST PRACTICE 3:

Shock and Awwww - Surprise them with radical course corrections

The Action:

Surprise is not always a party. Teams get a project, become excited, and start to create something wonderful. They achieve flow, put their thought into a product, start building and learning, feel some professional satisfaction, and start to gel as a team.

Then someone steps in and surprises them. They redirect the project, add a new equally difficult challenge to their workload, or kill the project outright...with no consultation with or discussion from the team. Managers tell them the change is a "company priority", which is exciting to the manager, so they expect it to motivate the team.

The Reaction:

The team, however, sees their plans, their work, their energy lost forever. Their hard work is negated, their learning lost. It's not the first time this happens. In fact, for many teams, this is the status quo.

The team watches as their workflow becomes the diagram on the right.

They rightly ask themselves:

▸ *What the hell was I doing the last two months?*
▸ *Why should I put my effort into this new thing?*

We see not just learned helplessness here; we also see Loss Aversion, a reaction people have when they start something, invest themselves in it, and then would rather complete it than change. Loss Aversion often promotes the status quo in unhealthy ways, but in this case it is simply the team wanting to finish what they started. The team has put effort into the original project, and even if the second project is awesome, they are still suffering a loss. The more time, effort, or enthusiasm the team and the individuals invested in the project, the greater the loss.

The System is Being Jerked Around

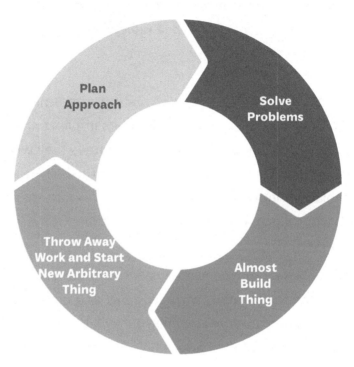

The Residue:

If these course changes are frequent, unanticipated, and poorly explained, the teams will lose faith that their work will be completed, let alone valued. Agency is quickly destroyed. Why would anyone act in a system that produces no value?

ANTI-COLLABORATION WORST PRACTICE 4:
Judgement without Information—Have demeaning performance reviews

The Action:

If we don't provide professionals with real-time information about what work is in flight, who is doing the work, and its implications, they are left in the dark. We have built a system that guarantees they will be underinformed and therefore underperform. Ignorant of the hell we are subjecting them to, we blame them for underperforming. We want them to perform, so we have performance reviews. We can't fine tune the system, but surely we can fine tune the people.

Performance reviews are considered necessary because we have historically lacked the ability to create a professional and collaborative working environment. They are an indicator that our ability as individuals, teams, and a company to know what is happening on a daily basis has utterly failed.

We resort to sporadic check-ins between two overwhelmed people (reviewer and reviewee) who only remember the systemic bad things that happened, and then they co-conspire to figure out ways the reviewee could improve their personal performance, magically saving both people from having to think about that bad thing for up to a year. It's basically waving a dead chicken in a confessional.

The Reaction:

The system (yes, this is true for 360 reviews too) requires both reviewer and reviewee to create lists of successes and failures, most of which are systemic happenstance, all of which are blamed on and internalized by the individual. Goals met are lauded; goals not met are fretted over. Both people come away, even in the event of a "good review", with largely inactionable recommendations concocted by two people trying to fix a person who is simply reacting in a broken system.

The Residue:

People *internalize* unsatisfactory work that they helped create. Inside, they feel they *know* they were responsible for this flawed work, and they inappropriately hold themselves *accountable*. This false accountability means in the future they will seek assurances that their work will be successful. They will over-define work to be done, over-plan, limit options, and try their best to hope that problems that arise will go away. When they don't, they, in turn, will look for the people *accountable*. It will not occur to them that their rigid plans caused the failure, because their plans were *flawless*. They will unwittingly play a game that protects them from their next annual review, because the goal is to have a good review...not be attentive to the needs of the work and the people around you.

The individual nature of annual reviews in a largely collaborative environment always works to the detriment of culture, product, and quality.

The Systematic Structure of Siloed Sub-Humanity

If we are to build these collaborative systems and they are to work, it is helpful to look closely at how the typical corporate organization destroys individuals, teams, and value as a matter of course.

Let's do this quickly, by discussing the org chart, perhaps the most abused worst practice of them all.

Organizational charts have been around for over a hundred years. They are generally cascading diagrams with a super-powerful person at the top and then graduated steps of increasingly disenfranchised people.

They were originally created to understand which people in the organization were under the control of specific managers and how information flowed through the company. Those are information and organizational silos.

The kind way of looking at this chart is to assume that information was gathered by the people working or by the managers and efficiently distributed up and down the silos. However, this 19th-century level of efficiency was created when the cost of information exchange was incredibly high. People and paper were the network.

Over the course of the 20th century, this previously efficient system became the embodiment of bureaucracy and sluggishness. Here in the 21st century, it is counter-productive and simply an excuse to continue to create and promote silos.

The hierarchy of the org chart provides natural bottlenecks for information, decisions, and action. The necessity of the four anti-collaborative best practices become clear.

What we see in this diagram are the surface or official silos, each with barriers for information flow, accountability cascades, and pre-designed bottlenecks. We see the power dynamics. We see the dysfunction. We can see where agency stalls and learned helplessness takes over.

Infantilization: The system invents a role of silo-keeper, an *infantilizer* driving micromanagement. This role is not necessary for the healthy operations of a 21st-century business but was crucial in the industrial era.

Asphyxiation: Silo-keepers benefit from their darker boxes, requiring that people in their silo talk to them first before talking to their peers in other silos if something needs to be done. This is where *asphyxiation* was born. Information, expectations, and context get stuck behind organizational bottlenecks—hindering the flow of vital oxygen for the system of work.

Shock and Awwww: Silos create massive communication and information bottlenecks that drive lopsided funding, political squabbles, and sluggish and annoying barriers to company success. The results are unexpected directions (*Shock and Awwww*) to the team that create avenues for failure, cost overruns, and rework.

Judgement without Information: When the negative impacts of these silos become evident, we find silos not to be self-healing but self-preserving. The cascading blame trail allows the (mis)identification of a scapegoat who is then dealt with to save the silo-leader (*Judgement without Information*). These actions centralize information, slow improvement, and frustrate work completion. Silos generate fear.

Silos always limit agency.

The Final Residue of Worst Practices

Each of these worst practices is a system in and of itself and becomes part of a "wrong environment" of working. They are extremely common; every company has at least one of these active right now, and almost every company has all three. Performance reviews being the most obvious, these are all expected parts of a management system and primary actors in destroying agency and stopping individuals in teams from creating value.

How might we avoid this trap?

CHOOSE AGENCY

At Turner, Kevin's sense of agency was boosted by the format provided in his Obeya. He and his support network were able to transform from a person doing work and some bosses into a team, where people, regardless of station, knew when their input was *required*.

Collaboration happened not because Kevin was deficient, but because the work required it. Kevin did not have to make a humble request to his superiors; they were part of the team. There is an inherent respect that is generated when work is being done in an understood, professional, and coherent way.

We can build architectures of agency.

Our call center team were all expert problem solvers and customer relations ambassadors stuck in an environment that stunted their every action. Yet they were reviewed, graded, and reprimanded on their performance individually. And while the system was dehumanizing, they were ironically evaluated as individual humans.

No incentives, no negative reinforcement, no threats to their livelihood, can get people to perform well in an environment which does not give them the freedom or even the ability to perform well.

When Kevin and the TLC'ers were individuals, they were silos of one. A single unit fighting to provide value against a tsunami of anti-collaborative practices.

The moment they were in systems designed to promote good collaborative work, they performed better because the system supported, expected, and rewarded it.

With TLC, the moment they understood they had agency, they built a system. They gathered into teams and focused customer service as a coordinated group. Sometimes that involved training, sometimes it involved more than one person, sometimes it was assignment. The work, not the silo or the title, dictated the appropriate response.

The TLC team went from focusing on one metric and considering themselves as failures (when they were not), to having a real-time, always-on Obeya, constant collaboration with their team members, and a mutual training program that let nearly everyone work together. Increased communication and respect allowed them to build the relationships necessary to achieve flow and engage in PDSA.

The team had architected a system that provided agency through collaboration. This is how value is truly created.

TOWARDS A COLLABORATIVE ARCHITECTURE

We've seen how anti-collaborative systems entrench themselves, yet also how simple they can be. The good news is, as we could see with Kevin's example, there is a place for leadership, for new workers, for experience, and for professionalism. We don't have to go full-on anarchy or holacracy or multi-million-dollar restructuring. We just need to *see* where information, work, and agency are impeded and remove the impediments.

Balancing Structure and Agency

The Two Painful Truths of Working Together:

1. The stronger the silo walls, the higher the costs of doing business.

2. Lack of team (silo) definition leaves people uncertain how and when to act.

These two painful truths often work together to withhold information, ensuring people are underinformed and don't know how or when they can help. Collaborative systems must provide appropriate and immediate information to professionals so they know when they can help and act with confidence.

In West Virginia, access to one simple piece of information led the new teams to rapidly solve a problem. The Obeya screens for the support team showed them, in real time, their shared work and shared responsibilities. Once, in a call with their CTO, Jabe, I said, "Hey, I noticed that there are some really old tickets in the system, can you put an aging summary on the support board?" It was all digital, so he simply said, "Sure." He typed for a minute, and then I saw it appear; the team in West Virginia saw it appear as well on their Obeya screens.

It was ugly. There were tickets in there that were incredibly old, some marked urgent.

I said, "Hey, that's ugly; how should we discuss this with the team?"

He said, "I don't know, we could…"

Then one of the entries disappeared, then another, then another. One was checked out to a person and immediately annotated. Yet another was combined with a current issue for the same customer. They disappeared so fast that this screenshot missed the very old ones.

Communication and Triggers: The professionals saw something they were responsible for and that they were professionally dissatisfied with. They immediately and effectively pulled this new information into their existing work. They were able to do this because they had the structure of their new teams and roles, control over their flow of work, and a desire to make customers happy.

Before their collaborative system, if someone noticed there were old tickets in the system, they'd say, "someone should fix that crap" and go back to rapidly answering calls. They would have waited for a command before action.

Their new flexible structure and agency was obviously more responsive than the rigid silos. Value creation was immediate. Acting with confidence wasn't just doing what you wanted; it was doing what was needed, when it was needed.

Agency suddenly becomes something more. It's not merely professionals acting of their own volition; it becomes your company being instantly able to seize opportunities as they arise.

CREATING VALUE THROUGH TEAMS OF INDIVIDUALS

Individuals in teams create value.

We've taken a look at how we create value. We discussed what the creation of value looks like structurally—how we can build our own systems of creating and providing value that reflect our context and change based on our experiences and learning.

Design-Build: The TLC team showed us that success didn't lie in industry best practices, but easily stemmed from knowing what roles, responsibilities, and reactions the work required. They reorganized in their own way, meeting the specific needs of those individuals in those teams providing that value.

Old Systems Reimagined: Their Deming Meetings were quality circles. Their teams were work cells. These were inventions of theirs with precedent. If we had taught them about quality circles or work cells, they would have constantly asked, *are we doing quality circles right?* As it was, the systems they created were entirely theirs, and those systems existed, improved, and evolved through the creativity and professionalism of that TLC support team.

Informed by Industry Standards: Their teams' focus on continuous improvement and the advent of the Ticket Slayer and Smooth Operator created a minimal structure that increased every industry performance metric while focusing on none of them in particular. The collaborative system met the metrics in a way no demand from on high ever could.

Agency is the Prerequisite: For the TLC team and for Turner, agency created through collaboration makes the actions of value delivery clear. They removed the impedances of information flow, decision making, and action. This wasn't empowerment; it was simply allowing good professionals to be good professionals.

The Next Step: Now our favorite management buzz words can start to be realized for perhaps the first time. We can pivot, continuously improve, self-organize, actualize, achieve flow...all those things we talked about previously without context, now have context. They are all just decisions or outcomes from a healthy system of professionals learning together to create something.

We need to bring these components together in an Obeya that serves our Right Environment. This requires deeper dives into both Obeya and Right Environment construction. But before we do that, we need to cover the system itself. There are some common derailers of collaborative systems, functional roadblocks we commonly see in the most earnest of teams and orgs. They are bottlenecks, feedback, and complexity.

Collaborating in the Real World

BOTTLENECKS, FEEDBACK, AND COMPLEXITY

SEEING THE PRISON THAT IS OUR SILO

On a drab Seattle morning, I sat in a conference room of a company we will call FungiCorp with 16 scared product managers. They were despondent, worried, fearful. They were drowning in unrealistic demands, slipping schedules, cost overruns, and simple work left incomplete. Their project plans showed they had enough staff, enough time, enough money, but nothing was getting done.

Blame was a commodity in highly active trading. The PMs loved each other as people but were fed up with each other as professionals. It was exhausting listening to the litany of crimes against humanity charges the room was dredging up. Everyone was angry and feeling personally attacked.

It was a fight or flight playhouse, with no option for flight.

After a few hours of this, we broke for lunch. Amusingly, they all went off to eat and laugh together because *they liked each other*.

We needed to change the conversation from blame to the work that needed to be done. While blame was easy to generate, the only real fault

Kanban

Just My Team 10	Team One Shared 2	Team Two Shared 2	Team Three Shared 2	Team Four Shared 1	Database Team Shared 13
Recreate margin system	Baker model engine	Deliver results to customer faster	Submarine Functionality System	Increase revenue from upsells	Disperse Junk Data
Return to 2017 Functionality	Project Kirkwell	Integration with Venmo	Integration with Visicalc		Catalog More
Interior logic					Gather data
Solve the crashing on enter					Interior accounting tasks
Dipole Dipswitch Deprecation					Distribute More Carothers
Depreciate Downward					Manage binary choices
Payment system upgrades					Pescatore Divisions Update
Integration with Paypal					Distribute monthlies
Integration with Stripe					Gordian Knot Routine
User data leakage					User data available for public download
					Get db crashing issue solved
					User data corrupted
					User data disappearing

here was that each silo (strong team) believed they were the most important silo, and the others were somehow conspiring against them. Strong teams led to tribalism, where their team's needs were more important than the company or other teams. This is how isolationism works. Success is over-defined in your silo, every other silo is a threat.

When they returned, each team visualized their work: what they were doing on their own and the work that relied on other teams. The first column shows work they did alone, the other columns held tasks that were shared.

Immediately it became clear that everyone was relying on one team: their database group. The room immediately pounced on the database group. Aha! We have finally found the end of our blame trail...IT IS YOU!

Tribal behavior became a call for justice. Why was this team so terrible and awful?

Accordingly, the database group at the center of the blame, just as we saw in West Virginia, had already internalized the failure and was quick to own how awful they were.

We're sorry we're so slow, we've tried to raise our velocity/throughput/ productivity, but we're just so slow and we don't know why...

Needless to say, the database group was not awful. They were a bottleneck in a system.

They were the bottleneck because there was an overwhelming amount of work blindly pushed at them. **Blindly pushed work** is work assigned with no understanding of capacity or ability to complete the work. Push was not a problem with the database team; it was a problem with the way the company structured its work. The business priorities of the company inadvertently pushed too much work at one resource at one time.

The database group was never consulted when new projects started but were always there to receive surprise work requests with short deadlines when the other teams finally figured out what they thought they needed from the database group. The other teams were then annoyed to find out that the database group's professionals had questions about what they were being asked to do, why, and if that was the best way to structure the work.

Common anti-collaborative patterns like not paying attention to what others are doing, not visualizing work, and not planning together created an undue burden on a team. Unexpected work piled up and created a bottleneck of underdefined work. That bottleneck was then personified as a problem with the people. The systemic problem became seen as a personal favor.

Bottleneck 101

Bottlenecks are common and *almost always* come from poor planning, emergent workload, or lack of communication. They are also almost always blamed on a hapless manager or other scapegoat who happens to be holding the work at the time. Blame feels right here because we expect work to be done by individuals, and when something collapses, it must also be the fault of *an individual*.

Businesspeople call this institutional scapegoating as **accountability**. The rush to judgement is wrong; this is dangerous, and it is a root cause for most inhumane businesses. It's also, unfortunately, all part of being human. In behavioral economics, this is known as **Fundamental Attribution Error**: attributing the success or failure of a system to an individual. Its fundamental tool is blame. Blame is a false solution born from a lack of desire to actually solve problems. Fire or discipline the person "accountable", and the problem will magically disappear. Blame seems easy and logical, but it provides false certainty, makes it seem like we've acted, and leaves the root causes of our problems active and festering.

Responsibility, as we've discussed, is the professional response to any given situation. When change happens, problems arise, or opportunities present themselves, responsible behavior triggers *a group of people* to look for root causes and find solutions.

Eliyahu Goldratt was the patron saint of bottleneck relief. His book, *The Goal*,[26] showed us that our capacity overall was equal to the capacity of our tightest bottleneck. He let us know that when faced with a bottleneck our primary job was to understand it and relieve it.

When we find a bottleneck, Goldratt told us to *exploit it,* by which he meant making the most of or getting the most value from something. Our problems reveal weaknesses in our system that we can fix. When we fix bottlenecks, the system that was a liability becomes an asset.

We have a choice. **Status Quo:** We can ignore bottlenecks to and deal with the perpetual, predictable, and pointless failures. Or **Professionalism:** we can acknowledge they are natural developments in any system and simply address them honestly and collaboratively.

Pro Tip: It is nearly impossible for one person to single-handedly solve a bottleneck.

------

26 Goldratt, E. M., & Cox, J. (2016). *The Goal: A Process of Ongoing Improvement.*

Bottlenecks Do Not Happen in Isolation: It turns out that solving problems like bottlenecks requires psychological safety (you need to be able to act with confidence) and, almost always, *collaboration between different parts of the company*. You see, we *want* so desperately to be able to take the lazy path, blame someone for it, have them "shape up", and make the bottleneck disappear.

Bottlenecks Are Part of Your Job: If we are collaborating with others and continuously improving, we will *want* to not only see where the bottleneck is, but how it is being solved. We want the discovery and the removal of bottlenecks to be a natural part of doing our work better. They are not to be feared.

Using Bottlenecks and Visualization to Help the Database Group

Now that we have identified the bottleneck and can view this problem as something that has been created by the system, we can work as a team to make things better.

In the big collaboration image exercise, the Fungible PMs could see that the database group was overloaded. They could see that other teams are available for work and were relying on that work getting done. Surely, that would inspire collaboration.

Here's the sad thing. Everyone, including the database managers and the database team, wanted the database group to solve the problem **on their own**. The database professionals thought that they were failing because they couldn't do the work. The other teams thought they were just stupid database people.

So, we changed the visualization.

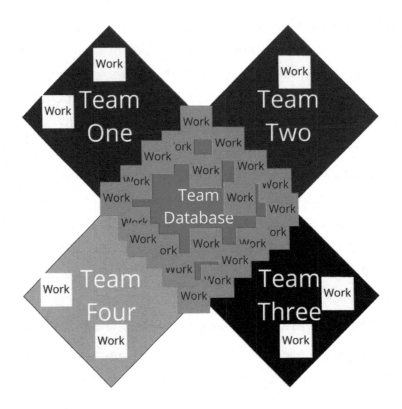

The team rearranged the work by placing the Database team in the center. They put the bottleneck in the middle of the diagram.

The focus of the work went from "what each team had to do" to the *impact on the database group by the other teams*. The change in perspective was an instant and embarrassing epiphany for all.

They all realized they were holding the database team *accountable* for unplanned and underexplained work that was killing the database group.

By the nature of the work residing both in Team Database and the other team's space, *responsibility* for that work became clear.

Very quickly, blame-happy product owners looked at the table, the wall, out the window...or in some general direction not populated with the database team. Toxic blame was shifting; productive collaboration was now possible.

Everyone could see the impacts of the anti-collaborative system. They could see the isolation of the database silo, the lack of cross-silo communication, the horrific lack of workflow planning, and the unreasonable expectations of an underinformed system. Everyone was ready to stop focusing on "my work" and begin on "our work".

Collaboratively Exploiting and Relieving the Bottleneck

Exploiting a bottleneck is a period of extremely heavy collaboration. People come together and swarm on a problem, keep the system running while it is being fixed, and end up with a better way of working. Kim, Behr, and Spafford wrote a beautiful little novel called *The Phoenix Project*[27] about this.

FungiCorp has a huge bottleneck that is greatly hindering the progress of everything in the company, and they have two choices.

1. Continue to force unhappy professionals to do more under-planned work than a group four times their size could handle? Or

2. Ask almost everyone in the company to focus on the bottleneck for a few weeks, get a vast majority of the work done, and plan a better way to hand off work in the company going forward?

Everyone wanted option one, but we were able to finally argue for option two.[28]

---

27 Kim, G., Behr, K., & Spafford, G. (2018). *The Phoenix Project: A Novel about IT, DevOps, and Helping Your Business Win.*

28 Everyone wanted option (1). Business is, and indeed human beings are, that stereotypical guy who will drive for hours the wrong way rather than stopping to ask for directions. We are ruled by sunk cost fallacy—a cognitive bias that says if we sink a bit of ourselves into something, we are very reluctant to stop to improve it or switch to something better. In this case, every person on every team who was working on projects would have to interrupt their projects to fix this bottleneck. That is a lot of cumulative sunk cost fallacy.

Make the System Work: In the Lean Startup[29] world, there is a concept of *concierge service* when inventing a new product. Say we want to create a system that automates filling out mortgage forms for borrowers. First, we'd test the market by hiring a bunch of people to fill out the forms for people. During that time, we could offer an expensive-to-provide service that provides the same value as our assumed product, but we would learn what the market really wants, what the market really needs, what parts of the process are easily automated, and a whole lot about the snags you might find in filling out forms for people.

The concierge service for fixing this bottleneck was to swarm on the work, plan it jointly, and to be there the moment the database team needed them...no matter what the request. And yes, they would be giving up headcount to the database team during this exercise.

All that work that touched multiple teams needed to be jointly planned, jointly defined, and scheduled in a way that made more sense than "the CEO demands that you satisfy Team Two now."

Build the Obeya: Planning and day-to-day operations of organizing disparate work, figuring out who would pair or mob on what work, and how this experience would result in a workflow that didn't let this bottleneck re-occur required an Obeya. We needed a conference room, where the work be clearly visualized and all the individual challenges of the work would be clear.

See Problems Immediately: The group made a rule that that all challenges would have strike teams of at least two people, whose work would be visualized. As these teams worked, they, of course, found new problems that were so significant that they became known as "LittleNecks" or problems that could be their own mini-bottlenecks. The team agreed to be on the hunt for other LittleNecks that, when found, would be immediate news

---

29 Blank, S., & Dorf, B. (2012). *The Startup Owner's Manual: The Step-by-Step Guide to Building a Great Company.* Pescadero: K & S Ranch Press.

for all and the group would visualize and swarm on.

Use the Obeya: Visualizations must be seen to be valuable. The Obeya had to be used. All meetings happened in the Obeya, where some visualizations were placed on rolling white boards and moved during working sessions to other conference rooms or places around the office because there was that much collaboration going on. People and teams actively updated visualizations in the Obeya as they worked.

No Professional Left Behind: No work was assigned to an individual, and no teams were pervasive, meaning that strike teams always had different people. The volume of work and the focus on the mission-critical part of the company meant every morning there was a huddle with all involved (over 75 people). In that huddle, architecture and issues being tackled that day were reviewed.

Keep Work Humane: Watching the teams, you could see that they took regular breaks and walked the floor to see what others were doing. There were bottles of water on the tables, people were always getting snacks for each other from the kitchen. Humane work created safe focus and a sustainable pace.

Acknowledge Progress: Slowly, just like with TLC, the tickets subsided, and, as they did, we learned how the company as a whole could collaborate better. Boards appeared showing the "burndown" of their shared backlog. The percentage of the backlog complete was a primary metric, but so were bugs and rework. The team wasn't just progressing productively; they were progressing effectively.

Increase Professionalism: The teams created new collaborative but stringent rules around quality control, review points, and education of colleagues. Pairing, mobbing, and peer review became not just necessary, but comfortable. Because the work *was focused*, it became easier for everyone to learn. The experience no one wanted to tackle had become fun and productive.

Evolve Tasks and Work: They started to gear the tasks to improve the operations of the database group and their processes overall. Better schemas, tighter security, ease of integration, etc. These historically sticky problems became easier to solve and implement with the corporate focus.

After three weeks[30] of grueling work, the bottleneck had been solved. The database team (and everyone else) were heroes, the customers had a better experience and greater security, and new collaborative planning routines helping discover and relieve other bottlenecks around the company had been implemented.

WHY THIS IS INCREDIBLY RARE

Most bottlenecks we discover, even ones more obvious and destructive than this one, remain long after we depart. There is simply no will to solve these big problems because they involve interrupting *schedule*. Schedule becomes the greatest barrier to psychological safety ever devised. Professionals fear it and budget much more than retribution.

> SCHEDULE BECOMES THE GREATEST BARRIER TO PSYCHOLOGICAL SAFETY EVER DEVISED.

This is also rare because so few of us have any real experience in problem solving as a professional activity. We are much more focused on "getting things done", not getting the *right* things done or making sure the right things *can even be done in the first place*. The allure of wasteful productivity always seems to win over the sure win of effectiveness.

---

30 Three weeks doesn't sound like much, but getting the C-Suite and Board of Directors to essentially take the entire company off the product development path for an entire month was a monumental achievement.

Visualization Ensures Professional Action

No one in this chapter's story, not even the database team that was the victim of the process, had the internal political will to solve this bottleneck. There were plenty of MBAs in the company that read Goldratt and had to regurgitate his words on paper to get their degree. Still, they didn't recognize a painfully obvious and easily solvable bottleneck as it slowly tore the company apart.

They saw the work, but not the broken system. They blamed the people, while ignoring and neglecting the broken system. The broken system thrived while they scurried around looking busy.

Their professional neglect allowed a small problem to scale into a nearly fatal one.

It wasn't until the problem was visualized in an undeniable way that the teams and management agreed to do something about it. Before we fixed this, there were security breaches, system outages, schedule delays, people were fired, consultants were hired, paid, and let go...simply because productivity always took precedence over effectiveness. They spent a lot of money and disappointed a lot of people.

With the initial visualizations, we were able to see, understand, and share (sell) the narrative of the problem. We were able to give it visual weight and then convince others that all those sticky notes represented risk.

Triggering Action

In Lean, there is something called an Andon. This is a tool and a behavior from manufacturing where, when a problem is spotted, stops the line. And by that, I mean it physically halts all production. The problem is then quickly and collaboratively solved or escalated, and the line is started back up again. You can imagine how this increases the urgency to solve problems.

Think of this as a moment where productivity is forced to wait for effectiveness.

It can be a button, or it can be a cord, but sometimes you have to stop the line. We are singularly unwilling to do this in knowledge work. On an assembly line, we can *see* the impact of a defect, and with the Andon we can see the urgency. In knowledge work, problems pile up, cost money, time, and professionalism, and simply fester.

There is an oft-told and perhaps somewhat apocryphal story about the Andon. General Motors learned about the Andon cords used at Toyota. They had some Toyota people come and coach them. GM put up Andon cords, line workers started pulling them, all looked good.

Toyota consultants came back a while later, and the GM plant manager proudly told them, "These things really work! When we first installed them we were pulling them hundreds of times a day. Now we are doing maybe one or two pulls a week!"

The Toyota consultants looked at him sadly and said, "We pull ours thousands of times a day."

Each Andon pull is a *feedback loop*. When you stop the line thousands of times a day, you learn thousands of times a day. The Andon is a shared, collaborative mechanism that triggers us all to look for things to improve, see problems early, and solve them. The mechanism is key to a culture that values responsible professional behavior over mindless negligent productivity.

The database team's massive bottleneck was due entirely to negligence. A lack of collaborative planning, collaborative staff allocation, and collaborative learning meant that silos kept churning when the overall system could not produce anything of value.

Here is the thing: the more the problem grew, the more pressure grew on the woman who led the database group. The more people blamed her, talked about her lack of leadership, her prowess, etc. The more that happened, the more it was impossible for her to ask for help or act with confidence. Like any other person, she began to blame herself for the problem, which opened the door for others to do so even more. The feedback she was receiving was 100% negative and 0% collaborative. No one offered to help.

She was at the end of what disaster experts call an **event cascade** or a **failure cascade**. A lot of little events and some dumb luck led to a large amount of work in the company as a whole requiring substantive changes or time-consuming work in a single department.

For her sake and for the sake of the company, we needed to transform this systemic victim into a hero.

USING FEEDBACK AND PDSA TO SOLVE BOTTLENECKS

If you read *The Goal*, *The Phoenix Project*, or *Learning to See*,[31] you will find passion plays about people facing not only bottlenecks, but the predictably ineffective way that business responds to them. In these cases, problems are solved by collaboration. The specifics of the Theory of Constraints or A3 thinking are extremely important for solving their particular problems, but in each case the *collaboration* between people is the secret sauce.

Collaboration is entirely the action of professionals working together to create value, in this case solving problems and creating more stable ways of working. Stability makes work more predictable, deals with issues honestly as they arise, and works to avoid issues from happening in the first place.

---

31 Shook, J., Lean Enterprise Institute. (2010). *Managing to Learn: Using the A3 Management Process to Solve Problems, Gain Agreement, Mentor and Lead.* Cambridge, MA: Lean Enterprise Institute.

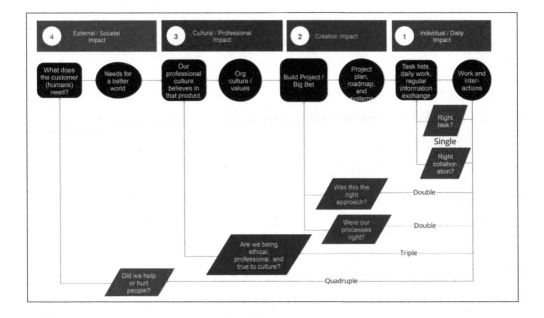

Management theorist and organizational development trailblazer Christopher Argyris[32] teaches us that there are levels of learning loops that provide different feedback to professionals so they can act with confidence and make good decisions. These loops have different impacts on our work and must all be present to do daily work, and certainly to solve a crisis like the database team's catastrophic bottleneck.

Loop 1 (single loop learning): Individual/Daily Impact: Work and interactions provide immediate feedback to question if work currently being done is appropriate and being done in the right way.

Loop 2 (double loop learning): Creation Impact: Kanbans,[33] roadmaps, dashboards, and our Obeya give us constant project-level feedback on the progress being made, the approach we are taking, and the processes by which we are collaborating and producing.

Loop 3 (triple loop learning): Cultural Professional Impact: Are we

---

32 https://www.gse.harvard.edu/news/13/11/remembering-professor-chris-argyris

33 Benson, J., & DeMaria, B. T. (2011). *Personal Kanban: Mapping Work, Navigating Life.*

being true to our culture? Is our way of working stopping us from achieving our Right Environment? What are we doing regularly that undermines our culture? How is our culture helping bolster our professionalism?

Loop 4 (quadruple loop learning): External/Societal Impact: How is our product helping or hurting our customers? How is our product helping or hurting the world at large?

Feedback is not Comments

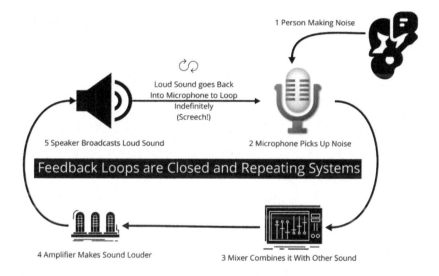

1 Person Making Noise

Loud Sound goes Back
Into Microphone to Loop
Indefinitely
(Screech!)

5 Speaker Broadcasts Loud Sound

2 Microphone Picks Up Noise

Feedback Loops are Closed and Repeating Systems

4 Amplifier Makes Sound Louder

3 Mixer Combines it With Other Sound

We fundamentally misunderstand the word **feedback**. Feedback isn't comments, constructive criticism, or one person simply responding once. Feedback is when you have a signal that is broadcast and reintroduced into the system that provides the signal. It is recursive. It builds. In the music studio or an auditorium, it can be painful to hear.

But feedback can be controlled. It's used effectively in nearly every rock album produced since proto-punk Gary Burger of the Monks dropped his guitar in the 1960s.[34]

---

34 Shaw, T., & Klemke, A. (1994). *Black Monk Time*. Carson City, NV: Carson Street Pub....And yes, there are a million artists that claim responsibility for doing feedback first, including John Lennon and Chuck Berry. So, just give Gary props anyway.

More than a response: We believe we can do something until it is almost done and give it to someone else for comment and that is feedback. That is wrong. That is reaction. Feedback is when we set up a recursive system of signal generation, response, signal alteration due to the response, and over and over again until we release the sound. This book had commenters, and it had people giving feedback. The difference? We sent the book to commenters, and they provided comments. Feedback, with Tonianne and Tom, was one-on-one, reading and editing the book with very tight cycles of work/response/alteration. Both have a place, but if you don't have true collaborative feedback, you are merely fishing for compliments.

The System of Professional Feedback

The Plan-Do-Study-Adjust (PDSA) cycle is unfortunately most often seen as the outmoded Plan-Do-Check-Act (PDCA) cycle. This can be called the Deming-Shewhart cycle, co-named for W. Edwards Deming and his mentor Walter Shewhart. The cycle tracks anything we do from doing the dishes to building a rocket through four concurrent stages of visioning, action, reflection, and improvement.

What PDSA Means:

Plan: *The period between the inception of a potential action and the beginning of carrying out that action.*

Do: *The period where you are taking conscious and concerted actions to get the work done and achieve the goals of the plan.*

Study: *The act of being thoughtful about our plans, our actions, and the results. How close did we come to achieving our goals?*

Adjust: *The act of improvement.*

PDSA Is Simultaneously Single, Double, and Triple Loop Learning: The PDSA graphic above shows a simple and misleading loop that waits for a stage to be completed to engage learning. Human beings can't operate like this. Learning isn't a scheduled event; it happens all the time.

In knowledge work, we have different opportunities to deploy the results of our learning. Sometimes we'll have to wait to engage in an improvement, but often professionals have the ability to engage in change at any time. With discretion, learning and improvement can happen, which the context allows.

How PDSA Impacts Decision Making

PDSA, as both a system and an ethic, urges us to build ways of working with rapid feedback loops and opportunities for immediate change that provide an effective treatment for Generalized Annoyance Disorder. We build the single, double, and triple loops to simultaneously improve product, process, and culture with minimal effort.

This means that any decisions we are making will naturally become more collaborative and better informed. *We are paying attention. We have a system to keep us present, professional, and connected.*

Why PDSA and Not PDCA

Plan/Do/Study/Adjust versus Plan/Do/Check/Act Words matter. They are psychological triggers for action or reaction. Therefore words are also an integral part of systems. There is a huge difference between "check" and "study", which is why Deming changed it 30 years ago.

"Check" is a mechanical and scientific action of externalized observation. You check your oil levels on your car. You check your temperature. You check the box on the form. Check is an action that can be fulfilled with a casual glance.

"Study" is active investment in the work at hand. The professional that is studying is closely observing, watching how changes occur, and gaining an understanding of the relationships between their actions and the quality of the product or service.

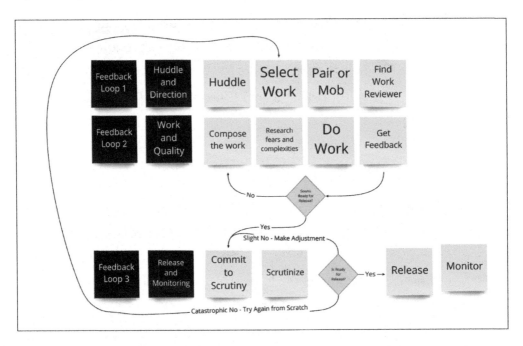

Because FungiCorp's crisis was so extreme, we had to create an effective, but costly, collaborative solution. A more collaborative and visual planning system up front would have easily avoided this whole mess because people would have *seen* the bottleneck before it started. The sentence, "Hey, in Q3 it looks like a huge amount of work relies on the database group. Maybe we should spread that out," would have been obvious.

Here we see the workflow during this time of crisis. We knew that acting with confidence required everyone on the team to understand the systems of their work. Feedback loops (single, double, and triple) are explicitly designed into this system, making it a good lesson for how they could solve this problem together and work better together (and avoid these situations) in the future.

The database group was a bottleneck for everyone's planned and unplanned work. The amount of work they were required to do that focused on a handful of political, legal, and technological systems created even more complexity and opportunities for both technical and political[35] failure. The fact that data is at the heart of all digital systems meant that every decision that they made had ramifications in the overall architecture and growth strategy in the future.

The Database Group were hardworking professionals stuck in what business calls a **cost center**.[36] Their work did not directly sell the product, so they and their mission-critical work were demeaned and sidelined during planning and strategy meetings. Their work touched every aspect of the company, but they weren't sexy. The corporate priority of strong data should never have been in question.

To professionally respond to this crisis of complexities, the database team became **the emergency database team**, now roughly the size of the company. This new collaborative and temporary team needed to solve all the problems (known and found) with people they hadn't previously worked with and in configurations that would change from day to day.

This new collaborative group required the following:

‣ **Have group focus:** everyone needed to stay informed,

‣ **Plan like it was important:** plan upcoming work as a group (the more often you plan, the less time it takes),

‣ **The right work at the right time:** select specific work from the options,

---

35 Politics is when two or more people have two or more ideas of how to approach a problem and then entrench over conflicting options. Usually, these conflicts are irrelevant and don't enhance solving the problem logically. Politics is abated when people collaborate to find mutually acceptable solutions.

36 Cost centers are seen as pure overhead even when they are a crucial component of a healthy organization. Because they are classified as overhead, their budgets and headcounts are held to a bare minimum, and their actions are scrutinized heavily. Almost every cost center is abused in this way, stifling their ability to increase the value of the company as a whole.

▸ **Create dynamic "tiger teams":** teams composed of people with the knowledge to deal with specific work (no more dependencies),

▸ **Feedback:** have ample feedback and QA while designing and coding (through pairing or peer review),

▸ **Get fixes active:** release into a live environment,

▸ **Test immediately and often:** test in a live environment,

▸ **Get more feedback:** get feedback and QA while doing so,

▸ **Pay attention and learn things:** learning is visible and a core component of the work,

▸ **Pay attention and do things:** spot new emergent work and get that work into the planning system,

▸ **Pay attention to your surroundings:** stay abreast of everything happening on any other tiger teams, and

▸ **Visualize the work and stay connected:** build a single Obeya that would provide all this information in a coherent way.

Does that sound difficult and convoluted? This is how Turner builds buildings, how crisis teams respond to emergencies, and how good software gets built.

This is what they should have been doing every day before the bottleneck occurred. If they had been operating in this collaborative of a system, this large-scale costly systemic failure would likely have never occurred.

We want to build systems that provide the information individuals and teams need to work together in a composed and professional way. This is the nature of collaboration.

The Planning Loop

When you have many people working towards a common goal, they will invariably have different roles and responsibilities. If that goal is in any way pressurized by time, budget, or political weight, it is also necessary for these roles and responsibilities to change regularly.

Knowledge work does not have the predictability of an assembly line. The nature of the key Lean concept of variation is wildly different. In knowledge work, the rate of variation in our work is significantly higher. We are starting with more vague directives, learning more, and our products are less standardized. In the service of improvement and innovation, variation is more acceptable in knowledge work.

This means that during a project our quality is defined less on the relationship between quantity and quality (productivity) and more on the relationship between suitability and quality (effectiveness).

However, to think that this means there is nothing we can learn from the assembly line is dangerous and self-defeating. We do need a process, we do need predictability in product creation, we do need the brains brought to bear on the problems at hand to communicate, collaborate, and create in concert. If we do not strive to calm our work, we will be rewarded by unnecessarily complex work.

We need to prepare with **collaborative planning** and execute with collaborative process.

In **collaborative planning**, everyone knows what is going on, decisions are informed, and course corrections are logical. Teams plan their work fully informed by work happening in other teams. Work that changes the structure of part of the system is discussed with those who would be impacted, causing collaborative solutions through greater perspective. Decisions that would alter the architecture of the product are displayed and discussed with a map of the architecture; ramifications are collaboratively redesigned. This collaborative model keeps everyone informed, involved, and inspired.

Anti-collaborative planning is born of the silo and creates workflows that try to conform to the structure of the company and not the needs of the work. Changes made by one team often impact work done by another, but those impacts may not be realized for months or years. Work that changes the structure of part of the system often negates other work, causing rework and infighting. Decisions of architecture go undiscussed and radically shift other solutions already being planned. The anti-collaborative systems we have in place are always keeping teams on the defensive as they struggle valiantly to get their work done while unknowingly destroying value elsewhere in the company.

FungiCorp's Collaborative Planning Loop:

Huddle Structure: Every morning, the FungiCorp team (about 60 people) would meet in the Obeya and, using the visualizations, would discuss learning from the previous day, how complicated or complex work was moving along, acknowledge the "easier" tasks that were completed, and enter new tickets into the backlog.[37]

In the beginning, they were adding more tickets than they were completing. This was a demoralizing illustration of how deep the hole was. As the days progressed, this dynamic changed as they found the areas of higher complexity and solved them, turning the initial demoralizing growth in complexity into a motivating problem-solving experience. Every day, the huddle saw measurable impact.

Dynamic (Tiger) Teams: After visually seeing the undeniable fact that work was *shared between* the database team and other teams, it was equally obvious that no task could happen in one team or even by one

---

37 Note here that the huddle structure provided avenues for single, double, and triple loop learning by opening up the discussion beyond simply assigning tasks or asking for help.

person. All work took on the people the work required. This mean pairing, a few people, or mobbing as appropriate. Pairing, at a minimum, happened on all tasks during the crisis. These groups of two or more were called Tiger Teams.

A Tiger Team Board used magnets with faces of all the team members to show which people were gathering to work on which problems. Since everyone was gathering in open spaces in the office, this board also started to show where that group was sitting (Large conference room, Dev area, etc.). This made people easier to find in the organized chaos.

At the board, people who didn't have an active task to work would gather up and select tasks that best matched their shared skill sets or learning they wished to achieve. This created a dynamic opportunity to upskill. Why would this be natural? Because every emergency provides opportunities to learn.

The role of **Reviewer** was established. This is a person with a lot of experience in the codebase, the operations of the business, the customer demands, or legal implications. Most had a mix of backgrounds; all had been with the company over a decade. That's right, the most experienced people did not do the active work to fix this problem. Why would this be natural? Because every emergency provides opportunities to learn.

The pairs selected a reviewer or reviewers as their work demanded. As time went on, reviewers would select themselves. Often, they would review work that didn't logically fit with their skill set to get new perspectives and to learn from each other.

Architectural Awareness: Tickets that were pulled all had systemic implications. The teams needed to look at the huge architecture diagrams in the Obeya for impacts or opportunities. Any change could derail another's solution or might provide better alternatives. The former was the fear, but the latter ended up, excitingly, becoming the norm. A pair would pull a ticket, and someone else would be like, "Hey, come work with us this morning and help us finish our thing, and it'll make that task a lot easier!"

Not wait for us to get done…but *come help us*.

They had established a real-time collaborative planning system that allowed for short-, medium-, and long-term solutions. Now, they just had to do the work…

The Work and Discovery Loop

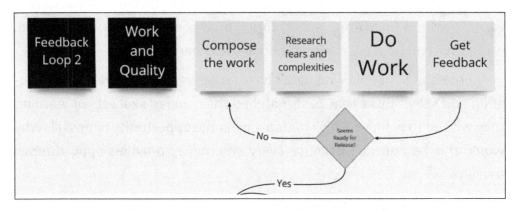

We need to prepare with collaborative planning and execute with **collaborative process**.

Process is how work gets done. "Working" on something is transforming it from a plan (expectations) into a product (reality). No plan fully survives contact with reality. There is always an arc of starting the work, discovering things about it, changing your path to suit the discovery, and then finishing the work. Even in simple tasks like turning off the lights before bed, you might start towards the switch and have to step around a box, a cat, a rat, or a suddenly opened pit of lava.

David Snowden and his team at The Cynefin Company are the inventors and standard bearers for the Cynefin Framework,[38] a complexity model that fits that list. When we are working, tasks fall into one of five domains of *complexity*: Confused, Clear, Complicated, Complex, and Chaotic.

---

38 Cynefin can be found in depth at The Cynefin Company, www.thecynefin.co.

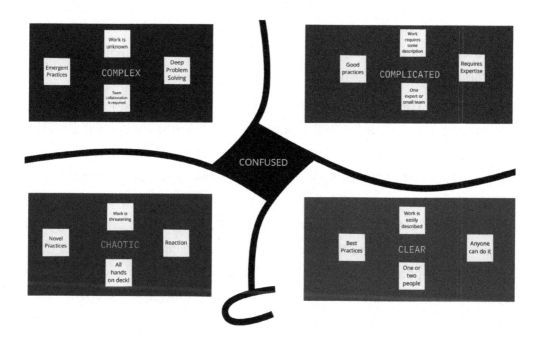

Confused: What is that Thing?: We first note that there is a thing at all. We aren't sure what or how complex it is. We perceive *object*. Then, we do a quick evaluation; depending on the level of complexity, that evaluation may take longer, be easier to overlook, or be more stressful. We'll cover this more at the end of this section.

Clear: The Box: Stepping around the box requires no additional information. The box is there, you step around it or move it, and turn off the light. This is a task you can do *alone (no collaboration)*. This type of task is easily described and can be done with little or no training, usually by one person. Clear tasks use *Best Practices*, which are practices where if you follow a set of rules, you will get a predictable outcome every time.

Complicated: The Cat: Stepping around the cat requires you to not step on the cat while the cat keeps moving to where you were going to step. You, however, have had this cat in your house for years and have become an expert in moving around the cat. You use this expertise to safely shut off the light and go to sleep. This is a task you can do *in concert (working with a small team, in this case you and the cat)*. Complicated tasks require some expertise and employ *Good Practices*, which are practices where if you appropriately mold rules to your context, you will often get a favorable result.[39]

Complex: The Rat: The rat, on the other hand, is new and weird. Why the hell is a rat in your house? You jump straight into the air, land on the bed, and wake your spouse, saying, "OMG Totes Rat!" and your spouse is all like, "Dude, whence doth yonder rat hail?" and then you go into a mode of solving a problem you didn't know existed and will have great impact on your ability to get your work done (sleep). *Complex issues are best solved by groups* because of multiple perspectives, in this case, initially, your Californian 1990s person and your Californian Shakespearean person of significance. These tasks are often problems to solve and have *Emergent Practices*, meaning it is your job to work with a group of people to understand the complexity and tame it by creating reasonably predictable good practices for them. As this understanding *emerges*, you will become an expert in this new practice.

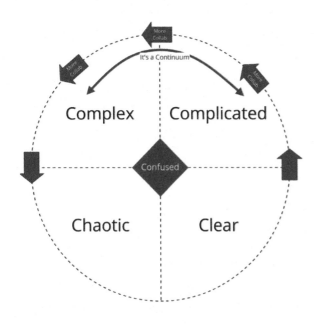

Chaotic: The Lava: It should be clear that a lava pit opening in your bedroom would be a state of chaos, in which case you and your spouse would run screaming into the street, then upon arriving in the street you would calm down (stabilize) and start to figure out what to do next. Solving this problem will require, likely, many

---

39 Most "Best Practices" today are ill formed and overly prescriptive "Good Practices" mistaken for a best practice.

people and will spawn multiple complex, complicated, and simple problems. Here we have *Novel Practices*, things you will do once or a few times to cope with the situation...like *push the dresser into the lava so we can use it to jump to the other side*.

Think of the domains as a continuum. As the work becomes more complex, it becomes more collaborative. Something kind of complicated would need an expert (leaky faucet needs plumber); something really complicated would need a team (colonoscopy).

Each domain comes with different expectations. As your team's work moves **through** the clear, complicated, and complex domains, your teams' response to work changes. The need for collaboration, expertise, customization, and experimentation increase. This is why it is crucial that modern knowledge workers have a basic understanding (box/cat/rat/lava level) of complexity. Otherwise, we assign work to individuals that should be done as a team.

This illustrates why we avoid change. There are two moments of fight or flight response we have when confronting work, a problem, or change. (1) **Confusion** *Oh god, what is that? Now something else I have to deal with?!* and (2) **Increasing Complexity** *Oh no, that new thing came up and it means I'll have to change my plans, budget, schedule, etc.* Both of these moments represent the unknown, which makes our amygdala go crazy. We don't want to calculate the unknown, and the more complexity...the more unknown.

A System that Processes Complexity

The FungiCorp Tiger Teams had some serious challenges; work was already visualized by assumed complexity, but it was not uncommon for even tasks that seemed simple to erupt with unexpected complexity. Complexity, by nature, is emergent and difficult to plan for.

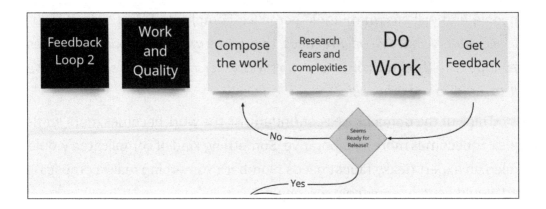

Since there was a lot of work happening in the same domain at the same time, work often collided with other work. New complexities of work integration, technology selection, newly discovered defects, architectural issues, and more created a need for people to be very clear when work required more than one person.

Compose the work: Tiger teams select a ticket and begin work composition. The started by defining the problem the work was trying to solve (what), they people impacted (who), and the business case (why). They ensured they had all the right people involved or informed.

During work composition, teams began root cause analysis of the work. While this seemed like an extra step at first, it took about two minutes for a clear problem, maybe 10 for a complicated problem, and became a research assignment (its own task) for a complex problem.

Root cause analysis was the first gatekeeper to exposing complexity and, therefore, exposing how much collaboration, attention, and time a particular task would take. Arguably, it also elevated the importance of a task as complex tasks tended to have impacts the bled into other work.[40]

---

40 Full root cause analysis for knowledge work would be a book on its own. Learn more with *Finding Solutions, Problem Solving for Knowledge Work,* Modus Institute. Modusinstitute.com.

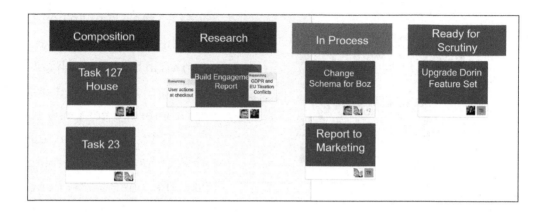

Research unknowns or fears: Research is a hedge against complexity; unknowns (discovered during the early root cause analysis) and fears (professional concerns) were warning signs that the team was not yet ready to act with confidence on this particular task. Professionalism required research.

Note here, that this step, like the questions for the World Bank team and the upskilling for TLC was an *explicit step* and therefore an expectation. It encouraged the behavior of professionally understanding the work before undertaking it. Decisions improved with this type of **immediate feedback**. The professionals questioned and researched their own assumptions, and therefore were more honest with themselves about what they did and did not yet know.

This expectation that research was a crucial part of the workflow meant that in the root cause analysis part of work composition, since research was the next step, there was no harm in calling for deeper research (finishing the root cause analysis). In any other system, people would have naturally tried to solve the complexity with little or no research or tried hard to make every work item be clear or complicated. That would have resulted in improper work, quickly completed.

Why is Research its own step and not just part of composition? Because anything in research is either complex or requires special attention. Above,

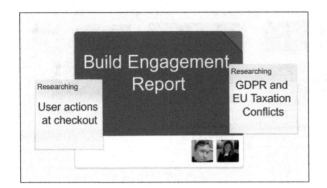

we can see a kanban board for this phase. The tickets shown in the Research column are clearly called out for the entire company to see. Let's say that a real ticket looked something like the one to the right: they would see who was working on it and what the problem was they were currently trying to solve, and everyone would know if they could help. The column itself is a call to action, without anyone having to call a meeting and beg for attention.

Do the work: Here the pair, group, or mob sits down and creates an informed solution. Because they are working collaboratively, they are giving each other feedback constantly while working. Because this work is happening with an Obeya, the work is being conducted with constant feedback as to what decisions are being made by other groups. While creating their product, each team is aware of the actions around them.

The work items have been discussed, categorized, and largely understood. Clear tasks are completed quickly and largely without incident. Complicated tasks are given more scrutiny but also tend to pass without much fuss. Complex tasks are taken on by a group that largely understands the issues creating the complexity and works on solving for them (often creating new tickets for the backlog along the way).

Get feedback: Throughout this system, we see real feedback being given in planning, design, and (in the next section) release and monitoring. Between pairing, peer review, and making sure that everyone knows what research is being done, everyone gets the best possible opportunity to provide input, expertise, and energy. This type of real-time and consistent feedback changes what we receive from a lot of comments after something has already been built (noise) to active signals that guide quality product (music).

Throughout this process, the workflow at the top might be repeated many times until the product was deemed "ready for scrutiny". This meant that other pairs would pull the ticket (usually with a Quality Assurance or a customer support team member) and declare it ready for release.

Remember, this company was dealing with extremely sensitive personal data. The cavalier Lean Startup release-first test-later approach would not work. If the work was deemed stable and responsible, it would move forward.

Quality and Completion Loop

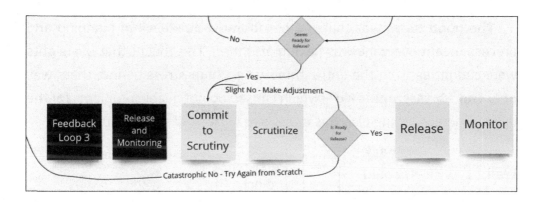

Quality is crucial to a profitable and successful business, but it isn't sexy. There was a limited amount of time before the company and its customers would start to notice that nothing "new" was happening. The group was working on a "boring" part of the business called *infrastructure*. No one wants to pay simply for infrastructure. Like the chassis of your car, you never buy the product for it, but you notice it when it is defective.

Customers had been noticing for years that there were increasing issues like slow information retrieval, erroneous reports, and the occasional notice of a security breach. Still, telling them that they couldn't get the new features they wanted because we were "upgrading data services" wasn't exactly a customer pleaser. Quality had to happen fast.

Professional Scrutiny: We needed to make changes extremely quickly and professionally. After work was accepted in the work phase, "scrutinizers" would check the work to make sure it was readable (often software developers are focused on speed typing and not code other people can understand) and that it operated as expected. All work was under scrutiny for several hours to several days.

Simple work would get a quick check, while work that had higher complexity or less confidence was treated as a proof of concept and watched very closely.

This seems like a lot of work, but this phase ended up being a revelation for the company as a whole.

The good news was that the collaborative feedback in planning and process meant everyone was paying attention. This meant that oversights were caught early. In the entire three-week, high-stress period, there was **only one "Catastrophic No"** (which caused no noticeable problems for the users), and everything else was either fine or needed slight adjustments.

The Feedback Wall: I wish I could show you the real feedback wall. Just like Turner has blueprints of the building in their Obeyas, this was a software architecture blueprint. The teams put sticky notes of work or research that showed real-time 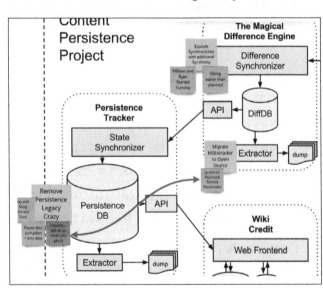 learning directly on the part of the system they were working on.

When someone was pulling tasks that next day, they could see the parts of the systems their work would touch and could see the work that had touched, learned about, and evolved that system. They knew who had been there, what they did, and what impacts that would have on new work.

This completed the loop back to the planning and huddle.

THE COLLABORATION EQUATION OF BOTTLENECKS AND LEARNING

Seeing the Bottleneck * Seeing the Impact = Rapid Relief

> BOTTLENECKS IN INFORMATION, DECISIONS, AND WORKFLOW BECOME COMMON WHEN WE ORGANIZE OUR WORK AROUND SILOS AND NOT AROUND THE CAPABILITIES NEEDED TO DO THE WORK.

The Pain: Bottlenecks in information, decisions, and workflow become common when we organize our work around silos and not around the capabilities needed to do the work. Decision making, problem solving, and quality become domains to be fought for, while deadlines, new features, and "autonomy" become political weapons. The teams' required collaborative structures to do quality. Without those structures, professional work suffers, ultimately costing customers and careers.

The Collaboration Equation: We must create, on the fly, new structures of work that meet the demands of the work at the time. The flow of work required should always supersede the false divisions created by our shortsighted team silo definitions. Collaboration should always supersede political organization.

See the Bottleneck: We could see the bottleneck, as a group. There was resistance to accept the bottleneck for what it was, which meant the visualization needed another format. The narrative needed to be communicated in a way people could comprehend. Once that was done, the need for the Andon-style response was clear, even to upper management and the board.

See the Impact: No one wanted to pull the Andon and pause existing work; they rightly feared political reprisal even though the impact of not pulling the Andon was clear. This, however, is not the end of the story. Relief comes from being able to *complete the relief effort*, not from starting it. Any relief effort has a window of opportunity in which change is welcome; after that, it becomes ineffective and an increasing political liability.

Rapid Relief: Seeing impact wasn't just seeing the impact of the bottleneck on the database group or on the schedules of the company as a whole; it had to include seeing the impact of fixing the situation and the likelihood of returning to normal (or better than normal) operations. Visible rapid relief was necessary to reassure people that suddenly halting normal operations for this fix was worth the stress.

Operational Relief: Visualizations in the Obeya and beyond gave standard formats for assembling teams, exchanging information, pulling work, investigating problems, solving problems, creating quality work, releasing quality work, and sharing/utilizing learning in real time.

Strategic Relief: It didn't stop there—those same visualizations allowed for frequent reports to leadership and the board, many of whom stopped by and just sat in the Obeya. They read the boards, watched the work being done, and knew the company was acting with confidence.

During this experience, work was constant, directed, serious, and frenetic. There was a deck just outside the Obeya; at one point, I was getting some air and one of the company's board members walked up and said, shaken, "It's like an OR in there. The company is on life support and we didn't even know it was sick." She didn't question what we were doing, because the need, the professional response, and the value were all visual and understood.

CREATIVE COLLABORATION CREATES EXPECTATIONS

In knowledge work, bottlenecks are created from simple missed signals in planning and team structure. They rapidly scale when ignored. This would cause many a limited thinker to want to tell managers to look for bottlenecks, but managers end up being the worst people for this task. Managers are tasked with the success of their teams, productivity, and quality within the confines of their team's definition.

The Andon is a powerful lesson for us all. It works precisely because it is distributed amongst *everyone*. It gives us Argyris feedback loops of every type at every level and allows us to see emergent complexity. That is an academic way of saying that people can see, quickly report and act on anything that would interfere with their quality, their Right Environment, or their professionalism. That is a collaborative recipe for acting with confidence.

Building a Practical Right Environment

Turner cares about every project they take on, quality professionals working together to safely build a quality building on-time and on-budget. Humanely completing a difficult project on time and on budget requires a Right Environment. Turner project starts with a Right Environment Exercise where the team discusses what they need to get their work done. The project team designs their own preferred professional environment. They decide together how they will communicate, reduce stress, ensure impact, and improve.

This is culture.

In business, we stress the importance of culture, but we can't define it. Culture is nebulous, organic, elusive. We are frightened of its lack of definition, and yet it lacks definition because we don't have a system to define it. We don't even try, leaving it up to chance. Just like hope isn't a strategy, chance isn't a culture.

HOPE ISN'T A STRATEGY, CHANCE ISN'T A CULTURE.

The culture of your project, your team, and your company is the foundation of how you work. Your culture defines how people work together.

How they learn, how they support each other, what they *value*.

Value is another nebulous word. People feel that it is *what you like*, but every like is a need. The values of your team are the needs of your professionals. They are the prerequisites of your team members being able to act with confidence. So, your culture is the system of the team's combined professional needs.

These needs can be: tangible ("I need two monitors at my workstation"), procedural ("We need to plan our work together so we know what we are doing and why"), tactical ("Onboarding should always include time in the Obeya")—and they can be comforts ("We need a real espresso machine"). They are all *practical* ways to make sure that the way your professionals are working is the way they *need to be* working.

One thing is certain: **without understanding your culture, you will never obtain a culture of continuous improvement**. You and your team must discuss what you do, how you do it, what you need to do, and why you are all there to do it. Understanding the who, what, and why gives everyone **a definition of your culture**, process, and professionalism. With those definitions, we can agree on ways to make sure they all happen and continue to happen in the best way possible.

This chapter answers two key systemic questions:

▸ How do we practically build the Right Environment so we can have a culture that we can define, maintain, and improve?

▸ How do we ensure that our professionals have the tools they need to act with confidence?

THE MODUS RIGHT ENVIRONMENT EXERCISE

For well over a decade, Tonianne and I have refined a one-week engagement designed to help teams visualize and understand their current state, discover their own internal culture, and build a roadmap to an improved future state. Most of the teams in this book went through parts or all of it. We call it our Right Environment Exercise (REE).[41]

Our exercise is both intensive—*and intense*—often involving some uncomfortable discoveries as members of presumably high-functioning and cohesive teams surface and confront how far their beliefs, assumptions, and ways of working stray from their reality.

Nota Bene: *Pay special attention to what the individual activities are designed to do. They themselves are not sacred. We alter how we do them with every team we work with. Again, this isn't a recipe, it is technique. Take these, experiment with them, and show us and the world how you extend and evolve the whys, whats, and hows of the REE.*

The Problems We Need to Solve

The REE helps the team define, maintain, and improve their Right Environment. This is a process of revealing the culture of the team to everyone and showing how that culture will be leveraged to allow people to work together professionally and humanely.

Basic problems the Right Environment Exercise addresses:

▸ **Teams tend to focus inward, becoming silos.**

▸ **Teamwork tends to be designed for productivity and not completion.**

▸ **Individuals in teams are given direction and directives that thwart, rather than reward continuous improvement.**

▸ **Individuals cannot act with confidence.**

---

41 This is not the exercises that Turner staff use, but the results are similar. Again, the goal of this chapter and this book is not to provide recipes, but techniques. Start with this, understand the why, and then build your own.

The Promise: Breaking Out of the Cycle

At the heart of those four problems is a simple question, *"Why don't we solve these problems already?"*. I have seen, over the years, many teams that felt like they were continuously improving were merely talking about their problems, not actively solving them.

The Eternal Problem Loop

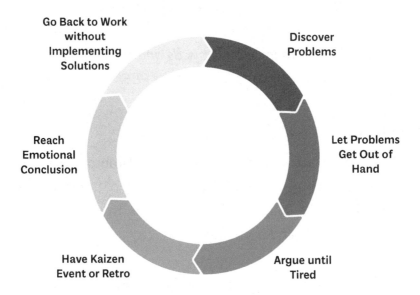

They were either Lean or Agile teams falsely engaging in continuous improvement. Lean teams had Kaizen Events; agile teams had their retrospectives. The rhetoric behind both methods is solid, but the results are very often depressingly the same: the Eternal Problem Loop.

A defined Right Environment ends this loop. The simple failing of traditional process improvement methodologies is they discuss culture, but **they don't make continuous improvement a cultural asset**. With our Right Environment defined, we create systems that reward good culture, professional growth, and quality product by ensuring that continuous improvement can happen in the first place.

Focusing on Root Causes

Teams come to us for REEs because they have dug themselves into a hole. They have trouble with prioritization, delivery, operations, or office politics, in general. They call for a REE because they want to solve these "problems". "We have a problem with prioritization," they will say. These are what we call their "known problems".

Curing The Symptom:

What they think are problems are most often symptoms. Symptoms are seen as the problems to solve because symptoms are the pain the team directly experiences. They are seeking relief from what is hurting.

Use the REE to remove that pain, noting that success will remain elusive as the team tries to solve their "prioritization problem" (observed pain) and not the bottleneck problem causing it (root cause).

Curing the Root Cause:

Just like with FungiCorp, this recurring frustration can, itself, be fixed. When a team collaborates and makes a commitment to understand the root causes of their pain and solve them, this situation reverses. They find ways not just to end the pain but show themselves that improvement is possible. A commitment to finding root causes must be part of their Right Environment.

To this end, the REE is built to have the teams either find these root causes or recognize there are deeper problems that require a stronger root cause analysis (which would become a task for the roadmap). The team will also develop an ability, or at least a desire, to see issues easily in the future. The value stream mapping exercise helps teams see the true impacts of their culture and their operations as a system.

THE HOW: THE RIGHT ENVIRONMENT EXERCISE

The REE is a weeklong event which has evolved over the years. When we work with teams, our goal isn't simply to complete these exercises, but to make sure the team knows how they want to instantiate their culture.

Every weeklong Right Environment exercise joins culture and process by having the team detail where, how, and why they collaborate...and where they do not. We want to clearly understand our culture, our processes to support that culture, and what we need to do to get from the team we are now to the team we want to be.

If their culture is unique, it stands to reason that each REE will have unique element. In every REE, additional activities surface which are tailored to the team's needs. The REE has four elements: the Value Stream Map, the Charter, the Communications Agreement, and the Roadmap. These are the core that we do every time. You will find that your team will have a sticky problem that requires a new, unique exercise.

You should not only feel free to extend this format; **you _must_ extend** this format to suit your context.

Collaboration is nothing more than a healthy culture engaged in a flexible and effective process. Every anti-collaborative problem in chapters one through four directly resulted from a lack of cultural clarity. Each solution resulted from providing clarity.

▸ **Clarity is co-created in the REE** by getting the team to visualize, confront, discuss, and align around:

▸ **Standard Work:** How their work flows routinely,

▸ **Non-standard Work:** How/where their work surprises them,

▸ **Problems:** Where their work is duplicated, breaks down, or is ill defined,

▸ **Fixes:** How they can correct those redundancies / breakdowns (together),

▶ **Silos:** Where they are denied the opportunity to collaborate,

▶ **Expectations:** What they need from each other,

▶ **Information Flow:** What they need but is often unavailable or hidden, and

▶ **Impact:** How they remain aware of where and how they can provide the most impact as professionals.

When we have a shared understanding of these key elements of being a team, we can then create a **roadmap of improvements** that will immediately and continuously make their work life better.

The Flow of a Right Environment Exercise

The exercise is designed to last five days. It is important to invest the entire five days in the exercise. Each activity is designed to look at work from a different perspective. If you rush through, your team will not have time to discuss, to process, and to change. The exercise is one in which the team comes to alignment about commitments they are making to each other, the company, and the customer.

Just like with bread, this is a proofing process that cannot be rushed.

The Structure

There are four main stages in an REE: a value stream mapping exercise, a charter, a communications agreement, and a roadmap. Each stage allows the team to dive into culture and operations from a different perspective.

STAGE ONE

The Question: How Do We Work?

The Action: The Value Stream Map[42] (VSM): A Lean exercise for your team to understand its culture, process, and collaborations. For many teams, this will be the first time they have ever considered their work in relation to other people.

STAGE TWO

The Question: How Do We Relate?

The Action: *The Charter:* Builds on the Value Stream Map, helping a team to fully define their desired professional and collaborative culture and take steps to make it a reality.

STAGE THREE

The Question:
The What Information Do We Need?

The Action: *The Communications Agreement:* The team discusses their information needs, where information currently hides, and agrees to honor and implement improvements.

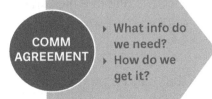

STAGE FOUR

The Question:
How Do We Build Our Right Environment?

The Action: *The Roadmap:* The agreement of how the team will implement and maintain their culture of professional collaboration and improvement.

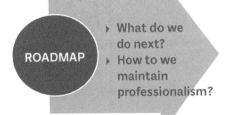

---

42 Rother, M., Shook, J., & Lean Enterprise Institute. (2018). *Learning to See: Value-Stream Mapping to Create Value and Eliminate Muda.*

The Professional Is Personal: During each stage, the team details deep and sometimes emotional conversations where they plan out how they work, interact with and treat each other, help each other become the best professionals they can be. Each REE day, teams confront and tend to their professional pain. They solve problems that have been plaguing them, make decisions that have lasting impacts, and build a collaborative and professionally satisfying way of working. This can be draining.

The REE is a system. All four components are instrumental in understanding culture, process, and information flow. Each of the components provides crucial information which in turn informs the others. If you only focus on the VSM, charter, or communication agreement, you will only be optimizing part of the system, which means you will be ignoring crucial conversations. You can add to this system, you can change the questions, but always be asking yourself if you are getting the real information you need to build and maintain a healthy, collaborative team.

Why This Structure? Culture is a System.

We are here for a reason: Individuals work in teams to provide value, and their Right Environment (a known culture) amplifies that value.

Work, being the reason for being together, cannot be extracted from the culture. Culture and process are parts of the same system. Therefore, any Right Environment must begin with a key understanding of how the team works *together*. The team needs to see their culture and work through these lenses:

Five Lenses of Humane Management

1. **Communications:** Does the team agree on how they communicate with each other, leadership, and the client? Does the team have the information they need when they need it to act with confidence?

2. **Relationships:** Does the team understand how it relates to other team members, other teams, customers, and the way the company creates values?

3. **Respect:** Does the team know when good work has been completed and who was responsible for the work? Does the team know where and when problems were solved? Does the team know when team members helped solve or avert a problem? In short, does the team see *why* their team members are worthy of respect?

4. **Flow:** Does the team work with minimal interruptions? Does the team understand their predictable work? Does the team have agreements in place to process complex or difficult work? Is the team visualizing their work so that actions and reactions are logical and clear? This leads to both smoother workflow, but also psychological flow.

5. **PDSA:** Does the team have enough structure for continuous improvement to happen? What are the impediments to PDSA? How is it built into or out of their existing processes? Has the team built an environment where PDSA is possible?

These are the key components of a Right Environment. It is the full integration of a professional human system of work with a clear, manageable, and sane workload. It is culture and operations operating together.

There are specific activities we structure a REE week around. And yes, as you would guess, we've had no two REEs go the same way. Every team needs at least one specific conversation or exercise not on this list that responds to their specific needs. Every REE has about 80% of this format and 20% unique activities.

Again, that's a long way of saying...do the REE, but don't ape the REE. Make sure it meets your needs. As your team discusses their work, see what they are saying through the five lenses, and let that guide you to directed activities your particular team might need.

STAGE ZERO: RECOGNIZING VALUE

These exercises are the first steps a team takes toward becoming individual teams to create value. This is also the first experience many will have at self-defining value simply by making decisions about how they work. Before, these have always been wishes, but now they are structural...they will become the actions of their Right Environment.

By the end of your REE, the team will be exhausted, mentally and emotionally. They will also still be skeptical: they've had improvement sessions before that felt great and achieved little. As a change agent (regardless of your company role, you are now a change agent), make sure that the effort everyone put into the REE is respect in both word and deed. Behavior modeling is key here.

Be Grateful: Make sure that people recognize the effort put in to reach conclusions. Call out improvements you, personally, are excited about, and set an example for others. Be clear when you see emotional investment, process improvement, and have a better understanding of why the people on the team gave a damn.

Be Visibly Active: Call attention to what you, personally, will be doing to move the roadmap forward and help maintain the newly defined culture. You are invested; show it. Let others know, so they have someone to work with or reassurance that the improvements will get done.

Schedule Things Now: Make sure that people schedule collaborations or that follow-ups make it to the roadmap. Don't say, "we'll met weekly" with no date and time, because you won't meet weekly (and you know it). Put dates on the calendar *immediately*, right then—make the commitment real.

Schedule Breaks: Make sure people have ample down time; these are intense sessions.

Don't Let Schedule Kill Conversation: Some conversations *need* to happen so the team can process together. It might feel counter-productive or adversarial at times, but let the conversation happen.

Don't Confuse Complaining or Deflection for Conversation: Yes, conversation is important, but you can only complain so much. Look for ways to use the momentum of frustration to create a solution.

The Right Environment Exercise

See Results Immediately

Individuals in your REE are teamed to create value. Value that is seen creates momentum. The team begins creating momentum and value from the first minutes of their REE. Visually acknowledged momentum builds; unacknowledged momentum weighs you down.

As your teams work on the exercises, they create decisions, ideas, wishes, and action items (value) for how the team wants to structure its future. They are building a roadmap of decisions and activities that will make their right environment actionable. If the team can be honest about the culture they require, they can also be honest about the work required to get there. They are building a team structure that is ready to act. They are building a team that is primed to improve.

During the week, starting on the first day, have a box where everyone can record Decisions and Actions.

Decisions are small changes or agreements the team makes that impact workflow, culture, quality, or anything else. It is easy to make cavalier and logical decisions during any of these exercises and then forget them as we are working. We must capture them as they happen. This is a primary role of any facilitator, but everyone should be watching for them.

Actions are larger items that will require work outside the REE. These will become tasks in the Obeya. These will often involve time investment from team members and those outside the team.

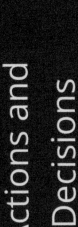

Actions and Decisions

Decisions and actions must be captured at the time they are made; don't worry if they are half-baked or require further discussion. Just capture them. When we get to day 5, we will use them to build our roadmap and improvement plan. They will be discussed and used, modified, or rejected.

Pro Tip: This is collaborative, remember, so everyone needs to be adding decisions and actions; not just the facilitator and certainly not the manager. When a decision is made by the team or someone has an idea, make sure they put it in this box.

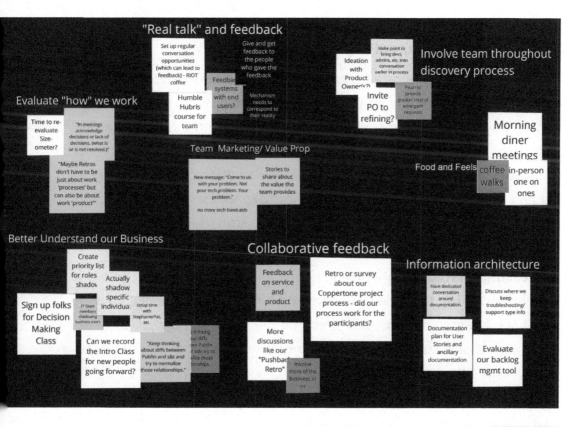

Go Deeper

Stage One: The VSM—the Foundation of Your Collaborative Architecture

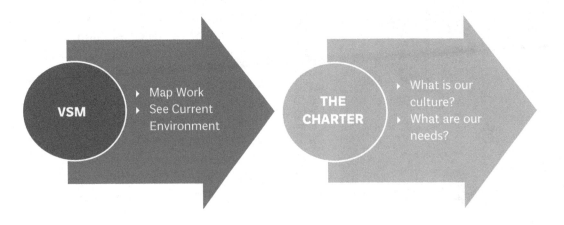

What Is a Value Stream Map and Why Start Here?

Culture is never separate from action. A value stream map (VSM) is an exercise where a team charts all the actions of their work in an open and honest way. What happens, who is involved, where things break down, what fixes might be applied, and where they could collaborate better are all scrutinized. The exercise creates a shared definition of work, highlighting and curing areas where the team lacks alignment. In this beginning, the team learns very quickly where work flows smoothly and where team members unknowingly hurt each other.

Seeking Shared Insight: Most teams are simply drowning in work. They haven't taken the time to understand how their work really flows; all they have are assumptions, and these do not serve them well. They become used to inaccuracies, incompleteness, and a certain level of institutional incompetence.

Building a VSM is often a team's **first glimpse into how they work and how their work impacts others**. Individually, as a team, as part of the company, with customers, those **relationships** become clear as they *see* the impacts of each sticky on the board.

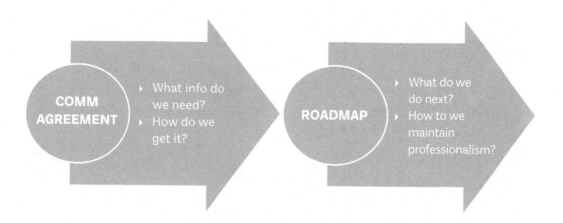

Creating Clarity: The VSM exercise gets the team to map every element of *their* work, every issue, every potential solution, every collaborative opportunity, every exchange of information or input, and every frustration.

The team can see the system for the first time, together.

Creating Respect: This shared understanding of culture and process is rare, it is often emotional, and it is rife with opportunities. As they build, their gain **respect** for their role in the team's work and for the real roles and professionalism of their teammates.

Forward Thinking: The VSM is simply a statement of how your work flows. It doesn't care what anyone's assumptions were when they entered the room or what the internal politics of the company are. It is merely interested in seeing work for what it is and allowing the team to correct for how they wish it could be.

Start With The End in Mind

Value Stream Mapping starts at the end. In this VSM for a copywriting team, the end is **Release to Client**.

The team then works its way backward throught the flow of work.

What do we do before Release to Client?

Well, we do the last legal check. Then before that we do editing.

Wait, what about Sign Off?

Oh, I was trying not to think about that painful step...

The team collaborates, learning and defining their work as a shared conversation. They celebrate work they are happy with and confront work they have issues with.

The team continues to work backwards until they have a full value stream that includes work as it flows now, as they wish it happened, where there are issues, and different ways to solve those issues.

Every step of this journey is an opportunity for improvement.

Current State

The team is mapping its current state, the way work is actually happening. Every team will come in with understanding and assumptions. Much of your current state as you know it, you will find happens in many different ways.

The team will be constantly negotiating what is really happening and what is an assumption. Through these conversations, they will be very honest about what is happening (current state) and what they wish would happen (future state / right environment).

Every VSM conversation will include a decision. The team will find something difficult, talk about it, argue maybe, align, and then decide *something*.

Those decisions are often **Quick Wins.** A simple agreement like "I will help you with that next time" or "We will talk to Johanna before we start that kind of work."

Quick Wins show up on the VSM as a "fix", but they should also immediately go on the **Decisions and Actions** board. They are Right Environment actions.

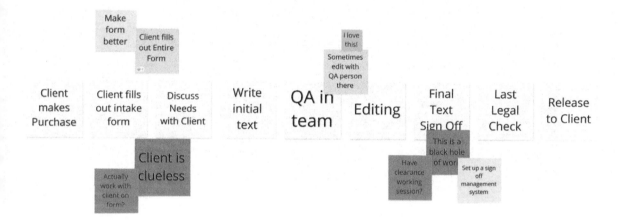

Future State

Each element shows how much of our Right Environment we already have and what we are still needing to work on. We have stickies that show workflow, problems, and fixes.

Each fix is something the team would like to see.

Don't lose sight of these: they are the value and the product of the VSM and should be used to inform every other stage of the your REE.

This is where your team identifies how they want to work and how they want to be treated.

Do not let people settle for historic mediocrity here. Look for ways to do inspirationally better.

Go Deeper

VSMs Build Shared Understanding

You do not work the way you think you do. We are always surprised by the perspective of our peers; we always find improvements when we look closely at how we collaborate. Your value stream map will be the most practical activity your team will ever undertake.

Teams think this will be a short exercise, because, they "know what they are doing." Every team assumes this. Even teams with great quality, rapport, and output are surprised by what they find in a value stream map. Taking the time to examine how we work with each other, seeing where we succeed and where we are challenged, is always illuminating and often emotional.

The goal of the VSM is highly practical: Build a visual map of how work flows through the team, from the planning of work all the way to completion.

Build Relationships

VSM results are often very personal. To have a right environment, your team needs a shared understanding of what you do, how you do it, who you do it for, how you work together, and what you need to improve.

This is what the VSM exercise does and why it is invaluable to true collaboration. Human beings relate to our teams and the value we create. Relationships are the essence of humanity and our work.

Collaboration hates ignorance. Mediocrity loves it. We must know how we work together in order to be highly performing professionals, teams, or organizations.

> "Collaboration hates ignorance, mediocrity loves it.

We are always surprised by the perspective of our peers; we always find improvements when we look closely at how we collaborate.

Coaches' Corner

We are working backwards intentionally. When we tell a story forwards, we skip important details. Our brain builds a quick, convenient narrative and runs with it.

When we work backwards, we question each step. "Does this really come before that?" "Is that really the earlier step." We have to slow down and engage our rational brain, we analyze, and we discover.

Teams will be very anxious to "finish" because value lies in completion. So they will rush through if you start at the beginning. We want them to realize the most value from the VSM, which means we want to invest time in processing together how we all want and need to work.

FAST EXAMPLE

We worked with a team that had been together for 25 years and felt they knew their process and culture. They figured they would be done with their VSM in a few hours. It took them over a week.

Their process had been around for so long that they all had built different assumptions and work-arounds. Showed them issues that were difficult to see, but strangely easy to fix.

END STATE IS YOUR BEGINNING

Start with the last ticket and move backwards, asking the question "what came before this?" lorem ipsum parabellum.

YOUR END STATE WILL CHANGE

As you build your VSM, your team will discover that their end is never really the end of their work lorem ipsum parabelllum.

SEE AND SOLVE THE PAIN

Look for where work is painful and find solutions. You aren't there to report process, you're there to improve it.

Key Elements

▸ **See the impacts of work in progress**

▸ **See issues, problems, and solutions in real time**

▸ **Discuss with future teams or leaders**

▸ **Build expectations of transparency**

▸ **Build expectations of quality**

▸ **Help future teams see problems very early**

Go Deeper

VSMs: Use Color to See Your System

Visualizing work shows us the our narrative. Color and shape surface patterns that provide instant context and greatly increase the speed at which we process information. We see the board, instantly see meaning, and get out.

In the VSM Exercise we make use of color or shape (if some are color blind) to call out different evolving stories from the board.

Functional Perspective Provides Safety

Each color is a perspective to view our work. They are functional, creating comfortable, practical, and unthreatening ways to express our work.

Surface Assumptions, Create Alignment

Colors are containers for different assumptions we think are facts. We need to see, discuss, and arrive at a shared set of truths.

Color In Action

Always (Yellow) - These are the steps in our work that "always" happen. This is the VSM's spine. We are focused on how work flows, where it slows, and where value happens.

ALWAYS

Tickets quickly appear in this category, many eventually change color to "sometimes" or "fix" or some other color. People put always tickets down, they are discussed and quickly show people that things they thought were happening (assumptions) are actually things they wish were happening (aspirations). As the tickets change in color, the group learns together that their individual assumptions were not valid and sometimes even toxic.

Sometimes (Orange) - These are valid steps in the workflow that don't always happen. This can be a rare event or an actual alternate path. We've had some VSM exercises where there have been so many of these that the "sometimes" streams eventually required their own, independent VSM exercise. In office settings, where people have rarely sat down and planned out how work is done, these conversations can get heated and filled with confusion. What is the right way?!

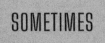

Coaches' Corner

Pain: Assumptions can be coping mechanisms used to navigate toxic work cultures. Each perspective can bring different epiphanies which, depending on the level of toxicity, can include tears. Always watch the emotionals of the team, they reveal where true dysfunctions hide in the work.

Payoff: Through shared exploration, the VSM creates opportunities. "*Hey, when you give me this form without the insurance info, I always have to ask you." "Oh! I thought you knew that already, I'll be sure to include that.*" These small agreements build, on the spot, better workflow and better culture. Call them out.

Pro-Tip: These are those micro-agreements that people often lose or forget. As a facilitator, you need to watch for these decisions and make sure they are recorded on the VSM and acted on. These are easy wins that create instant value from the exercise.

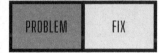

Problems (Red) – These tickets often consider pain points. Where on the VSM do things break down, where are there bottlenecks, where is there confusion, frustration, and fear? These red stickies generally appear slowly at first, then come in a tidal wave as professionals become more comfortable being honest with themselves about what is slowing them down or causing them frustration.

Fix (Green) - What might solve one of those red problems? While we try to avoid solutioning (the creation of a resolution before examining the problem), we do ask participants to suggest solutions for the problems.

Collaboration (Purple) – These tickets are used to show collaboration opportunities on the VSM board. Beyond a simple "fix", each purple ticket explicitly acknowledges existing silos and shows logical ways to move beyond them. Every time there is a purple sticky, you know that in your current way of working something (information, work, decisions, reviews, etc.) isn't flowing smoothly and requires collaboration.

Input and Information (Blue and Teal) show areas of collaboration we are routinely missing. Information (context, history, deadlines, prior work, politics, etc.) and input (feedback and comments) needs are noted at critical points where comments would be quick and savings would be impressive. These stickies show where collaboration is necessary and will be fixed with purple stickies. While these might seem redundant (they are problems that could be red stickies), we find that asking these specific questions through these types triggers people to look at the VSM from different and important perspectives.

FOR ADDITIONAL INFORMATION **HTTP://MODUSCOOPERANDI.COM/TCE**

Go Deeper

See & Build Collaboration

Value created by individuals in teams is improved by finding the best ways to collaborate. VSMs were created for 20th-century manufacturing, where value is created through the speed of assembling and standard work. In 21st-century knowledge work, value is created through quickly processing information into products or decisions. Collaboration is therefore crucial for modern business where the problems are more complex, the solutions more immediately implementable, and the payoffs are greater.

When we say **Individuals in teams create value**, we acknowledge that relationships are the nucleus of any working system. Traditional VSM exercises over-focus on the team (silo), shaving seconds off a mechanical process. In the office, we're not interested in shaving seconds off a task's completion time. We need to remove frustration that delays delivery by days, weeks, or even months. We want to see how we can and should collaborate.

Purple tickets explicitly show collaboration on the Value Stream Map. Beyond a simple "fix" each purple ticket explicitly acknowledges existing silos and shows logical ways to move beyond them. Every purple sticky improves communication and relationships.

Seeing Collaboration

This is the value stream of a global team. The circled stickies all have collaborative elements. You will find, as they did, that every VSM exercise reveals impedances and solutions. These are usually collaborations people felt were difficult to pull off. They involve other teams or work. They seem insurmountable or at least "not my job".

Despite our fears, solutions to these problems are shockingly easy to implement. Solutions are rarely invasive (involving a large change in process, tooling, or scope). Solutions are almost always perfunctory (can be done quickly, like a form, a simple decision, or an activity) or they are choreography (meaning they involve explicit collaborative actions of more than one person or groups).

This means that almost all problems are solved by understanding the impedance and agreeing to work smarter together.

We see in this VSM that the team wants to work more with marketing and to integrate with QA. They want a designer to be part of development and to involve other teams that they previously annoyed with requests. Previously they complained about those teams, now they know they can't live without them because the work requires them. They cannot have a right environment without those collaborations because they won't have the information and alignment to act with confidence.

Mark
Resea

Input and information are the raw materials of knowledge work, yet most teams work with very little.

We are routinely missing information (context, history, deadlines, prior work, politics, etc.). We are also routinely bereft of input (feedback and comments) at critical points where comments would be quick and savings would be impressive. These stickies show where collaboration is necessary and can be fixed with purple stickies. While these might seem redundant (they are problems that could be red stickies), we find that asking these specific questions through these types triggers people to look at the VSM from different and important perspectives.

We want these perspectives to reveal where feedback loops are missing. In manufacturing, this was less necessary because there is usually a large gap between the design and the production of something.

On the assembly line, you aren't going to complete assembling a car and have someone say, "Oh, hey, you know people don't get in cars through the roof, maybe you should move the door from the roof to one or two of the sides." Then the team says, "Oh yeah? Well, Batman does!" and then there is a big fight about different Batmobile configurations.

That feedback (input) would have been received back in the design phase, which is very distinct from the manufacturing phase. Increasingly, in all kinds of work, there is no distinction between the design phase and manufacturing phase at all.

In knowledge work, patently stupid things are produced every minute of every day because the teams producing the work are shy on information and input. These two stickies represent two triggers for the team to specifically think about input and information as core components to the flow of quality professional work. Again, do we have the information we need to act with confidence and do other people have our backs?

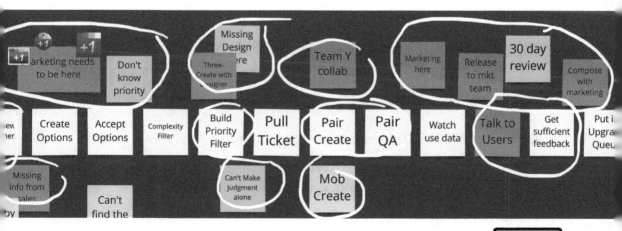

Go Deeper

Coaches' Corner: VSM Implementation Guidance

Value Stream Mapping exercises are incredibly powerful and emotional. The implementation guidance reflects this, so please read them carefully. At Modus Institute, we devote several classes to VSMs and include different aspects of VSM in every class we teach because of this depth.

Go Backwards or Go Home: Really, do this backwards. If you don't, the team will put up a "happy path" which just shows how they wish work happened or how they've been told it is supposed to happen.

You will feel pain. And it will be good. The VSM is first in the REE to surface not only issues, but the pain surrounding them. Pain shows up in humor, anger, sadness, withdrawal, resignation, or false stoicism. Many problems have become so painful and remained unsolved or unrecognized for so long that people identify the dysfunction as a healthy part of their process.

Take Breaks: This stuff is tough. Take breaks, of at least every hour. If you are live, take a five-minute break; if you are remote, take a 10-minute break. If you are remote...walking around is mandatory. Get up and leave the desk, go outside if possible. Get the body moving, the lungs working, the blood pumping. This recharges the body, clears the mind, and allows you to write some of what you were doing into mid-term memory. Sitting is forgetting.

Celebrate Moving Targets: In the beginning of this VSM, "Release" was the end state. Here it is "Put in Upgrade Queue." At some point, someone said, "That's not really the end, is it?"

Frequent changes to the end of the value stream are common, healthy, and *usually spark an epiphany* for the team. This is usually a first clue that their stated problem isn't really the problem. This is also an emotional moment for people who have spent time becoming increasingly agitated about a symptom.

Call Out Blind Handoffs and False Dependencies:

Blind handoffs require input from another team, but we don't tell them it is coming or involve them in any decisions we made to create it. It is a surprise.

Blind handoffs become work *the team* thinks is complete, because they finished it and handed it off. But that other group will invariably come back with questions because we assumed that just doing the work constituted completion.

We didn't recognize that collaborating with downstream teams was a major part of our job.

Epiphanies Drive Change: There will be *epiphanies*, or *difficult and emotional* realizations that spur change. People will realize that they have been negligent in providing a Right Environment for their team and that this has been systemic. This systemic dysfunction is now seen, recognized, and can be corrected in future onboarding.

Constructive Disagreement: Teams are making sense out of something they felt they already knew. Seeing the work, arguing about the work, and realizing that the issues the team was having was being caused *by the team* was tough. The different perspectives made these conversations easier. Rather than personal attacks, the conversations were...*what happens when work gets to this point right here?*

As the facts are discussed, people quickly see that a system, likely unintentionally, led to people doing incomplete work, having awkward handoffs, or becoming overloaded. That system created the problem with workflow, operations, delivery, and prioritization. They were able to slowly build their own visual depictions of the root causes, the system in which they operated, and fixes.

Stages Two and Three: The Charter and the Communications Agreement

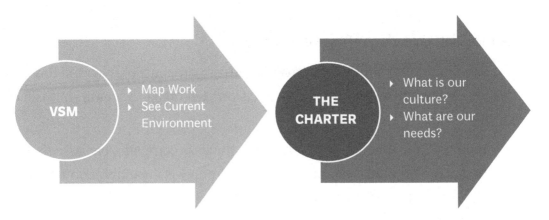

The VSM exercise led the team to tell a coherent story of what is (current state) and what they would like to see (future state). That is where most continuous improvement exercises end. We want to go further and *build a culture* that will *truly continuously improve.*

They aligned around the structure of their work and what stands between them and working effectively. They are aware that they are not alone, no longer isolated individuals or as a team from the rest of the company. They've seen the practical need to collaborate, and that is professionally exciting.

In stages two and three, we take on two exercises: **The Charter** (designed to create a practical and rewarding culture) and **The Communications Agreement** (designed to better provide the right information to the right people at the right time).

Both exercises build on the momentum of the VSM, and also its practicality.

The team has begun to see the relationship between culture and process. They've discussed their professional desires, things like: *we believe we should have clean handoffs, we should let each other know when a change has been made, we respect our customer,* etc. When these desires are clearly stated, they become **cultural norms**.

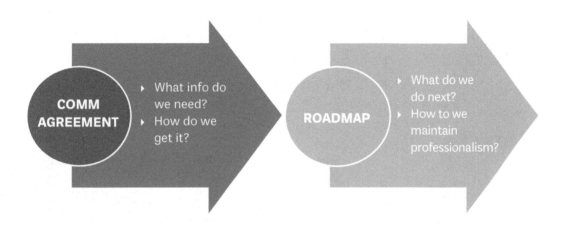

We can now discuss the team's professional culture and information needs in an informed way. They will be honest needs and not whims.

The Charter provides a framework for a team to examine and clarify their culture. It reveals a team's Right Environment by getting them to express and align around their individual and shared professional needs. The goal of these exercises is for the team to generate as many ideas as they can in a very short amount of time. They can then see (visually) where there is alignment, where there are novelties, and how they describe similar things differently.

How To Affinity Map

The results of an affinity mapping exercise are grouped to show alignment and the subtly different ways people can give definition to a similar problem. In the case to the right, members of this team felt that there was considerable and painful time pressure for their work.

They used words like "busy", "pressed for time", "time pressure"...but also words like "underappreciated", "needs to be reminded and prompted", "busy lives", and "lacks time"...all of which combine to tell a much deeper story than simply "busy". We can feel the isolated professionals on this wall.

HOW TO AFFINITY MAP
A Modus Cooperandi One Sheet

Purpose

▶ To understand the breadth of a complex problem.
▶ To discover major and minor themes.
▶ To create vast options.
▶ To begin to see the system.

How to

1 **GENERATE** On super sticky Postits, participants write down everything they think about the given problem or issue.

2 **POPULATE** This should generate a lot of Post-its. Put them on a wall.

3 **GROUP** Without talking, group Postits into cohorts. Anyone can move any Post-it, even if it has already been moved or grouped.

4 **OBSERVE** The result is thematic groups of Post-its. What is expected? What is a surprise?

5 **SELECT** Pick groups for further discussion. These become the topics for your Lean Coffee.

Why?

1 **OPTION CREATION** Develop the broadest possible set of options for discussion and consideration.

2 **UNDERSTANDING** Think of the problem (i.e. what is the problem?) before thinking of any solutions.

3 **EMERGENCE** Allow patterns to emerge from observations and intuition. Avoid cognitive biases toward premature defintions of the problem or the solution.

4 **EFFICIENCY** Quickly generate options rather than have long drawn out periods of investigation.

See also Gamestorming by Dave Gray, Sunni Brown, James Macanufo

THE CHARTER EXERCISE

Seeing and Acting on Your Culture

1.

3. Col

Own Your Right Environment

The Charter is a four-step exercise that uses an affinity mapping to surface ideas and highlight ones that require attention. The charter examines vision, expectations, collaborative needs, and victory conditions.

This gives teams a foundation to begin to understand their culture, needs, and expectations for a right environment. This is a mix of current state and future state.

The four activities happen in succession, each building on the one before, and shaped by the epiphanies and practicalities from the VSM exercise.

The team completes one activity, discusses it, and moves on to the next. Each stage brings new learning and insights; the professionals gathered are slightly changing their perspective and gaining alignment on their culture and their right environment.

The team gains shared insight—a powerful and rare commodity in business.

The Four Exercises

1 **Vision**: The vision exercise asks key questions to get the team to define what they are doing and why.

1. Vision

We ask:

▶ What is the value of our service?

▶ How does this service improve the lives of our customers?

▶ How do we help the company?

▶ How do we help each other?

2 **Expectations**: We want to know what we expect from each other as professionals. This is deeper than roles and accountability.

2. Expectations

We ask:

▶ How do we make sure our team supports each other?

▶ What should people expect from us?

▶ What should we expect from each other?

▶ What should we expect to have as professionals?

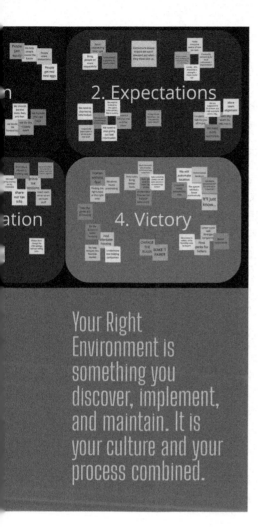

2. Expectations

4. Victory

Your Right Environment is something you discover, implement, and maintain. It is your culture and your process combined.

Time is on Their Side: Each affinity exercise should last as long as necessary. Some will go very quickly; others will go long. Root causes and hard-to-implement fixes will take time. Don't time-box these.

It's the Team's Right Environment: We want the team talking about acting collaboratively with confidence. Their Right Environment is not defined by you or me. There are no best practices (rote things to do), only good practices (examples or guidelines to be informed by).

When You Go Long: Individual exercises are optional, the need for their information is required. Skip one or merge two if needed. Watch the conversations in the VSM exercise closely. They will hint at where the team will be spending extra time.

Learnings and Action Items: There are two goals of these exercises: (1) to get the team to agree on their cultural and procedural right environment and (2) to generate a roadmap at the end of the week of actions to implement and maintain it.

3 Collaborations:
Look for people to start reaching out and thinking about what is stopping them from working together.

3. Collaboration

We ask:

▶ What professional boundaries exist on our team or in our company?

▶ Who needs to be informed, included, or involved?

▶ What triggers those actions and their related behaviors?

▶ What triggers or information are missing?

4 Victory:
Ensure that the team has a shared or at least coordinated future state.

4. Victory

We ask:

▶ *Do we agree on where we are going?*

▶ *What would it look like if our product or service was completed perfectly right now?*

▶ *How would the world change?*

▶ *What would our customers have that they don't currently have now?*

▶ *How would things improve?*

Go Deeper

The Right Information at the Right Time

The communications agreement is focused on the key struggle of any team or organization: Do people have the information they need to do a professional job, when they need it?

Given that the answer to this question is always "no", there is always room for improvement.

The right environment is a mix of cultural and operational elements. Almost all successes or failures are based on the flow of information or the communication of need.

In this exercise, we are teasing out the root causes to many of the issues found or discussed in the VSM and Charter exercises. The results will help us refine our possible solutions. Often problems that seem very deep and complicated in the VSM, are solved with an epiphany here. People will realize this insurmountable problem all boils down to simple information being hidden, routinely lost, or miscommunicated.

The Four Exercises

1 Information -

We lose information and decisions in our tools. To compensate we ask others...repeatedly. These manufactured interruptions slow delivery and distract us.

We ask:

▶ What info do we regularly search for?

▶ What info do we regularly lack?

▶ What info do we often interrupt others to get?

▶ What info do others seek from us?

▶ What necessary information is simply unavailable?

2 Tech - Teams

use tech to process, store, transfer, and display info they need. We want to understand where information lives, hides, or dies.

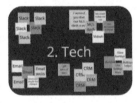

Tech is: transport (email, Google Docs), conversational (phones, Slack), collaborative (whiteboards, flip charts, Miro), work flow (online kanbans, CRMs, ticket systems), or etc.

We ask:

▶ What tools do you use to store information?

▶ What tools do you use to transfer information?

▶ What tools do you use to talk to each other?

▶ What tools do you use to create information?

▶ Where does information go to die?

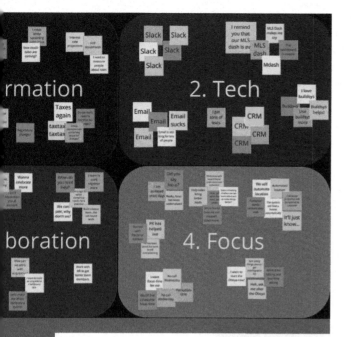

Information Conversations: We want to gather many types of information the team needs. Get the team to vote on information that is important, let them see they value it. When discussing, the team should note on the board which information needs are dire and, as always, potential improvements to solve that problem.

Tech Conversation: What tools do people enjoy? What tools hurt them? There are no "right tools". We have worked with teams who despise MSFT Teams one week and then another that loved it. Your team decides what works.

Collaboration Discussion: Broken meetings often ground this converstion, shift focus to how to collaborate. Put collaboration and information squarely together. For the first time, the team can see an entire working process.

Focus Conversation: Conversations here revolve around "me" and "we". The team begins to look at healthy ways they can focus and finish work. Sometimes this is solo, but increasingly it will be collaborative working sessions with others. Pairing, mobbing will become a staple of focus, not seen as an interruption.

3 Collaborations-

Teams require information flowing to maintain and support healthy relationships. List at all the ways that the team already collaborates.

We ask:

▶ *What do we do to collaborate now?*

▶ *What regular collaborative events do we have?*

▶ *What do we do to respond to change or problems?*

▶ *What triggers or information are missing?*

4 Focus- We

want the right information at the right time. The team sees information and work flows that are open to visualizations and sharing. They find ways of communication that thwart hoarding and bottlenecks.

We ask:

▶ *How do you get time to focus?*

▶ *How do you protect yourself from interruption?*

▶ *What can we do to visualize or exchange information without interrupting each other?*

FOR ADDITIONAL INFORMATION **HTTP://MODUSCOOPERANDI.COM/TCE**

Go Deeper

Stage Four: The Roadmap: Making Culture Actionable

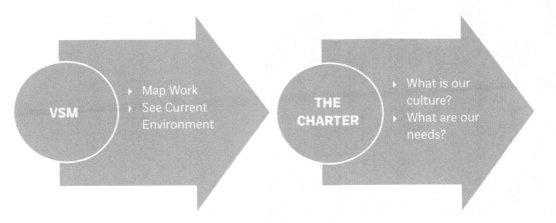

The team is now ready to create its roadmap. This is not a roadmap of tasks; it is a roadmap to create their collaborative structure. While these are actions, the team is building expectations that actions like this will continue and committing to a way of working that enables continuous improvement and underwrites professionalism.

The team has needs around workflow, culture, information, alignment, and direction. They have discussed what they are, what they want to be, and what they'd like to become. These discussions have all been practically grounded in the real work they do every day.

We'd like to avoid the common failings of Agile Retrospectives or Lean Kaizen Events where improvement items are created, but there is **no professional system** to drive the improvement work. At Toyota and a few other companies, continuous improvement is baked into the culture, an autonomic response. We are going to use this roadmap as a guide for our team's Right Environment to bake in continuous improvement.

The Eternal Problem Loop returns. Just listing arbitrary improvements and hoping someone does them never works. When team members go back to their day jobs, improvements *aren't part of their routine*. The system doesn't value improvement. With no system to check that the improvements were done, improvements are mostly always deprioritized or forgotten.

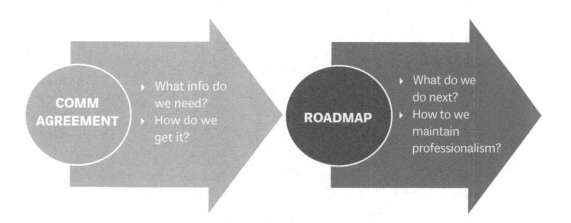

The Eternal Problem Loop solved. Our *Way* must have a clear roadmap between our current state (not so good at continuous improvement) and our future state (we are always getting better as individuals, as teams, and in providing value). The roadmap to our future state must be clear. It must have triggers that cause us to act and remind us of our commitments and the need to act on them.

This becomes a new actionable system and hopefully a fairly simple one. It sounds difficult because change *feels* hard. But, it's really unexpected change that freaks us out. Our roadmap takes "unexpected change" and turns it into improvements which are important to both solve and discover.

Our relatively simple roadmap might include agreements like:

▸ We will put improvement tasks on our kanban

▸ We will bring up issues and improvement opportunities in our daily huddle

▸ We will have a board of only improvements and select some to do every week

▸ 20% of our tasks should be improvements

▸ When an issue is causing a team member stress, we will talk about it

▸ If a problem is deemed severe, we will set aside time to swarm on it

▸ Improvements should be paired and immediately quality checked.

Our system doesn't need to require new tools or training; it simply needs to state the professional expectations for how problems are responded to and include the initial improvements.

REE STAGE FOUR:
THE ROADMAP
Your Roadmap Starts Rough

Slow Down & Do It Right

It is tempting to dive right into the roadmap, making a plan and acting. We are juiced on momentum and tired from the week. We want to *act now!*

But we need to slow down and build our roadmap deliberately. Just like we started from the end of the VSM exercise focus on the product, we to slow down here and make sure we understand what we are about to plan for.

The team has already done most of the work of defining their **actions** and **decisions**. They now need to organize these options into **themes** and see the acheivability of their Right Environment.

Build Your Options

For many on the team, this will be their first full-scale planning exercise. Keep the other exercises close and refer to them often.

First we take the items from the Decisions and Actions section and organize them affinity map-style. We can then label them into areas of need.

Those areas of need are made up of actions and decisions and will spawn more. There will be logical holes in the options that were created over the week.

As you come up with more complete lists, you build a full set of options for the Roadmap.

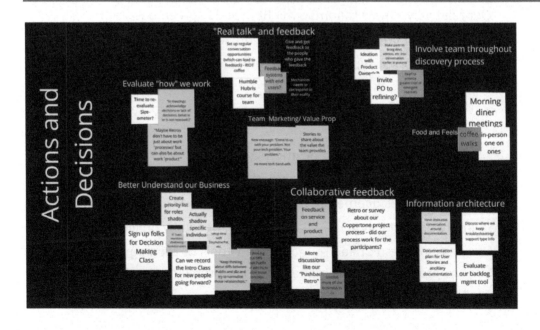

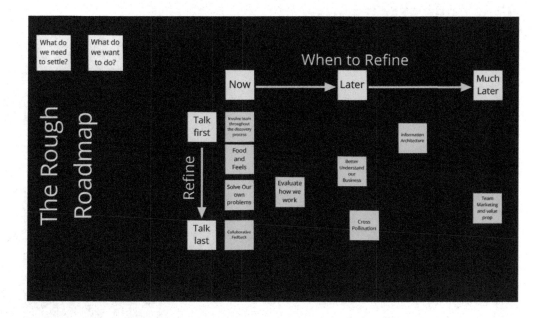

Building a Rough Plan

As an urban planner, I will tell you that **planning is not building**. Planning is also not scheduling or prioritizing.

Planning is taking all the things we want and could possibly have and creating a way to achieve several, but never all, of those things.

The team will have several themes (Food and Feels) that rise from specific action items and decisions (coffee walks, morning diner meetings, one-on-ones). These are groups of future state value that the team *wants to achieve*.

The Rough Roadmap quickly organizes poential work by what we'd like to tackle first. It does

not presume that we know all the answers yet. Using discussion for refinement, the team organizes the themes into things they can refine and agree on now, later, or much later. We don't care about specifics here, we care about quickly seeing how the work is organized.

The team then discusses the items in the Now column. *What action items and decisions are already there? What need to be added?*

The **Now | Later | Much Later** is intentionally vague. It is not a schedule, it is a statement of intent. If the items in the Now column are quickly solved, go forward. If people get upset because something is scheduled to Much Later; find out why.

FOR ADDITIONAL INFORMATION **HTTP://MODUSCOOPERANDI.COM/TCE**

Go Deeper

REE STAGE FOUR:
THE IMPLEMENTATION PLAN
The Detailed Roadmap

The team now has a loose roadmap for when they would like to tackle specific tasks and build their Right Environment.

The Detailed Roadmap is the structure of the work and a guarantee that the improvement work will be completed. This generates tickets for the team's kanban and sets an expected rate of completion of the improvement tasks.

This board lives in the Obeya and as tickets are completed they move from Yellow (Thing to do) to Pink (Done). The team sees their improvement commitments and how they are making them.

This is a project-level visualization that allows work to be tracked as it is completed, allowing everyone to see their commitment to their Right Environment realized in real time.

Do It Immediately

I cannot stress enough the importance of **immediate change** resulting from the REE. Teams create value and discard it all the time, making decisions and forgetting that they were made. Capturing them in real time and then acting on them is a crucial professional skill to model for all future planning sessions of any type. See the ROI.

Under **Do Immediately** are three projects: Involve team throughout the process, Food and Feels, and Real talk and Feedback. Next to these are tasks to be done to realize the goals of these projects. We can see several are already complete, showing ROI for the team. Many of these will be done before you leave the REE.

Pro Tips

Schedule Now:
If you don't do it now, you never will. Collaborative tickets require scheduling. It is no one's job to schedule after the REE.

Perfect is the Enemy of Progress:
There is no perfection. PDSA means things can always be better. The team must begin improvement paths immediately.

Lay the groundwork for the future:
You don't know the future, but you can see the first steps to get there. This group wanted better collaboration with stakeholders, starting with spending more time with them. They made that an immediate action that created a foundation for future improvements.

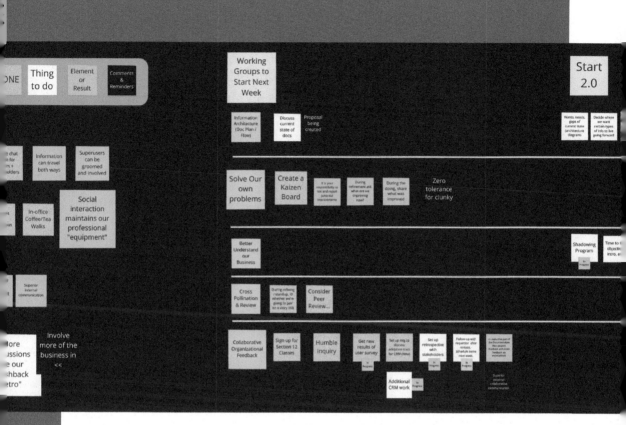

Future Value

This is deeper than just improvement. This is more than a retrospective; we are acting on our Right Environment. The team should commit to focusing some of their work on improvement.

This is a commitment: If reality makes you miss that goal, you need to make it up. If "reality" forces missing improvement goals for over a month, you have lost control of your work.

We want the roadmap in our Obeya to show progress and context, each ticket is part of our commitment. Completion shows commitments the team made to each other are respected.

Pro Tips

Keep it Alive:
This is the team's completion portfolio. As "Now" and "2.0" pass, new tasks and themes should appear on the board. You are building the start of something, not a finite scope of work.

Keep It Front of Mind:
Keep people improvement-focused. In your huddle discuss active improvements, who is acting, and celebrate completion. Remove any no longer relevant. This is standard work.

Regularly Formally Repopulate:
Retros or Kaizen Events are working sessions where teams or groups of teams discuss how work can be improved. Use these to quickly generate new projects and tasks for the board.

Beware of the Population Boom:
There is always more to improve than can be improved. Quality issues can be overwhelming. Remember to *solve root causes*. If you're overloaded with recurring "improvements", have a working session to remove the root causes.

FOR ADDITIONAL INFORMATION **HTTP://MODUSCOOPERANDI.COM/TCE**

Go Deeper

REE Implementation Guidelines:

REEs take human beings out of their comfort zones, divorced from their coping strategies, and thrust them into an environment that makes them honestly confront things that make them uncomfortable. While that might not be what we put on the sales brochure, these weeks are hard.

As such, if you are part of the team conducting these, there are some serious recommendations we've employed after doing these for well over a decade.

Take Breaks: Whether live or distributed, people have blood streams, hearts, and brains. Those things work by moving them around, not by sitting idly in a chair. The longer you leave people in chairs, the worse their performance will be.

Live: With Live events, try to get the room working at white boards and on walls as often as possible.

Remote: Alas, walking around on video is horrendous. We take ten-minute breaks every hour with an expressed rule that everyone should get up and walk around. Honestly, it is not hard to tell which people shut off their cameras and answer email...they are the ones that start to check out halfway through the exercises.

Provide Food: If you are live, get food, lots of food. Fun food. Healthy food. Human beings, strangely enough, need food in order to live. Food is also a short mental break. You want to grab some chocolate or carrots or something from the food table? Great, that is a micro mental break. It also gives people something completely different to talk about. "These cookies are great."

Provide Fidget Stuff: While we were at first horrified when one of our clients brought fidget spinners, pipe cleaners, and other toys to one of our events, it took no more than 30 minutes to see the wisdom. Many of us *require* something tangible to bend or roll around as we are bending and rolling around ideas in our heads. For remote events, curating and sending out a little gift box before the weeklong call makes the event a little more special and gives a bit of permission to not stare directly into the camera nonstop.

Seek Opportunity over Enforcement: We've all been on teams. We know some people talk nonstop and others don't. We know that some people are excited for change and others are jaded. We know that some people have a lot to say, but it's stuck somewhere between their brains and their mouths. We've seen some people say, "Jordan, we haven't heard from you, why are YOU so quiet?" And Jordan will usually talk and add value.

But Jordan didn't really get the opportunity to speak. He was ordered to do so. In Lean Coffees and affinity mapping exercises, you can create real opportunities for quiet people to speak that will create a precedent for speaking and make it more likely in the future. Commands will make it more likely that Jordan will wait for another command.

Use the tools at your disposal to create real times for people to add value. Let's say there are 12 clusters of stickies in an affinity mapping exercise. There is one cluster you'd like to talk about. One of the stickies in there that is particularly well-worked is Jordan's. Talking about the cluster for a minute and then pointing to that sticky and saying, "This one is really interesting; whose is this?" gives the quiet member a chance to pause, collect themselves, and speak about something they added to the board... something they already believe in and have put part of their voice to. There is context for the involvement.

THE ENDGAME AFTER THE REE

Pair Improve whenever Possible: Improvements need pairing, partially to make sure they are done, but also because they impact the entire team. Obviously sometimes you won't need to for super simple things like, "make reservation for team brunch," but for almost everything else...pair or make a team.

Reach Out Immediately: You should have many collaboration opportunities with other teams. **Do not wait.** Each day you wait drastically increases the likelihood that it will seem like too much trouble or some problem will come up that seems more urgent. Then you won't collaborate well with the other teams and, as you already know, that will create even more problems.

Follow Up or Don't Bother: If the team isn't going to follow up on the REE, then just don't have one. REEs are not free; they are an investment by both the company and the team. If you don't follow up, they will feel good when you are done, but lack any real commitment. No commitment means no respect for the work done. No respect for the work done means improvement and collaboration in the future will be even less likely.

Follow-ups are working sessions that can take many forms, which we discuss in chapters six and seven. There are three specific follow-ups that both show commitment and build the foundation of a Right Environment focused on continuous improvement:

- ▸ **Your Huddle:** Every day in your team huddle, you should review the roadmap and the active tickets. Celebrate things that are done and provide support to those that are not.

- ▸ **Completion Review:** You have a set of tasks under a certain family, and they have been completed. Take a look at how it went, and see what tasks might be added or were discovered that could make the improvement even better. This happens when work is done and, depending on the size of the improvement, could happen in the huddle or in a dedicated working session.

Quarterly Right Environment Sessions: Every three months, the team gathers, looks at the Right Environment tasks in flight and adds new ones. The team should look at the team's core values and goals and make sure they are still relevant, are being achieved, and that the team is comfortable with the current direction. Pro tip: Continuous improvement means things can always be improved, so the goal here is to find new improvements, not to say "Yay! We are fully improved!"

THE COLLABORATION EQUATION OF THE RIGHT ENVIRONMENT

Individuals in **intentional** teams create value.

We Have a Plan: Our Right Environment now has a shape, a form, and momentum. Our Obeya needs to respond, and quickly. Often the team takes a week off to form their culture or discuss how they work together, then they come back to their work and find a pile of emails, a list of new meetings, and many demands. They start to work satisfying those needs of others and quickly lose track of the commitments they made to themselves.

We Need a Structure: The Obeya needs to take shape immediately, to govern the work the work they've returned to and makes sure the improvements they agreed were necessary actually take shape. If the team does not see return on their investment, they will quickly return to their old ways of working and dismiss the event as a waste of time.

What Comes Next: To avoid this, let's talk about what really goes in the Obeya.

See Your Work

We need to see our work, the operative word being *our* work. Not a standardized assumption of what we *should* see, but a real set of visuals that show us what we *need* to see. Specific problems to solve, improvements to make, and work to complete. We want visualizations where professionals get the information that drives respectful relationships that result in learning and flow. We do this by creating *visual controls* (boards that guide action) that live in one place of professional focus (your Obeya).

In the REE, we created and elevated alignment around what the team does, how they work together, where/when/why they collaborate, and what information they need to act with confidence. Now we need to convert that into visual controls in an Obeya to make the Right Environment a practical investment that will yield returns every working day.

We've seen the ***similarities***: everyone needs information and to see their culture. Obeyas work in every area of human endeavor, from construction to research to software to manufacturing to producing a film to planning a wedding.[43]

We've also seen the human and collaborative ***differences*** between Obeyas, cultures, and boards. Kevin, TLC, World Bank, Coney Island, and

---

FungiCorp each represent different business cases for collaboration with considerably different visualizations and interactions.

You need to build visualizations that work for your individuals in your team creating your value.

With Kevin, we had a one-person team (initially) relating back to a company. With TLC, it was an established team with a short-term crisis, but a long-term need to improve. The World Bank team had a short life span. Coney tackled a massive project that lasted years. And with FungiCorp, we had a large company dealing with a crisis. In each case, replacing the isolation and assumptions that held back professionals with coherent and focused collaboration solved seemingly hopeless and entrenched problems.

In each case, organization facilitated by visualizations was required. The visualizations were the primary mechanisms to plan, work, study, and adjust. They facilitated conversations, kept professionals on track, showed progress in research and work, kept notes, spurred action, maintained alignment, and reminded everyone of their decisions and agreements.

We take the instrumentation on our car dashboard for granted, yet we operate business with far less information than we rely on to pick up a carton of milk.

It is time for us all to see our work and act with confidence.

WE LEARN WITH STORIES

Visualizations must be relevant and useful; otherwise people will ignore them. If people are ignoring the visualizations, it is likely they aren't getting information or value they need.

The boards need to tell a story *quickly*. A story has a direction and is interesting to us because **that direction might change**. Our boards and our Obeyas keeping track of stories we are *not writing* we are watching them unfold around us. The Obeya tracks subtle and gross changes in our work. This is crucial information that we often hide to our detriment.

Boards must be useful and easy to read. If the boards become difficult to read, people will be less likely to use them. We want our boards and our Obeya to be conspicuously useful.

The story your boards tell should be *coherent*: not dumbed down to one metric. Collections of single metrics or thin stories are called dashboards. Dashboards have their place, but we are after something of much deeper business, professional, and personal value. The world is driven by context (how and why are things evolving), not KPIs (how close are we to our desired guess).

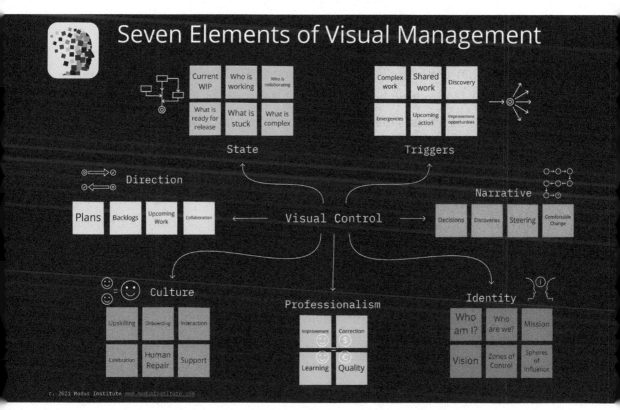

Context Visualized: Seven Elements of Visual Management

Visual controls in your Obeya need to give people the information they need to act. Context is a story: it has background, action, suspense, results, and meaning. Your boards need to convey this information in order to be useful and actionable. These are seven helpful elements for the visualizations you create (you can, of course, create more elements):

State: The visualization shows the state of something. (Car is going 60 KPH.)

Triggers: The team has agreed that certain actions are necessary at certain times; the visualization shows when some state has changed and requires action. (Car is going 60 KPH and approaching a school zone.)

Direction: We can see the plan, the goals, the direction of the team. What comes next? What's on the way? What is our shared story of what and why we are working together? (The map on our phone, the compass direction.)

Narrative: The learning and the value we've received from our Obeya, from our visual controls. What has happened? *What have we learned?* What changes in direction have we made? What do we still need to discuss or solve? (The deviations we or our mapping software have made to avoid construction, traffic, or road closures.)

Culture: Visual controls often fail to recognize culture or try to design it out of the visualization process entirely. This is the number-one failing of both tools and tool purveyors. Culture is also safeguarded in your visual control. We want to make sure that professionals have what they need to do an outstanding job. This includes commitments to each other to inform, help, or work together. The boards on the wall should *not* reward behavior contrary to your Right Environment. If you have agreed not to overload your team, not to commit to untenable deadlines, or to provide information to customers, your visual controls should not work at cross purposes to these agreements. They should work to support them. (Drive politely, stay in your lane, don't road rage.)

Professionalism: The visualization is there to drive professional behavior. *When can I help? How can I help? What are we learning?* Agency, autonomy, and mastery all fall into this bucket. (When you are driving, the passenger will be in charge of updating maps, engaging with phones, or otherwise avoiding distractions.)

Identity: Teams that have defined identities also have stronger identification of membership. Even something as simple as naming the team "The Radi8ers" drove stronger participation in the first Accreditation group at Modus Institute. The visual controls, and their architecture, in this way are respecting the efforts and the existence of the team. (Choice of the navigation voice, settings for screen brightness.)

YOUR OBEYA IS YOUR OBEYA

Remember when I said that the tradespeople on the Coney Island project were coming into the trailer to read what was in the Obeya? The elements in that room were so informative that people would walk a few blocks (it was a big site) just to look at them. The visuals at Coney provided relevant and necessary information that was unique to all the people working on the project.

When Turner built a second room so the trades could display their own information and have their own huddles (a second Obeya), it was clear that Turner's learnings and Right Environment had spread, not through coercion or demands, but through simple effectiveness. They built a culture of continuous improvement that extended beyond their trailer.

What made that Obeya work? Why was it effective? Why did it promote good learning beyond the trailer? How did the seven elements show up in their implementation and make it both effective and unique? What are good practices for building a visual control, and how can those seven elements guide us? Let's look at that Obeya and its elements.

Creating Intentional Visualizations in Your Obeya

The Coney team met before their project began and planned their Right Environment. From their first days of working together, they intentionally created a culture of professional respect and improvement by making sure that everyone had access to the information needed to make rapid decisions in the interest of all stakeholders. Intentionality is keeping in mind our goals and specifically achieving them. The Right Environment Exercise gave us specific cultural goals that required specific information that came from specific visualizations in the Obeya, around the trailer, and on the construction site itself.

If you start by asking what information your teams and professionals need, and create visualizations to provide that information, you win. If you

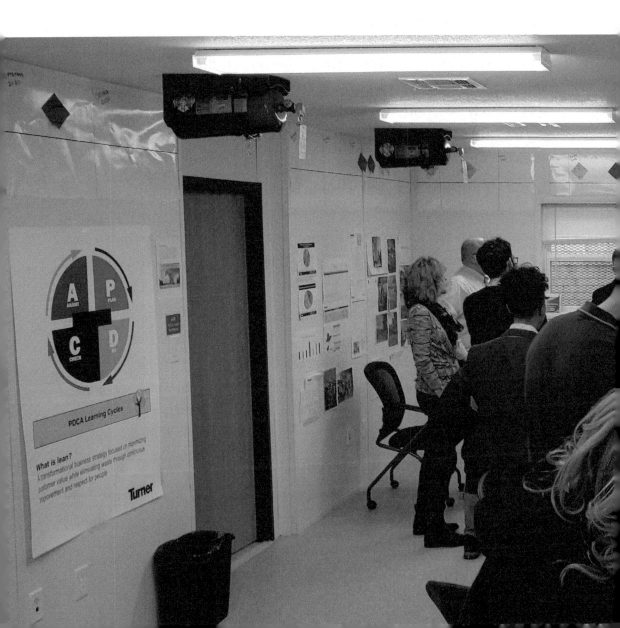

take other people's ideas of visualizations and copy them, you will most likely lose. Your visualizations need to respond to your needs.

The Two Pagers that follow talk about different types of visualizations I've seen and share some stories about them. Don't copy them; learn from them. There are many listed here—not to make you memorize them all, but to inspire you to see beyond a few popular visualizations and create truly useful Obeyas.

Giving Authority to Responsibility

We often assign collaborative work to a single unlucky dupe who lacks the authority to get other people to work on the task.

The unlucky dupe then becomes "accountable" for task completion. This makes them responsible for team work, while lacking any authority to get it done.

The rest of the team is focused on tasks they are accountable for and are therefore unable to help the dupe.

Assigning this work to a single wringable neck ensures that necks will be wrung and the work will not be completed.

To end this familiar no-win situation, owned commitment boards ensure that everyone remains focused on and completes this shared work.

Turner's Safety First

The Safety Officer owns the safety commitment. Every job site differs. These two visualizations create focus, every day. The safety commitment is clear (culture and professionalism). The daily safety plan (Direction), recordable injury rate (State), mitigations to safety issues (state and narrative) and specifics of safety-related issues or trends (trigger and narrative) are displayed in the Obeya right next to the door. You can't ignore them or the safety officer (owner).

Safety information is shared daily with the team and the trades in their huddles. Each trade on site every day has a Pre-Task Plan (PTP) that outlines any foreseeable safety risks they might face and mitigations for those risks. Those PTPs are also on their own visualization.

Safety is a shared commitment, with an owner. Daily safety information impacts how the engineers at Turner do their job. When displayed visually in an Obeya, the safety officer becomes collaborative, supplying engineers and trades with information they need to keep everyone safe.

MAN COUNT 5-22-19

COMPANY NAME	CONTACT	PTP/TOOL BOX	PEOPLE ON SITE
T/M/JV	917-587-6615 LYNN	Y/Y	18
RUTTURA	516-404-6600 Jeremy	Y/Y	31
F.T.C	919-993-1882 Michael		2
F.C. SERVICES	347-804-6667 Sammy		1
PIVOT	347-588-8583 Roman		1
F.P.S. SECURITY	347-723-1118 Carol		3
•EDC/PMX	646-648-1162 Julie Dan		1
STONEBRIDGE	631-275-3311		
ASPRO	516-418-9508 Paul Dan		
MORE TRENCH	201-709-1582		
UNITED HOISTING			
ISLAND		Y/Y	
VERDE	917-807-8328	Y/	

TOTAL

Turner Coney Island

WEEKLY WORK PLAN
PERCENT PLAN COMPLETE
WEEK OF 5/13/19:
81% PREVIOUS WEEK'S

How This Works

We demand accountability and assign goals without authority. Collaborative commitment owners must be able to guide and acheive.

ID an Owner: Owned commitment boards help steward a commitment of importance to the entire team. The role may not be permanent. *The need, the goals, and the requests must be of clear value to everyone involved and not undermined by management or other deadlines.*

Frequent Feedback: Owned commitment boards change frequently, often many times a day, as the state of the commitment changes. This frequent update of state provides triggers where the team will act in subtle or extreme ways. This isn't just the owner showing their work or reporting out; *this is information that guides the actions of the others.*

Shared Information Is Shared Success: Owners without authority end up chasing after the failure of the commitment, rather than organizing the success of it. At the same time, team members are never sure when and how they are supposed to act to support the commitment. *The boards must provide clear diretion and importance to the shared commitment.*

Outcomes and Metrics

▶ **Outcome:** Ownership becomes less "owner" (the only person who cares) and more "steward" (someone watching out for something everyone cares about).

▶ **Outcome:** Team culture rewards desired behavior; in this case safety, becomes standard work. People ask themselves, "Is this action going to increase or decrease safety?"

▶ **Outcome:** Language matches the team's Right Environment. The team begins to use the language of safety while planning and executing work.

▶ **Outcome:** Commitment owners build collaborative relationships with other teams to meet goals.

▶ **Metric:** The project meets or beats goals (in this case recordable injury rates and pre-task plans).

▶ **Metric:** The commitment owner or the steward feels like they are working with others and not policing.

▶ **Metric:** The team consults and uses the board without the board owner present and can present the board to others.

Go Deeper

Building a Project that Learns Together

Projects happen in succession. One person or team has work and hands it on to the next. A team that is currently leading sees a rise in their workload. "Productivity" becomes valued over communication. They rush to complete deadlines without communicating state or learning.

Teams down the line end up ignorant of, or at best re-learning, lessons the previous team did not communicate, which means they make the same mistakes.

Evolving commitment boards show work as it flows through a succession of owners. While work is ongoing, certain owners have primary responsibility at different times. Everyone can see work as it happens, they see workflow, mistakes, learning, relationships with stakeholders, changes in project definitions, and so on.

Future groups, which previously ignored the work of others as they prepared for their own work, now can start their work with a clear idea of the challenges and opportunities they face.

Turner's Quality Build

Turner wants to be known as a company that safely builds high-quality buildings (Identity). Images of current work being done on the site, quality issues, or quality successes are shown (state and narrative). Goals of transparency, low punch list, high quality, and high safety are all served in these images (culture, professionalism, and triggers).

These images focus on current work important to everyone. As the project progressed and different trades were active, concrete, structural steel, etc. created photos while their work was active.

These previously separate silos (you do your work and then I will do mine [anti-collaborative]), used the evolving commitment boards to see defects as they happened. Visualization makes everyone aware of the way defects occur (material handling, strange design elements in the building, location of loading docks or lifts) and allows for early solutions to systemic issues, and creates an expectation of problem solving and attentiveness, leading to a pervasive shared and evolving commitment to quality.

How This Works

We want to see work as it is happening right now, real work. Not simply post-it notes floating across a kanban or a status report. These boards show everyone the evolution of the project.

We begin to see how we are professionals:

What/how did we learn today? Something happened that created learning.

What made us deviate from our plan? An interruption turned planned work into unplanned work.

What improvements did we make? We made changes that will benefit the work and improve our right environment.

What problems did we solve? There was a moment where something that was an identified or emergent problem was solved.

What were the impacts of today's work? Today has outcomes that helped progress the team and their goals.

What were the artifacts of today's work? What we have to show from our work.

How can we help the next team? Events today that teams down the value stream will benefit from.

These boards are used in huddles for the team doing the work. Future teams or future team members should attend often enough to stay informed. The closer your team is to running the evolving commitment board, the more often you should attend.

This is similar to the owned commitment board in that someone owns a board that is valuable to all, with the key differences being that the ownership of this board will eventually cycle through all or mostly all the teams.

Outcomes and Metrics

▸ **Outcome:** Informed teams throughout the value stream.

▸ **Outcome:** Learning is acknowledged, shared, and benefitted from throughout the project.

▸ **Outcome:** Teams doing current work maintain greater focus by constantly scrutinizing and communicating their work.

▸ **Metric:** More, smaller problems are communicated and solved early.

▸ **Metric:** All teams are aware of current successes and challenges and discuss the project more often as a whole as opposed to their siloed part or specialty.

▸ **Metric:** When large problems arise, more teams show up to help solve them.

▸ **Metric:** Handoffs from team to team are smoother and more professional.

FOR ADDITIONAL INFORMATION **HTTP://MODUSCOOPERANDI.COM/TCE**

Go Deeper

Time and Trust Go Hand in Hand

Extremely long projects are planned and saddled with committments before any work has been done.

At the point where we know the least about our work, we build contracts, plans, and Gantt charts promising outcomes we cannot keep.

As work progresses, schedules and planning documents become difficult to read and interpret. Impacts of changes on schedule and budget interpretations and confusion between stakeholders is common. They become items to argue over, rather than see progress from.

Most of the Turner projects I worked on used this ribbon as a simple and effective way to see the current plan and discuss impacts of change.

When stakeholders would recommend or try to avoid change, the ribbon provides real deadlines and impacts for decisions. The board takes on the argument, not the people.

Turner's Deadlines Matter

The ribbon usually runs across the top of an Obeya, showing milestones and deadlines for a project. This seems like classic project management 101, like a Gantt chart on a calendar. The ribbon shows the current state (state) of the project's plan (direction) with rolling notations of change (direction); that's the easy part. The more subtle side of this simple visualization is when the team is discussing the project internally or with stakeholders, they can easily point at the ribbon when discussing impacts of proposed changes or unwillingness to change. *This allows everyone to see that the intangible decision you are making will impact a very tangible milestone.* (Triggers and professionalism).

The board takes time (which we all have a hard time grasping) and makes it physical. The stickies become easy to understand. Conversations become less emotional and more reasoned because we now have the ability to communicate and show impacts of changing or not changing behavior on the timeline.

Outcomes and Metrics

▶ **Outcome:** Better understanding and constant reminder of commitments

▶ **Outcome:** Tangible conversations show the impacts of change on schedule

▶ **Outcome:** Better plan for complexity and change.

▶ **Outcome:** Easy means to show stakeholders, the costs of new additions to work scope.

▶ **Metric:** Relationship between original schedules and actual.

▶ **Metric:** Shorter conversations about change, faster resolution of decisions.

▶ **Metric:** Greater ease between stakeholders and teams regarding change.

How This Works

In every project, we make commitments and would like to achieve our goals by a certain date. The dates, the design, the expectations, and the conditions of our projects can and do change.

Reduce Emotion: When we get together to discuss impacts of change, the conversations are usually going to be emotional. The Time and Progress Ribbon specifically reduces emotion by getting stakeholders to focus on the ribbon and see the impacts of an action or inaction.

Constant Reminder: When we are busy, it is easy for time to slip away from us. Even if our projects are not deadline-driven, there is always a cost of delay. There are trade-offs between quality and release.

Seeing Learning: As we move through a project, we learn. The ribbon shows the impacts on the schedule of that learning. Sometimes it's a delay, but often something is sped up. Seeing both helps people see the benefits of the learning.

FOR ADDITIONAL INFORMATION **HTTP://MODUSCOOPERANDI.COM/TCE**

Go Deeper

We All Build Together

There are many moving parts to any project. Busy people have commitments that come before the needs of others. How do we make sure that we know when we can collaborate?

This simple board is all about creating collaborative **Triggers** visualizing the immediate (up to one week out) **State** of availability and needs of delivery clear to all. It is intentionally short-term, providing small and highly coherent **Direction** and **Narrative** windows. The daily huddles focusing on this information create a **Culture** that looks for the right times to collaborate with others and underscores the need and expectation to collaborate.

Turner Works Smarter

The Team Kanban at Coney tracked team availability. The board was a weekly focus with columns showing the days of the week. Major deliverables, meetings, vacations, and other logistics that make team members unavailable to collaborate were shown.

The board showed one week into the future, so if it is Tuesday, items in the Monday column refer to next Monday. Every day, staff huddles to review the board and plan their collaborations. **The Team Kanban stops blockers from happening; everyone is always aware of the availability and needs of the team.**

If tickets are not completed, tickets will move from one day to the next, so this image was likely taken on a Wednesday morning.

Outcomes and Metrics

- **Outcome:** Availability is a focus.
- **Outcome:** Collaborative work is planned for every day.
- **Outcome:** Respect for other people's schedules and work.
- **Outcome:** Opportunities to help.
- **Metric:** Faster completion times for all tasks.
- **Metric:** Less interruptions.
- **Metric:** More issues caught and discussed early.

How This Works

Make it Coherent: Paul, the Project Executive, is leading this huddle. They are going over the work on that day (likely Friday because it has the most tickets in flight). The group is reviewing deliverables (things important to the project) and people are talking about how they can help remove bottlenecks or provide support on that particular day. That is a coherent system. It is small, it is understandable, it is effective.

Select The Right Detail: Way too often, I see teams try to put everything on one board...and it is always this one. Whatever the team calls their "kanban" becomes weighed down by all the information we've discussed on the other boards. Do not do overload the board.

Make it Visible to All: In this case, this board is pure logistics. It's clean, it changes, it is used every minute of every day by every person working in the trailer. When you make a board like this...make sure it is visible the entire time people are working. If people are working from home and it is an online tool, get them a cheap extra monitor and keep that board up all the time. Information radiators cannot radiate if they are unseen

Make it Relevant: These boards must tell a simple story. In this case it is availability and delivery. Who can help in what way today?

Go Deeper

FOR ADDITIONAL INFORMATION **HTTP://MODUSCOOPERANDI.COM/TCE**

Planning Alone Is Wishful Thinking

Our structure and teams often become silos that plan in spite of each other. This creates failures in logistics where we plan work that requires unavailable resources or happens at times where conflict with other silos is likely. Siloed planning is perhaps the largest cause of delay, defects, and defeated professionals in business today.

Regardless of what your company does, it can learn from an exercise common in Lean Construction called the Last Planner System (LPS), created by the Lean Construction Institute and Glenn Ballard and Greg Howell. The crux of LPS is a group activity called **a Pull Plan**. This is an exercise where stakeholders or groups that are going to be working apart, but rely on each other and can certainly mess each other up, get together and backward-plan upcoming work.

They plan collaboratively to avoid bottlenecks, dependencies, and other risks manufactured by siloed thinking. (You know, the "problems" we make for ourselves and then blame others for.) Pull Planning assumes that it is easier to get work done if everyone isn't in each other's way. While it might sound like trying to stay away from other people is not collaboration, it is the purest form of it. We are collaborating to get the work done by planning professionally up front and then allowing the work to flow smoothly.

How Pull Planning Works

Pull Planning creates a directed and collaborative tactical **Value Stream Map**. Stakeholders gather and backward-plan for the upcoming six-week period. Each stakeholder gets a color, say plumbers green, electricians orange, and drywall blue.

The format of the stickies is not set in stone: different companies add more detail (or sometimes less) to a Pull Planning ticket, depending on context. With software teams, information like availbility, complexity, or level of collaboration might be on the ticket.

> We will do...
>
> ---------------------------
>
> We need...
>
> ---------------------------
>
> Time | # Workers

1 **Start with the end**: Just like a VSM, the teams start at the end and work backward.

2 **Place Tickets**: Teams place tickets in the order work is expected to be performed in the upcoming six weeks.

3 **Evaluate:** Almost immediately, teams will see that their work is not achievable as laid out. *Why not?*

4 **Collaborate**: Work together to avoid unnecessary dependencies and collaborate on others. Schedule work to allow for smooth flow and execution. Destroy surprises before the ever happen.

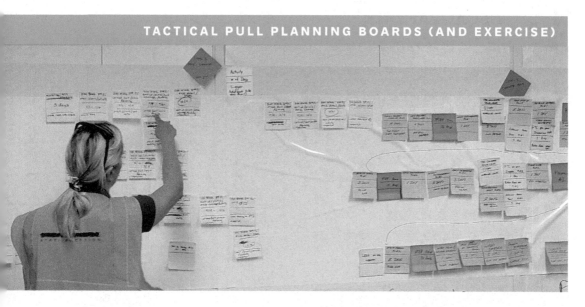

Outcomes and Metrics

- **Outcome:** Build new collaborative relationships between silos.

- **Outcome:** See the impacts of our work on others.

- **Outcome:** Better understand and improve the flow of daily work and the project as a whole.

- **Outcome:** Destroy the need to protect the team.

- **Metric:** Alignment and agreement on the board.

- **Metric:** Smoother scheduling.

- **Metric:** Mood of stakeholders and teams.

- **Metric:** Higher-quality work.

- **Metric:** More realisitic, on-time performance.

How This Works

Calm Conflict: In almost all Pull Planning exercises with first time participants, many arrive assuming they are combatants. This exercise is designed to surface future stress and relieve it early. When there is any conflict on the board, solve for it quickly and demonstrate the power of the collaboration.

It Is a Puzzle: When teams start putting tickets on the board, they are laying out puzzle pieces, but they don't know what the final picture is. The challenge is they often think they do know. This is threatening to some people in the beginning but soon becomes liberating.

The Collaboration Is Greater than Your Work: In the image above, we can see that there are three different groups working in a few weeks and that one group is extremely busy right now. However, everything this group is doing now impacts that later work. *How can later teams help ensure the effectiveness of the earlier teams and vice versa?*

FOR ADDITIONAL INFORMATION **HTTP://MODUSCOOPERANDI.COM/TCE**

Go Deeper

See What Holds You Back

Blockers, in this case, are those things we know are wrong or could slow us down, but we're too busy being busy to deal with them. We often wait until blockers are emergencies and experience unnecessary panic and stress.

This board lists any issues that are currently impacting schedule, budget, quality, safety or anything that might threaten the project as soonas it is found. No project is complete without one. This is common on construction sites, but rare in offices, even though *we all have routine problems.*

1	BG	7/27/17	C
2	AG	7/27/17	
3	AG/BG	2/28/17	C
4	Large ☐	4/15/17	L
5	Large ☐	11/14/17	L
6	AG/BG	10/4/17	
7	AG/BG	8/16/17	
8	AG/BG	12/6/17	
9	AG	12/6/17	
10	/BG	11/15/17	

What's in a Blocker Board

The blocker board captures date, title, description, impact, and current work being done to mitigate. There is additional room for notes or unique information. Teams review blockers at different intervals, but it is usually part of the huddle, keeping the team focused on finding root causes and solving them.

The board makes problems to solve conspicuous and, when combined with collaborative Lean problem-solving, can be an effective tool to acknowledge, promote, swarm on, and solve issues of significance.

The board creates an expectation that finding and solving blockers is part of a professional job; we don't hide them or ignore them. If a problem arises that is a surprise, it should trigger people on the team to be more vigilant.

Constraint

Coordinated Set [100 CD

Contract Terms Agree

Large ☐ Design Dwg

Large ☐ Final Dwgs

COR
STRUCTURE APPROVAL

TL
MECH EQUIP AWARD

How This Works

Embrace and Solve: Blocker boards are healthy failure demand in action. You have a system created to produce some product or service which has a set of problems that you are making known.

Solve and Eradicate: There are two stages of dealing with a problem: (1) make the current pain go away, and (2) make sure the problem doesn't come back. Stage one is dealing with the symptom; stage two is finding and removing the root cause. The blocker board should promote both stages.

You Need a Blocker Board: Almost no one has one. We hide our problems in tracking systems, spreadsheets, or reports that keep them out of sight and out of mind. We call these repositories because knowledge work projects tend to build up such insanely high numbers of defects that they wouldn't fit on a board.

Make It Central to Your Work: You must visualize your constraints; you must see as a group what is stopping you from being successful. Your boards must show the risks at hand, the investigation into the problem, the people that are working on it, and progress. The board must be discussed and used as a work surface.

Extend Your Blockers: If it is a rolling white board like this, have the blockers on one side, but keep the A3s or notes being used to solve the problem on the other side. Keep the report and the work together.

Outcomes and Metrics

▸ **Outcome:** Visible action on problems causing the team pain.

▸ **Outcome:** Direct support for the right environment, team sees commitment to solving problems.

▸ **Outcome:** Immediate attention when the cost of change is low.

▸ **Outcome:** Focus on culture of continuous improvement.

▸ **Metric:** Problems are solved.

▸ **Metric:** Negative impacts of problems are mitigated or abated.

▸ **Metric**: Less stress, greater focus.

Go Deeper

Without Kaizen There Is No Improvement

What's in a Kaizen Board

The blocker board captures big problems of immediate and pressing need. The Kaizen Board captures those smaller tasks that are easily thought of, but also easily dismissed. Individually, they don't have the weight or the fear-factor of the big problems. If consistently solves, these Kaizen tasks are those small changes that avoid blockers in the future.

The board is simply a repository of ideas. Your team should be dropping Kaizen Ideas into the board on a regular basis. The board should be reviewed whenever you are

改善

Kai = Change   Zen = Good

adding new work to your workplan or Kanban.

Kaizen tasks are often done during daily work. We see a need and deal with it. This board holds and remembers those changes where the work of the day won't allow a Kaizen task to be acted on but we don't want to forget it.

Opportunities for improvement are often voiced and forgotten. "We could do x" is often a lost opportunity for greater success, as there is no place to put those ideas and no mechanism to use those ideas later.

Change comes in two sizes, and two bits of Lean jargon: Kaikaku (large changes) and Kaizen (small, "easily" applied change).

At Modus, we Kaizen Boards. Each board holds options for improvements we can and should make. This Kaizen Board is for Modus Institute (our online school and community), LAVM (our visual management certification), our right environment (culture), and Future (what we want to do later).

This isn't a cure-all: it won't remove all problems, issues, or opportunities. The point is to be brutally honest about where improvement is possible.

At Modus, problems, opportunities, and continuous improvement are all parts of the same equation.

Outcomes and Metrics

- **Outcome:** Kaizen tasks are not forgotten.
- **Outcome:** The recording and acting on problems is rewarded.
- **Outcome:** Vigilance becomes part of the system.
- **Metric:** Problems are solved.
- **Metric:** Negative impacts of problems are mitigated or abated.
- **Metric**: Less stress, greater focus.
- **Metric:** Less issues make it to the blockers board.

How This Works

Embrace and Solve: Blocker boards are healthy failure demand in action. You have a system created to produce some product or service which has a set of problems that you are making known.

Solve and Eradicate: There are two stages of dealing with a problem: (1) make the current pain go away, and (2) make sure the problem doesn't come back. Stage one is dealing with the symptom, stage two is finding and removing the root cause. The blocker board should promote both stages.

Solving Big, Solving Small: For your kaizen boards, ask yourself: *What could be better? What is slowing us down? What is keeping us from our goals? How could we provide better service? How could work be better for all of us?* The blocker boards start filled with showstopping problems. As you collaborate to solve problems, huge problems will become less dominant, and this board of small improvements will take over.

These Are Backlog Options: When planning ahead, include some kaizen options. They must be serious commitments and, when completed, acknowledged not just as "normal" work, but as a commitment satisfied. This isn't just work, it's improvement.

Escalation Paths: Make sure urgent, tickets don't languish on the kaizen board. Everyone should expect that options that require immediate attention are more suited for the blocker board and that when solving a blocker, some of kaizen tickets are likely able to come along for the ride.

Go Deeper

THE COLLABORATION EQUATION OF THE OBEYA

Individuals in Teams Create Value

Establishing our Obeya creates a collaborative environment where everyone can get information immediately. No searching, no interruption, no pleading, no unanswered emails. In chapter six, we covered some generic visualization types nearly every project needs.

Proudly Personalize or Cowardly Copy: The way these Turner projects set up their Obeya visualizations is not *the way* to set them up. It is *a* way. These are **Good Practices** that you must mold to the needs of your professionals, your teams, and your stakeholders. Learn from Turner; do not copy them.

Create Visualizations Together: Learn from Pull Planning. The creation of the initial visualization is as important as using it in the future. Teams and stakeholders must come together, create and align, and build the visualization. *Hint:* If you do this, it is highly unlikely your end product will be a copy of someone else's work.

Be Creative and not a Pawn: It is common for teams to buy a tool that manages work, provides business intelligence, or displays information and then become pawns of that tool. Most tools don't do what you need. Creatively use your tools, but if they aren't giving you the information you need in the way you need them, find a way to see that information or get rid of the tool. You are more important than your subscriptions.

Outcomes and Metrics: The structure of the Two Pagers in this chapter each include outcomes and metrics. It should be clear that both can be as specific or as flexible as you need. You should always measure your outcomes and have metrics. You should also set **sunset dates** on them (like every three months or sooner) where you examine your metrics and ask, *Is this really giving me the information I need?* and *Do I need to know more?* If you do not regularly question your metrics, they will enslave you.

What Comes Next: We've covered how to find our Right Environment and collaborate on building and using our Obeya, but we do work together all day, every day. That means meetings. Now we'll discuss how to make the most of every minute we work together in effective, productive, and fulfilling ways.

Finding Your Way

We now have a collaborative structure. We explored the creation of a Right Environment in chapter five and how to build the Obeya in chapter six. We understand our professional culture, gave it a place to be expressed, and created ways we can gather to collaboratively focus.

We all go to work in companies to be in the company of others. It is through our interactions that we create value. It's time to get intentional about how we collaborate. We need a system, a predictable set of actions and responses that allow our professionals to act with confidence and respond to complexity with elegance.

This is **your "Way"**: *how you work every day to keep your culture and your process working together and continuously improving.* This is not something that can be commanded or taken from a book; it is, like your Right Environment and your Obeya, something that must be designed specifically for your teams, your organization, your customers.

WE ARE SPIRITS IN THE MATERIAL WORLD

There is no political solution
To our troubled evolution

— THE POLICE

The Right Environments at David Evans and Associates and at Turner were initiated by David Evans and Peter Davoren respectively, but the *ownership*, the implementation, the ongoing stewardship was and remains shared by the people in the company. Right Environments are opportunities for agency, not dictates for CEO wish fulfillment.

Let's be clear: neither Turner nor DEA are perfect. No culture ever is, but the goal here isn't perfection, but something far more attainable, and practical: to create a culture that is honest about what isn't working and strives to correct those deficiencies.

You are designing your Right Environment and your Obeya to celebrate routine victories and address what is lacking. Consciously break the hold of time-wasting complaints, complacency, and pessimism caused by focusing on what isn't fixed. Design and engage a new ability to fix things. Shift culture from "this doesn't work" to "this can be improved."

Build a clear understanding of what your professionals want and need collaboratively (the Right Environment), expressed in a way that reminds them of their commitment to each other and spurs us to action (visualizations of culture and work), located in an identifiable place (an Obeya), and part of a regular and predictable social structure (your *way*).

This is the full collaboration equation.

This requires us to have situational awareness, improve our work, inform our colleagues, visualize action, and give a damn. We need to care enough about our work, our colleagues, and our own careers to make sure that we are getting the most and the best experience possible.

You need a social system where the visualizations, the professionals, the stakeholders, and the product all interact in the best way possible.

This becomes *your* Way. Without it, agency and psychological safety are meaningless, and continuous improvement will be forced and unsustainable. Without a defined Right Environment, any system you build will always be susceptible to outside tampering.

> *Where does the answer lie?*
> *Living from day to day*
> *If it's something we can't buy*
> *There must be another way*

This is the Way: Building Collaboration into the Culture

The Nordstrom Way. The McKinsey Way. The HP Way. The Warren Buffet Way. The Toyota Way. "The <Insert Company Name> Way"....Faith in other people's "ways" has been with us since that first utterance of "Why reinvent the wheel?" Especially in business, reliance upon other people's "proven" methods is deeply engrained. While many are good, even a "best" practice needs to respect the context in which it is applied. Just think...none of these companies copied someone else's way, except for maybe McKinsey. They all did what they really needed to do.

We simply need to be thoughtful and ask, "Is this <canned process/ management fad/shiny new online tool> 'way' really compatible with how we actually work or want to work?" "What is our current *way*, and what *way* do we wish we worked?" "Is this thing really compatible with our Right Environment?"

Your *way* is functional: it is the rules for how you communicate, collaborate, and get work done. It's how you act with confidence and reliably improve. *Your way is a collaboratively defined and owned system of work that creates action in your unique situation.*

Three Ways from This Book:

The REDD+ Way created *a **definition*** *of work, processing, and relationships* guided by the collaborative system they participated in. They fostered a professional culture of mutual support, consistent product, and rapid delivery.

The Coney Island Hospital Way created *an **expectation*** that work would be visual, collaborative, respectful, and professional. Their Obeya promoted a focus on safety, informed decision making, and a professional culture of respect for all stakeholders.

The FungiCorp Way created *directed **focus*** on the need to collaborate and the results of that collaboration, making it clear that the long-term value of those results far outweighed the short-term costs of focusing the company on one piece of work for six weeks. Their Obeya nurtured a professional culture that valued information sharing, problem solving, and the power inherent to dynamic teams.

That **definition, expectation, and focus** created systems (*ways*) that were relevant to each of their specific contexts, where pathways towards team success were clear and actionable. This was true for a small, ad-hoc team like REDD+ and for a large, long-lived, or even dynamic team like Coney. All benefitted from individuals understanding their interactions **through** their processes and tools, valuing all equally. Individuals in teams, creating value.

Their Ways tailored ideas from Agile methodologies and Lean thinking and created specific visualizations and actions from scratch. They all built Obeyas to support their Right Environment. They all had specific ways of ensuring quality, providing feedback, and learning. All three resulted in professional systems of working, collaborating, and problem solving.

THE SOCIAL OBEYA AND THE WORKING SESSION

Our Obeya captures and shares information crucial to daily operations, investigation, and strategy for all professionals to create, track, learn about, and improve the products of the team. It is the engine of value, the seed of inspiration, the beating heart of agency, the town center of the team's community.

Engines must be maintained, seeds watered, hearts cared for, and town centers utilized. In return for the attention we pay to them, they give us transportation, sustenance, life, and connectedness. When we neglect them, they fall apart.

Laurie Anderson once said, "art is about paying attention." As the heart of our culture, the Obeya runs on attention. Attention is something we all have in very short supply. This means attention to the Obeya must become intrinsic to how we work. It must become a focal point for your Way.

Using Coney Island as a major example, let's look at different options the team can employ to make the use of the Obeya *standard work*, creating a clear link between collaboration and your Way.

Perform Rather than Inform—Let's Get to Work

The Coney Island Hospital team used their Obeya as a central location to keep everyone up-to-date, achieve goals, collaborate to create new visual controls, solve problems, have informed conversations with clients, and improve their work. This drastically changed the nature of *meetings*. When the team gathered it wasn't simply to inform about what *had happened* (low value), it was to perform: to create the best way for work *to happen* (high value).

What resulted were **working sessions** (a more apt term than meetings) where they focused on making decisions, solving problems, and showing respect to all stakeholders by demonstrating that everyone on the project deeply cared and could help. They were individuals on a team providing value, and that team included you, no matter who you were.

Working sessions can be divided up into four categories:

▸ **Routine:** Regularly occurring, quick, focused on alignment and direction,

▸ **Focused:** Directed, goal-based, and creates a definite product or decision,

▸ **Alignment:** Designed to group-process a problem, decision, or aesthetic, and

▸ **Restorative:** Creates a social, procedural, or cultural improvement.

The Coney team didn't spend any time thinking about these words: they weren't focused on *process*. They simply met to get things done. The working sessions they created were practical and just happened to fit these groups. You will, no doubt, invent or discover even more types of working sessions.

Let's look at some of their working sessions and see if we can spot some patterns (things you can do) and some anti-patterns (things that are done often, but should be avoided).

ROUTINE WORKING SESSIONS

A Routine Working Session happens according to a *routine*. A routine is something that happens consistently. These are a matter of balance. Have too many of them, time is eaten up by repetitive meetings. Have too few, your team will lack cadence or rhythm, which, even with the best visualizations, will make work seem chaotic.

Routine Working Session 1: Huddles

Professionals need to start the day informed. A team needs to start the day connected. If the team is the engine of value, think of the huddle as powering up that engine.

Huddles are short alignment meetings, usually at the start of a team's day. They should be informative and fun. They should inspire people to get to work, to start thinking creatively, and to know the expectations and limitations of the day. The Coney team had three types of huddles: Stretch'n'Flex, Team Huddle, and Engineering Huddle. Each met vastly different needs for the overall team.

Pro Tip: Note that huddles worked well at Coney because they had a strong Right Environment and these huddles were an expression of that. On other sites, these types of huddles were done with very different and less impressive results. Doing these types of meetings without knowing your Right Environment results in nothing more than empty rituals.

HUDDLE 1: STRETCH'N'FLEX

The Collaborative Pattern: Engagement & Collaborative Identity

Mandated by Turner corporate as a safety measure, Stretch'n'Flex was a few minutes of simple calisthenics to get people ready for a day that would both mentally and physically taxing.

The Coney Island Team's Stretch'n'Flex was a large, cohesive 15-minute event that started every workday morning at 7 am. Coney made this part of their Right Environment. It was early in the morning, with a new host each day. The host brought their own surprise music, creating easy cross-generational ribbing of people not knowing about artists before/after "their time", and personality. The team members got to show off, and the goal of getting people physically ready for the day was easily achieved. The group collaborated to create a social impetus for professional behavior and got the blood pumping to the brain. Every day started with action and laughter. Every person was invested in both the culture and the action.

The Anti-Collaborative Pattern: Collusion & Anti-Collaborative Identity

On other sites, where neither leadership nor staff there was less interest in Stretch'n'Flex, I witnessed teams engaging a in different type of collaboration: *collusion*. People would amuse themselves and each other by undermining the event, visibly and comically expending the least amount of effort possible to look like they were participating. This behavior was rewarded by management simply by allowing it, even though everyone knew that stretching before physical activity helps avoid injury. This anti-collaborative pattern is important: there was a mandate by corporate that was not embraced by the team, and therefore the team found ways to satisfy the brief, without actually engaging in the work, opening the door for other unprofessional behaviors through the day. Lack of investment in culture and action had its own impact.

HUDDLE 2: THE FULL TEAM HUDDLE

The Collaborative Pattern: Alignment

For Coney, their "Team Alignment Huddle" was an all-hands collaborative briefing held each morning in front of their Team Kanban. The Team Kanban displayed all the meetings, milestones, and items of importance for that particular day and the coming week, so they could easily be mentioned in a few short minutes. Both standard and emergent work was quickly described.

The safety officer would give a two-minute safety briefing (longer if context dictated), listing the trades on-site that day along with any safety trends or concerns that needed attention.

With visualized work out of the way, the group as a whole could then talk about anomalies. What weird things were coming up? What stakeholders, dignitaries, or media might be on the site? Were there upcoming interruptions in the supply chain? Were there major unexpected design changes? They could then figure out who should pair, swarm, or otherwise address the unexpected work.

The Anti-Collaborative Patterns: Pushing Information

Anti-Collaborative 1: The Briefing:

Even on sites with effective leadership and healthy culture, morning meetings were often a boring briefing delivered by one person reading from a sheet of paper or spreadsheet.

On the night before the meeting, the team had to provide information to the briefing owner, usually via email. When asked what should be reported, the response was often vague: "*What other people should know.*" This vague, inactionable direction meant that reports contained the minimum information possible or value-less information to meet the demand. The briefing became a perfunctory recitation of issues that were either obvious or not entirely accurate.

With no shared and regularly updated visual system, the briefing might feel organized, but it is misleading, spreading incomplete information to an inattentive audience.

Anti-Collaborative 2: The Report Out:

A common response to some of the odious outcomes of the boring briefing is the ridiculous Report Out. On some sites, team leads show up and report themselves what was happening that day. This means that the reports people received are directly related to the people talking. Some reports are overly verbose, some are grandstanding, some are the moral equivalent of "I'm fine, shut up and leave me alone."

To counteract the ridiculous Report Out, many teams replace it with a variant known as the repetitive Report Out by introducing a format of "What I did yesterday, what I'm doing today, and if I need any help." This works nicely for a time, but in the end doesn't focus on collaboration, so people spend time listening to and eventually tuning out work that doesn't concern them. Requests for help go unasked; actual work in progress becomes hidden. It is lone gun thinking, not developed professional collaboration.

HUDDLE 3: ENGINEERING TEAMS HUDDLES

Collaborative Pattern: Coordination

Every day, Coney's active engineering team (supers with work happening on site that day) would assemble before the engineering kanban. This huddle focused on the specifics of who needed what from whom during the day. How would the team collaborate professionally during a chaotic workday? They talked about the complexity of certain tasks, who had deliverables, what deadlines were in peril. This was a highly tactical meeting, not just informational, but allowing the team to plan their days in concert with their colleagues.

Anti-Collaborative Pattern: Willful Ignorance

Simply not having this meeting at all. All supers or engineers are considered in control of their own work; collaborative opportunities are assumed to happen without structure and are subsequently lost.

Routine Working Session 2: Lean Coffee
Changing the Perspective with Lean Coffees

Jeremy Lightsmith and I created Lean Coffee over a decade ago to answer a pressing need we saw everywhere. Meetings tend to be run either by chaos (people gather and just start talking) or by fiat (strong agenda with a meeting overlord).

Lean Coffees are structured conversations that break up the affinity mapping, provide opening for different styles of communication, allow the teams to more deeply discuss specific issues, and raise new ideas and opportunities. We often insert Lean Coffees throughout a REE to vary the types of discussion.

A Lean Coffee is a working session where professionals gather, democratically create an agenda together, and talk about topics of importance to the people gathered at the time they are gathered.

Lean Coffees are great for:

1. Unearthing latent frustrations, things that people might not bring up in something as formal as a value stream map or as diffuse as an affinity map. We often see completely new issues arise on a Lean Coffee on a REE's Thursday that receive tons of votes and are discovered to be a root cause for other problems that have been discussed.

2. Finding "weak signals": These are trends or items that have been touched on or overlooked during the other exercises that have grown in importance over the course of the week. "On Monday, Julie mentioned that we have a problem with feedback, and we sort of skipped over it...." Weak signals start weak and will die without a mechanism like Lean Coffee to bring them out.

3. Giving quiet people the stage: Conversation in a Lean Coffee is initiated by people whose topics get the most votes. This means that items are voted for how important they are to the group, not because they belong to a certain person. Since the person who place the ticket kicks it off, they also end up speaking. Because the topic was important enough to get votes from their peers, they instantly have authority when speaking.

4. Diffusing power distance: We have seen organizations with extreme and toxic power distance have open, honest, and equal conversations during a Lean Coffee. Senior Vice Presidents and Young Upstarts simply talking about the topic with each other without fear. The structure of the Lean Coffee makes the collaborative conversation an expectation that often overrides cultural toxicity.

5. Rapidly creating learning and actions: The group records, in real time, everything the group thinks is interesting (learning) and action items in the Learning column. The value of any meeting is its outcomes. Often we can't see other people learn or find something valuable. This column lets us all see that people did, indeed, get something from the meeting together. As this column is understood by the team, it becomes the point of doing Lean Coffee...*how can I make sure I and others got value from our time together?*

6. Giving structure to our time together: The minimal structure and rule set of Lean Coffee makes it a quick and easy way to collaborate in a meeting, as opposed to sitting through someone else's agenda.

HOW TO LEAN COFFEE
A Modus One Sheet

Purpose

To generate & discuss a diverse set of issues specifically tailored to the group.

The Lean Coffee Board

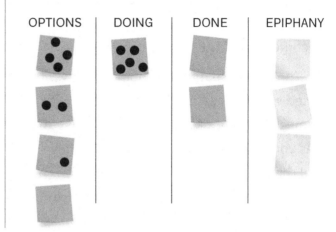

OPTIONS	DOING	DONE	EPIPHANY

How to

1 **CREATE** a Personal Kanban with an Options, Doing, Done, Epiphany value stream.

2 **WRITE** whatever you want to talk about on Post-its.

Making Better Decisions

3 **PLACE** Post-its in the Options column.

4 **GROUP** common themes by clustering similar Post-Its.

Making Better Decisions

Decision Making

John Makes The Decisions

5 **VOTE** for topics you wish to discuss. Each person gets two votes.

6 **PRIORITIZE & DISCUSS** topics in order voted, pulling the topic with the most votes into Doing, and moving it into Done when finished. Repeat until Lean Coffee ends.

7 **DISCOVER!** During the discussion, capture any realizations, action items, or topics for future inquiry into the Epiphany column.

FOCUSED WORKING SESSIONS

Focused Working Sessions achieve results. They set a goal, achieve that goal, and create an artifact to remember that goal. They are truly creative and productive. The visual results of these working session products then become part of the Obeya.

They can take minutes, hours, or days. The REE, in fact, is a five-day focused working session. As we've seen with Gamestorming and Innovation Games, entire books can be written just about possible *formats* for these. [44]As your team begins to *expect* that they should expect ROI for their time and that visualized/collaborative sessions are the best way to achieve this, work can happen quickly, effectively, and collaboratively. Your Way will naturally rely on these focused working sessions as a primary mechanism for the individuals and teams to create value.

Let's look at a handful of these. Remember, the narrative is more important than the format. The results are what is important. You will come up with your own visualizations to solve your own problems. When reading these stories of actual working sessions, watch for the learning. Watch for what the original assumed problem was, when learning changed the professionals involved, and why visualization and collaboration were crucial for an effective outcome.

I am also going to start with an example very few people will ever need, specifically to underscore that this section is about *technique*, not about recipes.

---

44 Luke Hohmann. 2006. *Innovation Games: Creating Breakthrough Products Through Collaborative Play.* Addison-Wesley Professional.

FOCUSED WORKING SESSION 1: THE DOOMINATOR

The Doominator is a visualization borne of frustration that revealed to a group of professionals their unconscious disregard for extremely risky behavior.

Stated Problem: This software company was plagues by bugs in their software. They felt the trouble rested in *prioritizing their work*, which led to them fixing too few defects. If they could find a prioritization scheme to help them raise the priority of the bugs, then everything would be fine. They were convinced that better prioritization would set them free.

Initial Response: The team examined how they had been prioritizing. Stack ranking wasn't working. They then went to work finding a different form of stack ranking. Each time, they would create a set of cascading zero-sum games (each defect must be more important than another one).

Observation: Their planning meetings were exercises in frustration, arguments, and time wasted. Every defect had an owner or group advocating for it. Stack ranking left everyone feeling robbed.

Realized Actual Problem: Everything about their planning was political. Loud voices dictated priority. Unheard voices grew resentful, withdrawn. Angry voices criticized or exploded.

The teams were brought into prioritization meetings and roundly ignored, while loud middle managers made questionable or uninformed decisions. Alignment, for them, meant people had become too tired or ran out of time, to argue. The teams in the room spent most the time texting friends outside of the room about how horrible the meeting was. Work was then parceled out to people who firmly believed different work was more appropriate.

Reality: We couldn't just tell the middle managers to be quiet and listen. Telling loud people to stop being loud makes them louder. Asking quiet or abused people to speak up only adds to the abuse. This couldn't be solved by just saying, "Come on you introverts, just say what's on your mind!" This required a visualization that would both increase professional participation and result in meaningful improvement.

Focused Working Session: The Doominator is an exercise that uses two perspectives to see the context of something. Remember when we were talking about Paul Nutt's work with decisions and how adding even one perspective greatly increases the likelihood of a good decision? The Doominator was designed to create two obvious perspectives (time and risk) and draw from many more.

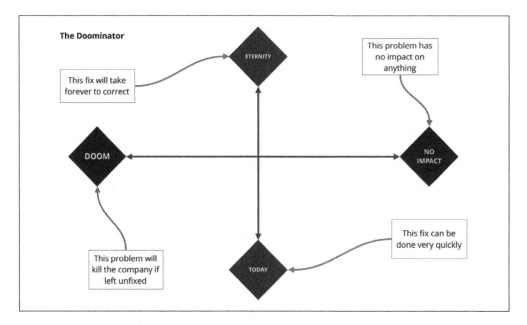

Here we see the Doominator as we laid it out on a large conference table. The long side of the table measured risk, placing tickets from two perspectives: the problems (No Impact to Doom) and the assumed fixes (Today to Eternity). Previously, these people had a meeting where they sat around and stack-ranked 200 things from 1 to 200. They **wasted time arguing** about things like whether item 24 was truly more important than 25.

With the visual exercise, the argument became a working session. The team collaborated, removing the need for false certainty, and focusing instead on alignment. They printed the 200 stack-ranked tickets and laid them out on the table silently—just laying out the tickets within the grid.

The individuals used their professional judgement (perspectives) to move tickets. Many times, a loud person would place a ticket and a quiet person would calmly move it to another location. We replaced combative conversation with collaborative action. Individuals at all levels of the company, coming together as a team to create value.

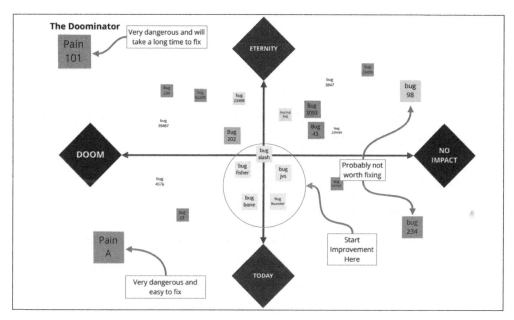

Tangible Results: The Doominator ended up looking like this, except with 200 tickets. This arrangement clearly showed that the stack ranks had nothing to do with either risk or ease of implementation. The tickets with the most risk (Pains A and 101), which could kill the company outright, were never highly prioritized. They were too scary, too politically sensitive, or would take too much time. No one wanted to touch them (even the easy one).

Ripping the Bandage Off: Pain A was quickly dispatched after a very emotional meeting. Blame, yelling, confrontation, acceptance, and finally alignment. Confronting that easy fix *and the reasons for it being ignored* was extremely helpful in breaking through long-standing cultural barriers and getting the company as a whole to start focusing on improvement. You will have similar results.

Confronting the Elephant: Pain 101 was a little different. The team called it *The Locus of Evil*. If that system failed, it would take their entire company down—not just crash, but destroy. Everyone knew it was there, but there was zero planning for its repair or replacement. The investment for this small company would be millions of dollars, and it was a lot less interesting than doing something new.

Lasting Structures of Improvement: They needed to address the difficult bugs, but also build a culture of improvement to make sure they didn't find themselves in this situation again. This used the stickies in the Start Improvement Here circle. This created a three-step plan to build a true culture of continuous improvement:

▸ **Focus on Completion: Built an improvement strategy and road-map**—Take the Doominator results and look for *threads*. The circled bugs were a thread. They were all about the same difficulty and required roughly the same effort. This helped create focus by scheduling work together that meets the same strategic need. This was an effort/impact theme, but others could include:

  • Narrative: Improvements for the same issue or root cause,

  • ROI: Improvements that have a high return and acceptable investment of time and money,

  • Upskilling: Fixes where we can pair and train people, or

  • Client Frustration: Fixes clients were begging for.

▸ **Respect Each Other: Built an improvement agreement**—No system means no commitment. The team created a Way that required:

  • a certain percentage of time would be invested in improvements/fixes,

  • fixing things while building new things would be rewarded,

- the team would alternate between improvements and new features,

- when doing new work, you always left the code better than you found it,

- the team would write clean code and test before handing it off, and

- everyone would participate in a stronger peer review and pairing system to avoid future defects.

▸ **Respect the Customer: Built a team to destroy the Locus of Evil**—The Locus of Evil was truly evil. It would be an expensive and complex fix. In a way, it was its own type of bottleneck, infrastructure that had been neglected, then worried over, and now outright feared. Years of development had built on the poor design and technology decisions of that part of the system, and now any change to the Locus of Evil would require changes in every other part of the company. The only difference now was that professionals were paying attention to the issue. It was no longer ignored. This team added new improvement tasks into the queue and prepared the system for outright replacement, but in the safest way possible.

From Exercise to Obeya: This board became a rolling exercise as the company moved into a less defect-prone and more professional and collaborative Way. The main metric was not the number of improvement tickets: it was **the migration away from the "doom" end of the table**. As with the Andon story, the goal is to catch defects when they are new and relatively harmless and to not let them fester into a Locus of Evil.

This "board" lived in the Obeya, but also fed the roadmap and the backlogs for a variety of Team Kanban boards. The migration of the tickets on the Doominator to the "right" showed the team that they were being successful at curing harmful defects and were being vigilant about noticing and acting on new ones. This visualization was so important that one of the conference rooms was dedicated to keeping it right there, on the table.

FOCUSED SESSION 2: THE I AM ANGRY EXERCISE

Stated Problem: Client leadership of a small startup in New York City said the company had good people, but they were all very angry with each other. Work was falling apart; everyone was blaming everyone else. They needed to get a handle on why people were so angry all the time.

Initial Response: In initial Lean Coffees with individual teams, people talked about how much they hated *the other teams*. In one-on-ones, the animosity was more concentrated, *blaming specific people*. Frustrations in delivery, direction, coordination, decision making, all created a huge circle of blame. The company itself had been a management merry-go-round with three CEOs, two CFOs, directors, investors, and corporate goals all changing at a bewildering rate.

Realized Actual Problem: Lack of coordination in work, coupled with frequent changes in corporate direction and leadership, led to a high-pressure, high-confusion environment. This was causing staff stress and making them blame each other. Their initial frustration with each other must be addressed and ultimately dispelled in order for progress to be made.

Reality: Telling people they didn't need to be angry with each other would make them *prove* why they should be angry with each other. We needed them to *see* it, to show themselves.

Focused Working Session: I Am Angry: These people were unhappy and isolated. The culture of the company was so stressful, their Way had become simply, "shut up, hate everyone, and do your work." Nothing was coordinated; no one trusted anyone else. This company needed to vent, come together, and rally. In classic management-ese, they needed to Storm and Form.

The entire company (about 80 people) got together in front of a very long wall and had the largest affinity mapping exercise we've ever run. On the top of the long, glass wall (which happened to be the wall of the CEO's large office) I wrote, WHAT PI**ES YOU OFF? (This was New York City...).

I specifically used "unprofessional language" to get people to not hold back. We wanted a wall of pain.

They filled the wall. Top to bottom, side to side with their frustrations. Across the wall, the CEO's office door, and beyond.

As the wall filled up, people started laughing and crying. People started staring at certain clusters. People started seeing their system. The realized they weren't isolated, that these frustrations were shared by all.

Tangible Results: Standing there, surrounded by the others, hearing the people you were so angry with talking, and *seeing* that your stickies on the wall were surrounded by dozens of others in the same world of hurt...is powerful.

One woman was shaking, just staring at the wall. She said, pointing at a cluster, "I have been so angry about this, but no one would listen...but... everyone knows it's a problem...everyone is angry...I thought it was just me. I thought...really no one would listen!"

Someone else said, "This wall is too big, too daunting, no one wanted to even think about improving all this. Now that we see it...we can't unsee it: we have to act."

The team then used this visualization to rally. Some clusters showed specific items to improve, but the weight of the wall, the visual mass of the stickies, showed the team that their frustrations were shared and were deeper than individual annoyances.

From Exercise to Obeya: This board remained up for some time after the previous leadership had departed. When things became irrelevant, they were taken down. It was a rallying point for the team, but also showed, as items disappeared, that progress was being made. At some point, things were noticeably better and the wall came down. It also showed the new CEO that the team was serious about making their work more humane.

FOCUSED SESSION 3: CONFLICT MAPPING

The collaborative analysis/mapping tool used at FungiCorp was another focused working session. Remember that we were brought in for prioritization, the bottleneck was discovery, and corporate structure/collaboration was the cure. The understanding of the problem always evolves with collaborative investigation.

Stated Problem: Our teams are having a hard time coordinating and prioritizing work.

Initial Response: Product managers jointly examined and planned upcoming work. They had a Lean Coffee, did a quick affinity map to see things that blocked work, and started looking at how they prioritized work.

Realized Actual Problem: The group was collegial, but conflict-avoidant. The database group was on the defensive but didn't realize it. No team had any idea what work was required by other silos to get their work done, and therefore they were routinely surprising other teams with unplanned "simple requests". For the database group, those simple requests were well above their capacity to serve while still doing their other work.

Reality: Acknowledging the bottleneck bluntly would, and did, lead to blame cascades and buck-passing. Making this a *discussion* topic would, and did, lead to political entrenchment by already overloaded teams who knew fixing the problem would result in additional work.

Focused Working Session: We started with a visualization to list work teams had that was just theirs, and work that required other teams. The visual story of that first attempt was not clear enough for the PMs to see the narrative. The database group was just a column on a series of boards. They remained entrenched.

Pivot: Change the structure of the visualization to *physically show* the relationship between the work and the bottleneck. The database group at the center of an onslaught made a stronger case. They could see that the cumulative effects and realize they all added little pieces of work to a crisis-level result.

Tangible Results: This work caused them to appreciate the bottleneck. This experience also showed the value of the Andon event to upper management. The image of a team literally surrounded by work was compelling and immediately descriptive—we all understand being surrounded. The physical nature of the image, the visualization of a team in peril, and the understanding that the company lived and died by the quality of its data infrastructure let a very difficult and courageous decision get made.

From Exercise to Obeya: This particular board was the center of the original Obeya, but was quickly replaced by more tactical boards that helped teams form, track work, and highlight collaborative needs. It was important that this board showed up in the initial Obeya so the groups could build off its success and use it as an initial grounding of what they were there to do and why.

ALIGNMENT/STRATEGIC WORKING SESSIONS

Alignment is the number-one reason to collaborate with other people. Aligning around a decision, an understanding, or what constitutes quality. Strategic Working Sessions bring together people of varying opinions, build a common understanding, and/or launch a larger initiative. These often involve many stakeholders and include people who are unaccustomed to working collaboratively. It is assumed that if we are looking for alignment, people are likely to arrive *unaligned*. They will be in active disagreement or of varying opinions. There are Two Pagers from chapters five and six that cover the "hows" for these. Let's go deep into the "whys".

ALIGNMENT WORKING SESSION 1: VALUE STREAM MAPPING

We have discussed the VSM at length, but it is a primary alignment and strategy tool. Do not ignore its intricacies. Let's use the Turner Procurement Value Stream as an example.

Alignment Truly Evolves:

When setting up the initial value stream for Kevin, a team of seasoned Turner procurement agents gathered in a conference room and started working out the value stream for "the average project". We worked with them for a week, routinely inviting other people currently or formerly from procurement in to watch, ask questions, and participate.

After we "completed" the map, we showed it to others in Turner's New York Office, getting more comments. In every showing, the map was refined, discussed, and fretted over. Its length and the visual realization of the work made everyone who saw it pause. For nearly a century, people had been buying the elements necessary for a project to be built. No one had ever graphically shown the sheer volume of decisions, actions, learning, regulatory hurdles, policies, and commitments that went into building a project in New York City.

This experience highlighted several truths for all alignment and strategic meetings that you will need to keep in mind:

Everyone Says Everything Is Special:

At the beginning of any VSM exercise, people will routinely and unknowingly under- and over-estimate the complexity of their work. They will say they "already know how to do this" and that their work is "always unique". The fact is, almost no one in knowledge work knows what they are doing, and their work is *sometimes* unique. The exercise must bring this epiphany to them: the facilitator cannot smugly state this up front. This is an epiphany that can only be realized through information and interaction. (The facilitator will come with their own erroneous assumptions as well, even if they are an expert.)

Standard and Non-Standard Work Are Both Manageable:

> PEOPLE WILL ROUTINELY AND UNKNOWINGLY UNDER- AND OVER-ESTIMATE THE COMPLEXITY OF THEIR WORK.

When people say that their work is unique or that they are problem solvers, it usually means they have no process and routinely create the problems they have to solve. The notion of standard work is anathema to many knowledge workers because they see it as a boring routine, yet they are frequently frustrated by the number of interruptions they have in a day. The VSM exercise needs to balance this...to find the standard work to provide some predictability, so the team can have the bandwidth to pay attention to the non-standard work that comes their way.

Alignment Doesn't Mean Eternal Agreement:

While the VSM can be seen as an objective, it is like any other scientific device...it shows the world in the most practical way that can be currently proven. The goal of the VSM exercise is *alignment*. We want our professionals to discover and agree on a narrative of their work. They will always come to the working session with their own opinions and perspectives. If they didn't, they wouldn't be valuable professionals. While the VSM can be seen as objective, it is like any other scientific device...it shows the world in the most practical way that can be currently proven. We want the group to align around this workflow: that the issues with it are truly experienced and that the fixes to those issues are worth undertaking. As the work proceeds, the value stream will evolve; it will never be perfect.

Practical Experiments Outweigh Objections:

When a group decides on an outcome or a direction from the VSM, that is an *experiment* that will be undertaken to see if the fix works. If it is a dictate and not an experiment, those who object *lose*. This "win/ lose" over "experiment/try again" way of working will increase point-less bickering to find a perfect solution in a room where no one yet knows what perfect is.

Alignment Cannot Be Dictated:

Alignment comes from working together, discussing issues, and *seeing* a result that people agree on. It does not come from a manager or ap-pointed leader. Alignment comes from understanding at the personal and professional level and sharing that understanding with those you are with. This almost always comes from collaboration.

ALIGNMENT WORKING SESSION 2: PULL PLANNING

Planning together is one of the hallmarks of a humane working environment. Finding ways to ensure that everyone knows what to do, how they can help, and that they aren't being made a bottleneck is central to any Right Environment.

Pull Planning gets its name from the *act* of pull. There are two types of Pull:

Work Selection Pull: You can get work assigned to you (push), or you can be part of selecting your work (pull). Pulling your work helps ensure that you or your team (who know the most about current context and capacity) aren't overloaded, underinformed, or missing other opportunities.

Customer Pull: The customer is the ultimate agent of pull: they are *pulling* value from your company. If you make cars, they order a car. If you

are a consultant, they schedule time and define the need. The customer has asked for something from your company, and that creates the need for work in the first place.

Pull Planning avoids dependencies or conflicts in upcoming work by aligning around both types of pull. What can we do next and what is needed?

We do this to avoid what we saw with FungiCorp: myopic planning within silos led to misaligned team goals, uninformed decisions, naturally occurring bottlenecks, and emergent social breakdown (distrust, blame, and frustration).

Coney Island's Pull Planning sessions happened regularly in front of the Pull Planning board. The first few were marked with distrust and confusion (why are we here? What are you trying to do to us now?), but in every session the participants found ways to help each other succeed. As they received direct benefits from the Pull Planning alignment, they became not only more interested in the exercise, but in the work of the other trades.

The tangible nature of the Pull Planning exercise builds trust and alignment. Bottlenecks and conflicts become clear, but less threatening. Maybe there isn't time in the schedule for the work to be done in a safe and professional manner...*as currently described.*

The tangible system, however, takes the politics and fear (intangible threats) and turns them into visual objects that simply need to be rearranged (tangible items of work).

Planning now becomes not a set of demands to meet, but a puzzle to be solved. *A puzzle*...not a set of commands. Not barked orders. Not one person making another look bad, but an honest puzzle. Three or four companies, dozens of workers, heavy equipment, a certain optimal flow of work...and a deadline that everyone had already planned around.

Strangely, when you are all paying attention to something, it's easier to manage.

This activity, this visualization, and the products they promote (better schedules, more certainty that planned work will actually happen, less conflicts between teams) is a perfect intersection of the Right Environment and the Obeya.

In alignment and strategic meetings, we are raising the bar of professionalism by acknowledging:

Value Drives Commitment: When people come to any meeting, they are looking for value. Not necessarily *what's in it for me?* but more foundational... *how is this not going to hurt me?* Alignment sessions are often the melding of various perspectives, which is envisioned as negotiation (adversarial). In every Pull Planning session, the adversarial assumption of negotiation has been met with the collaborative reality of finding ways to help each other.

It's About the Best Way to Work: Pull Planning sessions must focus on *the best way to collaborate*. They will unravel when the hosts think it is about scheduling and logistics, they will end up starting adversarial negotiations themselves: "*Why can't you do that faster? Why do you need to be there that day? We require this...*" Everyone I have met, and you'll meet them too, who hates Pull Planning hates it because the hosts actively used the sessions to push an agenda, not find the best way to work.

Honesty Drives Results: In order for work involving multiple parties to flow smoothly, people need to be honest about what might stall them, what resources they require, and what risks are at play. This is true for any kind of alignment; you need a full narrative to align around.

RESTORATIVE WORKING SESSIONS

Culture and learning are crucial to our success. The seven elements we discussed in Restorative Working Sessions provide feedback loops that the team is working well, the Right Environment is still relevant and working, product is being produced to the team's professional satisfaction, and learning is shared. These sessions should happen regularly and directly feed new options to your team's Personal Kanban, but they should also be sessions where you recharge, make sure everyone is okay, and make adjustments.

RESTORATIVE 1: RETROSPECTIVES

A retrospective working session is a regularly scheduled event that looks specifically at continuous improvement efforts in flight and generates new improvement tasks. These should be held at least every month, if not every other week. They should be short, always review improvements completed or in flight first, and then look at new improvement opportunities. If you do not do this, your team has no continuous improvement regimen. Regular retros are the momentum of your team's ability to improve. They are where you spot improvement opportunities, evaluate them, and select the ones to engage in now.

There are thousands of ideas out there of how to hold a retrospective. The additional information for this section is filled with links to help you structure yours. I have just three pieces of advice:

Momentum: Every retro must show progress to have value. You need to see (in your Obeya) what improvements are needed, what are underway, what are completed, and what impact they've had. Without that feedback visually and in the retro, improvement will stall.

Acknowledgement: Celebrating, seeing, realizing that the professionals on your team are working to make things better for each other is a second kind of momentum. This can't be perfunctory. Make this real.

Reach Beyond: Improvements that only involve your team will, after a while, become the least of your concerns. Make sure that when issues involve other teams or the customers that they become part of your retro.

RESTORATIVE 2: KAIZEN EVENTS

Kaizen Events are problem-solving events that look at a specific issue. They are engaged to quickly find a root cause or a solution to a known problem. A problem might be of a size significant enough to warrant multiple Kaizen Events. These events should have a designated problem to solve, invite enough people to solve the problem, and be focused on both a solution and the measurement of that solution (know it is solved).

Like retrospectives, this is a deep topic with many ways of fulfilling the need. Indeed, almost every visualization in this book has been used in a Kaizen Event. The Kaizen Event is special in and of itself in that it recognizes the weight of the problem and dedicates attention for it. The Doominator and the Hate exercises are two cases in point: both were Kaizen Events.

Guidance for Kaizen Events:

Outside Voices Help: Bringing in people who are not identified with a problem or a solution is important. When problems get this big, they tend to come with politics.

Select the Right Outside Voice: Many consultants come with a particular solution already in mind and then force your problem into their little box. Make sure that your outside voice shows some flexibility and is inclined to listen and learn before helping find a solution.

Your Problem Is Likely Not Your Root Cause: You are swimming in a soup of actions and reactions. There are many root causes and even more symptoms. Always run Kaizen Events with the goal of finding the root cause, not finding the solution.

RESTORATIVE 3: OFFSITES AND RIGHT ENVIRONMENT EVENTS

The Right Environment isn't plug'n'play. You don't just decide to have one and it magically appears. Offsites and Right Environment events are important for ensuring that your culture is maintained and runs with, not against, your other working systems.

These events come in two sizes: Micro and Macro.

MacroEvents—Building

These are offsites, REEs, conferences, or other events that take the team off-line from standard work for a few days to a few weeks to focus together on their culture, learning, or some other shared deep work. It should be apparent that doing something like a REE every year is important for the definition of your team. Beyond that "practical" need, teams also benefit from simply getting out of their ruts and stretching their minds, creativity, and attention in other shared directions. Yes, vacations or holidays give them a break, but these events are shared focus in developing a product, learning a skill, or building their culture.

MicroEvents—Maintaining

One of the teams we discussed had set aside time for **brunch** and created expectations that the team members would have **regular coffees** with each other. These are informal time for the human side of the professionals on your team to interact and maintain alignment. Microevents give space to learn more about teammate's world-views and perspectives. They keep up with what is happening with them personally.

When you work with people, it is important to know why they might be on edge, what their outside interests are, what splinter skills they might have, when they might need help with, and so on. These are part of humane management; a Right Environment will flounder without them.

JUST PLAIN OLD WORKING SESSIONS

Sometimes collaboration is just working together. We get together and we get to work. These working sessions might be "Plain Old", but they are the daily driver of any collaborative system. These work sessions need be assumed ways of working with clear triggers (standarding work). When to pair, when to mob, when to plan must all be clear to the team to act with confidence.

Pairing

Your pairing regimen will have different triggers, many of which we've already discussed: complexity of work, upskilling, shadowing, risk mitigation, the desire to increase quality, familiarity, or lack thereof with the work, etc. Pairing for many teams will require being the norm rather than the exception. There also should be no barrier to asking other professionals to pair. If someone wants to, it is necessary.

Mobbing

Your mobbing regimen will be the same. Triggers will drive mobbing activities...most notably being complexity, problem solving, design work, planning, retrospectives, and crisis management. If work or a problem demands that people be present, then it is crucial that those people are present. Just like the mass-mobbing at FungiCorp or the evolution to mobbing on the REDD+ Project, the work drives the team structure and the collaborative need.

THE COLLABORATION EQUATION OF WORKING SESSIONS

Individuals in Teams Create Value

Planning for Results: Meetings historically have been about gathering to be told something or to receive direction. This is why they are hated. Lucky for us, our new Obeya handles much, if not most, of that information, leaving us open in meetings to achieve rather than receive. We are there to work, to collaborate. We enter a working session wanting to make a decision, create something, or solve a problem. These are *results*.

Parallel Processing: We use visual systems in working sessions to get everyone focused and active on achieving their shared goal. Parallel processing drives real-time constructive conversations, where the people gathered see the conversation taking place, and tangibly adds to it. Everyone learns and creates together. Everyone walks away with a shared resilient decision because they have directly participated in the same narrative.

Personal Perspective Beats Personal Priorities: In a typical meeting where everyone gets to "be heard", people are trying so hard to "be heard" that they aren't listening, processing, or actually working. People remain locked in their own narrative, trying to figure out the best way to state it. Their ideas are valuable, but ultimately lost in trying to convince other people while they, in turn, are trying to convince them of theirs. This is a combative "Convince me" meeting, and it is, unfortunately, the most common. Perspective, on the other hand, comes out naturally in a working session every time you *add* to the discussion.

Tangible Is Manageable: When we make our ideas into a tangible visual system, they become malleable. They are moldable by ourselves and others into means to ends. It becomes exciting to see the difference between "what you wanted" and "what you got" because you could *see* how those ideas changed and why. Seeing the logic is critical for understanding.

Working Sessions Have Rewards: So many meetings end with no decision or action whatsoever. That is a negative return on investment for those who gathered and invested their time. Collaborative working sessions are designed to have Return on Investment (ROI). Decisions, actions, momentum, product, learning... can all be types of return. They are value.

An Exercise: At the end of your next 10 meetings, write down the ROI for the meeting for you. Then next to that, write down the ROI you assume two or three others in the meeting received. Then ask them what their ROI actually was. ROI can be zero, negative, or positive. And, watch for people (yourself included) trying to justify a worthless meeting.

What's Next: The Shared Responsibilities of Confidence: "This lets me act with confidence," Kevin said in that wintery meeting room. Having defined what we want to be confident about and how we want to achieve it (the REE), how we will communicate our progress and learning (the Obeya), and how we will interact through meetings and agreements (our Way), we realize that we are missing a critical element of any endeavor... *leadership*.

What does collaborative leadership look like? If everything is shared and understood, is there such a thing as leadership?

The answer is yes, nothing happens without leadership. Someone or something always exhibits leadership. But in light of everything we've discussed so far, it shouldn't come as a surprise that collaborative leadership will be a little more advanced than our ordinary hero worship. When we act with confidence, we also lead.

08

Leadership Is an Action

"All the world's a stage,
And all the men and women merely players;
They have their exits and their entrances;
And one man in his time plays many parts,
His acts being seven ages."

— WILLIAM SHAKESPEARE, AS YOU LIKE IT

LET'S GET ONE THING STRAIGHT

L eadership is a trap. It's a concept. It's an expectation. No one is trained in it. No one can identify it. No systems are built to support it. Everyone is judged by it, on it, because of it.

We expect our "leaders" to know it all, to protect us, and to let us do what we want. We put them in no-win situations of over-expectation and under-definition. They respond appropriately to this system by overreaching and micromanaging.

All those books about being a strong leader, a fair leader, a compassionate leader, get this wrong, and they sell a lot of copies sharing this bland cop-out excuse for advice. They try to make leadership into a definable yet unobtainable set of behaviors that will **appear in one anti-collaborative**

person: an *ubermensch*. That person who can top down and bottom up, manage, inspire, fiscally calm, invent markets, immediately make right and hard decisions, listen, be decisive, and cure all the ills of everyone forever and always.

That's not how leadership works. It is, however, how we routinely end up with overpaid narcissists as CEOs and utterly terrified middle managers.

Leadership is real, important, and part of any successful team, company, or system.

That makes it even worse. It's a trap and it is necessary.

We cannot collaborate without leadership. Leadership must be expected, but not hoarded. Leadership must be defined, yet emergent and distributed. Leadership must be decisive, yet flexible. In the end, either we are all leaders, or no one is.

> *Leadership is seeing* necessary action and ***doing*** what needs to be done, when it needs to be done, by the person or people that need to do it.

This is the very nature of leading: we want our professionals to not hesitate to be the first to act. They have the information necessary to respond properly and with confidence. Leadership is the expression of agency and psychological safety.

If we are going to have a sustainable collaboration, **leadership must be a constant collaborative act**.

A PULL MODEL OF COLLABORATIVE LEADERSHIP

In the past, we've confused the act of leadership with centralized authority. Father figures, czars, the politburo of any soviet-style system, which many, if not most, companies are. These are classic Henry Ford push models of leadership *where a single person or group inflicts their leadership on others*. This is autocracy.

Leadership is not control. Leadership is direction. It is one person or group taking point on something of importance. It isn't rank; it isn't privilege. Leadership is everyone's professional responsibility. When we achieve this, when we make this type of leadership part of our business model—*when it is our Way*—then we have a pull model of Leadership where informed responsible professionals act with confidence every minute of every day to the benefit of the professionals, the teams, and the value they are creating.

Leadership is separate from valid business needs like financial management, regulatory adherence, and human resources, which have fiscal, legal, and other reporting requirements that must be respected in order for a business to operate. This is not leadership; it is **administration**.

Leadership is separate from project management or ownership. This is a role that tracks what we want, how much something will cost, when we've promised it, and managing the expectations of stakeholders while completing it. This is not leadership; it is **management**.

Leadership, we are seeing, is agency. It is the result of individuals and teams having clarity of state, triggers, direction, narrative, culture, professionalism, and identity. When this information is available, confidence ensues and the intelligent people working with you can *act* when necessary, which is leadership.

Leadership belongs to the team: it is the product of a shared awareness of what needs to be done and a professional approach that distributes authority to where it is needed when it is needed. This type of leadership is immediate and adaptive. It self-launches at the sight of opportunity or trouble. This is a pull system of leadership, avoiding the misunderstandings, frustrations, and waste of push leadership.

START WITH THE PRINCIPLES, NOT THE PRINCIPALS.

Everyone begs for the strong leader, that infallible authority who leads the led by their leading leadership. All very mystical and godlike.

But leadership, like planning, is an activity, it is action. A human action, we all lead. Different people find themselves in leadership roles every minute of every day. Maybe you are leading a working session. Maybe you are leading the team to use a new visual control. Maybe you are leading this team in all their work. Maybe you are leading several teams satisfying a single value stream. Maybe you are leading many teams and many value streams. Maybe you are simply seeing that someone needs a break and you can cover for them for a few minutes.

Regardless of your pay grade, station in the hierarchy, or certifications, you will be a leader at some point. All leaders need to remember the Five Principles of Collaboration:

Pay Attention

Leaders pay attention. They are aware of their surroundings. They see current and upcoming risks. Regardless of rank, they make a point of knowing as much context as possible and suggesting or directing courses of action.

People that suggest or command direction without paying attention are not leaders, regardless of their title. Being underinformed while calling yourself a leader is malpractice. Being willfully underinformed is negligence.

Give a Damn

Leaders must care about the product, the customer, the professionals, and the environment in which work is done. This includes a desire for things to be done in the best way possible. Quality product, happy customers, satisfied professionals, and a supportive environment are not just goals; they are inextricable from the Right Environment, which a leader always wants to support.

Improvement is Your Job

Leaders are interested in quality, happiness, satisfaction, and professional support, which will never be perfectly attained. There will always be improvements to be made. A leader understands this. The Right Environment, the visualizations, the Obeya, the way the team handles meetings, the way work flows, can always be improved. If improvement doesn't happen, leaders become uncomfortable. Mediocrity and stagnation are anathema to leaders.

Information Drives Action

The primary job of any leader is expressed here. When information is not distributed at the right time to the right people, projects fail. Leaders notice where there are impacts from information starvation. Those impacts are usually seen through actions taken or avoided (where people who should act with confidence, do not). Leaders see slowdowns, frustrations, recurring defects, or bad decisions, and gravitate toward those issues and find where the professionals acted without confidence and help correct.

Trust but Visualize

Visualization, as we've seen throughout the book, is a primary weapon against information starvation. Collaborative leaders will always be looking for impedances to workflow, quality, and satisfaction and find the information (state, triggers, direction, narrative, culture, professionalism, or identity) that is missing and visualize that information. Those visualizations will in turn become part of the Obeya (common knowledge) and the social system (use).

SHARE THE LOAD/DISTRIBUTE THE RESPONSIBILITY

Sharing the load often means sharing the toil: *everyone doing the same amount of3 thankless and often unnecessary "work" handed down by a gruel-slinging taskmaster with a Gantt chart and delusions of foresight.* Sharing the load is the epitome of drudgery and inefficiency. Centralized false leadership only leads to many questions, information- or direction-related bottlenecks, and tentative action by unconfident professionals.

Distributing the responsibility is the essence of professionalism. Every successful collaborative team I have seen shared not the toil, but *the responsibility*. They understand the Lean edict of pushing decisions down to the "lowest responsible level" (sic) and take that to heart. Work is created to serve a goal and the professionals on the team learn their way to a quality product. They do this for a practical reason: it's the only good ROI we get.

We have companies filled with professionals who *need* responsibility. They are paid money and want to deliver value. It only makes sense to let the professionals be informed, learn, and make decisions. When they do that...*they lead.*

When responsibility is held by one person, that is a **dictatorship**. When responsibility is distributed but with strict tacit (hidden) and explicit (known) controls on how it can be used, that is an **over-regulated environment**. When action is expected, but people are blamed personally for systemic failures or natural variation, that is called **accountability**.

When responsibility is held by more than one person and decisions are discussed, that is a **democracy**. When responsibility has structure and clarity that can help make good decisions be made in accordance with a shared strategy, that is **checks and balances**. When action is expected and failure accounts for systemic failures are in place, but destructive actions are defined and not tolerated, that is **professional responsibility**.

Turner, like all companies, was struggling with a history of a centralized control model of over-regulation and accountability and their newer, more democratic model of professionalism and responsibility. As we say in the Lean management world, they were on *a journey*. As they have progressed through this journey, the people I saw rapidly rise through the ranks displayed a higher degree of collaborative decision-making and planning. It will be a long time before this is pervasive, but the focus of the newer crop of managers is noticeably more open to sharing responsibility.

To see some of the steps in Turner's journey, let's look at how Kevin's purchasing project allowed him to act with confidence by distributing leadership, making both his team and management more effective.

Kevin's Responsibility: Kevin's ability to act with confidence was created by a social agreement to pay attention to the information in Kevin's Obeya. Kevin's role was to keep the Obeya updated and do the work to the best of his professional abilities. Those above him in rank agreed to keep an eye on the Obeya and to act appropriately when necessary. Because they were informed, Kevin knew that they gave a damn. Because Kevin kept them informed, they knew he gave a damn.

Management's Responsibility: Managers, who previously might have been seen as enforcers of accountability, became team members with authority. Their authority was real; they were legally able to make decisions or take actions that Kevin could not. Their role was to ensure that the project moved smoothly and that they didn't burden Kevin with unnecessary oversight.

Shared Responsibility: It was the shared responsibility of management, Kevin, and Kevin's team to steward the Obeya: update it, use it, improve it. At various times, almost every person who used that room was getting value from it. When Sal joined the team, the board guided his onboarding. About a month into his work on the project, he said he could see what needed to be done on the boards in the Obeya, but that he, himself, wasn't always sure what to do next. We clarified some of the information on the wall *and* made it clear that this was his (Sal's) room, too. After that, Sal showed leadership by bringing many changes to the Obeya.

Role Definition and Leadership: The Obeya made the roles and actions of the professional and management clear and flexible: *both management and staff could now be leaders.* Kevin and Sal led by controlling the project, making good and informed decisions on behalf of Turner Construction and the owner, working closely with the project engineers and designers, and onboarding new staff...all expressed in the Obeya. The visual system made the standard work clear, the unexpected work apparent, and the responses to the unexpected work measured and professional.

Frank and the two Charlies could stop dealing with the waste of chasing status reports and do the real work of upper management: clearing obstacles for Kevin, ensuring that Kevin got the right staff, making sure all the other projects were running well, getting new work for the business unit, mentoring staff, training, strategy, administration, and all the other things on their very full plates. This wasn't usurping the authority of upper management; it was allowing that authority space to effectively operate.

> THE OBEYA ALLOWED THEM TO ACT WITH MORE CONFIDENCE BY CLEARING UNNECESSARY WORRIES FOR EVERYONE.

As Kevin said, the Obeya allowed them to act with more confidence by clearing unnecessary worries for everyone.

THE LEADERSHIP OF THE CHANGE AGENT

Amanda Caso and Savanna Sampson were two young engineers in Turner's Architectural Estimation group. After learning about Personal Kanban at one of Turner's internal Advancing Lean classes, they realized their team was missing an opportunity to visualize their work, better coordinate their efforts, and help each other succeed.

Amanda and Savanna were also informed by *ambient learning*. Kevin's Obeya was just across the hall. His team's use of visual systems radiated information beyond just them and their needs. Other teams saw the use, the focus, and the professional benefit and wanted that for themselves. Use of visual systems inspires more visual systems. Acting with confidence was contagious.

Armed with the lessons from seeing Kevin's Obeya (seeing success), hearing explicit enthusiasm about its use (the narrative), and absorbing both permission and information from the Advancing Lean class (agency), they took over a conference room and built an initial Obeya.

Migrating from Accountability to Responsibility

Amanda and Savanna built a board and an Obeya in a small conference room used by many other groups. Their first board used Post-It notes and looked very much like a traditional Personal Kanban for a team. The conference room was used by many other teams. The meetings were often standing room only, as people would lean against the wall and leave with mission-critical Post-It notes attached to their backs and butts.

They then switched to using white board markers, but people ended up erasing the board simply by walking by and hitting it with their coat. Their final revision was to use wet-erase markers which could withstand abrasion, but were still able to be erased.

During those initial months of trial and error, Amanda and Savanna demonstrated for the team how continuous improvement worked. As professionals, they didn't try to re-engineer the room, put boards on monitors, or drive out other teams from using the space. They figured out *how to get resilient value from the board*, while still being practical as Turner Construction's other teams to operate in the space.

Despite this, the team called this board "Amanda and Savanna's board". They put it up, they were improving it, they ran the meetings, and when they were gone, people didn't use it. This fostered an accountability model. The use of the board had "owners", and those owners were chosen simply because they were the ones that started it. Tight ownership always decreases participation and stifles leadership.

They recognized very quickly that their quest for positive change had become an inadvertent power grab. The visual system they used was now managing the work, and they found themselves in charge of the system. Not the goal, but a predictable outcome. They needed to get the entire team to own, manage, and maintain the board.

Amanda and Savanna had exhibited leadership in creating, improving, and getting the team to pay attention to the board. Now they had to exhibit even stronger leadership to get the team and management to collaboratively manage and maintain the Obeya into the future. Strong leaders share authority, and they were strong leaders.

The management stack above them was Robbie, Tom, and Charlie M., in that order. Robbie was their direct manager and was uniquely skilled at giving a damn. Luckily for them, he was also skilled at seeing when others were engaged in healthy leadership and not denying them room to act, learn, and improve.

Every morning, Robbie, Amanda, Savanna, and the rest of the architectural estimation team would gather in the Obeya, review the board, and manage their work. Robbie always gave the Obeya and the two women the respect they were collectively due, demonstrating to the rest of the team that the board had value without specifically saying, "I'm telling you now to pay attention to that board." It was simply where the huddle was, and leadership valued it.

Their board was highly specialized. It had not only copious **state** information, but did an amazing job of tracking both **direction** and **narrative**. On the far right of the board were columns identifying constraints, parking lot, and notes. The board was always tracking not merely work, but also how intricate the work actually was. They began to value small learnings, see the complexities, and better appreciate what they needed to show others. This led everyone, in architectural estimation and otherwise, to see and appreciate the complexities the team faced.

The lanes in the visualization were all different. The team realized that every estimation project had variations in its value stream. There were generic value streams for different project type (GMP, SCA, and Lump Sum), but different customers required different processes beyond that. This meant

that the projects all had different value streams, even though they had the same kanban.

Through the combination of seeing workflow and the notes, the team began to see patterns in their projects' "discoveries". As learning was shared, their notion of standard work became more refined, and their reaction to novelty became more professional.

The fact that the board was evolving with the team, and wasn't forcing them into one specific workflow, gave the team reassurance that this wasn't a tool of over-regulation.

As they worked together to acknowledge the intricacies of their work, the team began to find their value from the board, finding ways to help each other, share learning, allow staff to help on problem projects, get the work done, and see the work change as projects were completed. This also helped them see what learning was really happening, so, after the project was ready for Purchasing, they knew what learning to share with the Purchasing agents.

For Tom's part, as the GM in charge of the group, he would attend their huddles from time to time, review the Obeya and how it was being used, and actively suggest ways to improve it. He was paying attention, caring, driving improvement, and gaining the luxury to trust through the visualizations.

Every day, Amanda and Savanna handed off running huddles to different team members, setting an expectation that everyone had the authority to manage, describe, and change the board. Other team members suggested changes, or outright implemented them and told others later, migrating the board from "Amanda and Savanna's board" to the "Architectural Team Board". When this happened, their cycle of leadership was complete. They launched, stewarded, stabilized, and socialized a better way of working.

HUMBLE HUBRIS

Amanda and Savanna's journey from seeing the potential in an idea to making that idea part of the collaborative structure of their team was not only leadership; their evolution was also a great example of what I call **Humble Hubris**. When you are a leader of any type, there is a balance between recognizing you have a direction you want others to heed (hubris) and getting them to see the value in it and bring their own creativity and perspective to its execution (humility). The goal is to see the need, suggest or create an initial direction, and then allow the others to collaboratively own and execute. To lead and not control.

The Architectural Engineering Obeya created an initial system for their peers and managers. The leaders were influencing from the bottom up. The strength of their character is important: they did not let this become a "this is how I get promoted" or a "this is how I take control of my team" event. They specifically collaborated with their group to build a system that not only worked but lasted beyond their tenure on the team. Both women moved on to other projects, but the board remained.

For a more top-down approach, Charlie W. (Kevin's boss' boss) was a General Manager and Vice President of Turner. He oversaw dozens of projects at once. At one point, Charlie's portfolio included a historic skyscraper in the middle of Manhattan with a problem to solve.

The curtain wall is the "skin" of a skyscraper usually made of metal and glass, comprised of individual panels that are lifted into place and then secured to the building. In this project, after the first six floors of curtain wall were installed, hundreds of dents and scratches appeared on every piece of curtain wall, requiring repair after installation. If these defects continued up another 40 stories, the scheduling and financial costs would be astronomical.

Charlie W. could have shown up on site and loudly berated the engineering team. Screaming, after all, is a time-honored construction management technique that yields predictably unsatisfactory results.

Instead, Charlie turned to a young engineer named Randy and introduced him to Lean problem solving. He asked Randy to watch and record the installations, and to discuss the process with the trades doing the work (going to the Gemba). He also asked Randy to manage his investigation using an A3, a one-page problem-solving format that records all elements of an improvement process.

When I first met with Randy, he was *very green*. Not only new to problem-solving, but also new to Turner and the workforce. He spoke tentatively, waiting for direction from Charlie, who was literally his bosses' bosses'

bosses' bosses' boss. The power distance would have been daunting for anyone.

Randy was about to have a baptism of fire in collaboration, except for one thing: Charlie had faith in him.

Randy went to the Gemba, where people were understandably not happy to see him. The curtain wall installers were distrustful of Turner (management) and of oversight. They knew about the damage to the curtain wall. They suspected that Randy was there to dig up dirt for future lawsuits—or worse, to get them fired.

In the beginning, Randy approached them saying there was a problem that needed to be solved. This created more distrust, as the tradespeople took that as meaning *they* were the problem. Charlie recommended to Randy that he counter this distrust with honesty and information. Give them something to use, give them respect by involving them in the solution.

Randy then went back to the trades, described the problems he saw, showed them the damage, and pointed out that if these recurring defects weren't fixed, those tradespeople would have to fix them and not get paid for that work. He was there *to help them* finish with zero defects.

As they began to collaborate, they warmed up to Randy. There was a rapid shift, from being adversaries and not participating, to collaborators sharing with Randy every problem they ever encountered. Randy felt the direct effects of collaboration in an environment starved of it. Turns out there was pent-up demand for collaboration.

He learned a tremendous amount about the issue at hand (the curtain wall), the deeper frustrations (adversarial relationships between trades), the variation in curtain wall design (the panels weren't always perfect), and about the amount of expertise these installation professionals brought to the project (what they adjusted, how they ensured water and air tightness, how they compensated for damage).

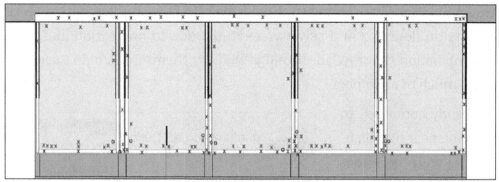

Scratches on panels before improvement

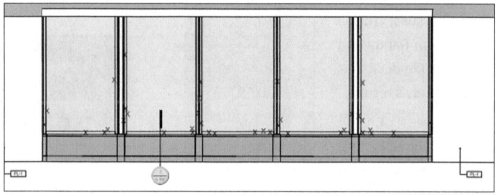

Scratches of panels after improvement

Table 5 - Punchlist by Area and Top Categories											
Area	Paint Touch Up (CW)	Paint Touch Up (Drywall)	Cleaning	Clean Caulk Residue on CW	Clean Tape Residue on CW	Caulk Deficiency	Mullion Alignment	Incomplete Installation	Repair Damage	Incorrect Material	Change Issue Other
Level 05	150	1	95	69	24	25	29	20	28	0	0	0
Level 06	391	2	117	99	36	71	13	21	19	0	0	0
Level 07	454	1	174	136	30	48	35	13	4	0	0	0
Level 08	260	0	79	98	7	9	13	6	10	0	0	0
Level 09	0	0	0	0	0	0	0	0	0	0	0	0
Total	1255	4	465	402	97	153	90	60	61	0	0	0

The numbers tell the tale

These were professionals, not just people with wrenches.

As Randy went through his A3 process, Charlie met with him regularly, guiding his learning and helping him see beyond the initial assumptions of why the damage was occurring (rough handling, unprofessional behavior). Through continued collaborative observation with the trades, they saw the multiple systemic reasons for the dents and abrasions (use of clamps, use of mallets, the mechanisms used to lift and place the curtain wall, hand trucks, unclean work surfaces). It became clear that the large number of defects on floors six and seven weren't just due to one action, but were a combination of a myriad of things that, by themselves, didn't seem to make much of an impact.

Randy continued to show respect by collaborating with the trades to find countermeasures (actions to remedy these issues). This is a slide from Randy and Charlie's slide deck that shared Randy's results.

Because Charlie built an initial system (hubris) and gave Ran-

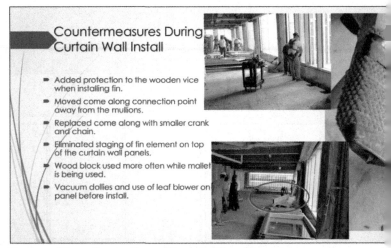

Courtesy of Turner Construction and Randy Castillo

dy the agency to fully engage, extend, and benefit from that system (humility), Randy gained confidence not just through the work, but through his own leadership. He took a VP's plan and made it reality.

By the time Randy made his final presentation to his team on the project and to other teams at Turner, he had become a professional who fully understood the narrative of his work and the impact he had in making it happen. The shy, stammering kid that started this project had grown into an extremely confident construction engineer.

Charlie had asked Randy to use a single sheet of paper that helps define the problem to solve, the current conditions, the experiments to cure, and the results of those experiments, called an A3. He did so with a clear goal in mind. This format helped Randy focus on the investigation and evolve his thinking, and the real collaborative leadership and therefore success came because GM Charlie had that perfect combination of humility and audacity—*humble hubris* to set a goal and provide a collaborative format for

Randy to try, learn, try again, and succeed. When Randy did prevail, Charlie did not grandstand or take credit; he gave all the credit to the person and the team who actually did the work.

Charlie gave a context where a new professional for Turner Construction who knew more just than curtain wall installation could actualize. Randy could now recognize the value of leadership in others and express his own. Randy knew the goal, had a collaborative system to work in, and received sufficient support to be successful and to professionally understand that success. He gave a damn.

THE EXPECTATIONS OF COLLABORATIVE LEADERSHIP

In addition to humble hubris and giving a damn, collaborative leaders also need to express **initiative**. Our examples of leadership so far all showed initiative to get a collaborative process started, but also provided enough structure to allow collaboration to happen. It's not just them. Before Amanda, Savanna, Kevin, Robbie, or Charlie were able to express their initiative, they needed **agency** and **psychological safety**.

The Battle of Brittle

We have a long history of modeling or misattributing leadership skills to people who were able to succeed *in* anti-collaborative systems. We use labels like "self-starter" or "works well under pressure", they are also generally gifted with the ability to see systems and exploit them for their own personal benefit.

Brittle management styles use fear as an anti-reward and cash or status as rewards. They generally lack clear definitions for success and intentionally hide information from professionals.

These management styles rely on rolling single points of failure, concentrating power in a Soviet-style management system of information and funding czars and alienating professionals from their freedom to act. When one single point of failure node in the system fails, the results are catastrophic. In many companies, these failures are happening all day, every day.

Resilient management looks instead for ways to ensure that all the wisdom, creativity, and giving a damn in a company is allowed to create value. Turner's commitment to a safe, effective, professionally run project started at the top, with their CEO Peter. But it didn't stop there. Everyone at Turner has an *expectation* that everyone is committed to that type of work and that everyone can, should, and will bring safety, quality, or other issues to a project's constraints board as soon as it is discovered. The Right Environment, Lean, and safety were expectations.

Amanda and Savanna had an expectation their team would use and maintain their Obeya, because it was a professional thing to do. Robbie had an expectation that Amanda and Savanna could build not only the boards, but also the social system, because they were creative and qualified. Charlie had an expectation that Randy would learn, would see value in the exercise, and would grow professionally without micromanagement. Randy expected that when he was given direction, he could run with that direction and make decisions to help solve the problem. They led the creation of resilient systems that would survive them.

Designing the Structure

We are seeing that **leadership both forms and is formed by the structure of your system**. If we want everyone to be leaders, our Right Environment must be able to self-correct when new people bring change. This change can improve something, or it might be counter-productive. To be resilient and foster healthy working, the system must have clear expectations, agency, flexible role definition, workflow, reactions to complexity, and initiative.

Expectations are the foundation of any collaboration. Your Right Environment is a collection of expectations your fellow professionals have for being able to do their work. They include professional expectations of each other, operations, and the company. Expectations drive behaviors while working:

▸ what triggers certain actions,

▸ what we can do with the information we have,

▸ when we should involve others,

▸ how to broadcast information and decisions,

▸ that situations honestly conveyed will not be punished,

▸ that avenues of professional advancement are clear and attainable, and

▸ that our system bolsters our professional growth.

Expectations of any Right Environment should be defined as a group, made visual, and acted on and improved regularly. Without expectations there is no collaboration, only arbitrary individual action.

Agency is having the ability to make good, professional decisions with confidence. The ability to act needs to be recognized, rewarded, and expected by all levels of a collaborative team or company. The expectation is the simple pre-requisite, but the design can be as subtle as it is complex.

A team must be working in a collaborative system with a defined culture that recognizes how they work together. Their Right Environment needs to be explicit, with visualizations that inform and trigger, and regularly deployed working sessions. The team needs to understand what they are building and why. These elements provide clarity, and clarity gives a foundation for every professional to have agency.

Flexible Role Definition is required. Whenever someone exercises their agency and becomes a leader, no matter how temporary, they invent a new role. Clarity of purpose and the ability to act not only provide role definition for professionals; they allow them to dynamically define new roles when unexpected events occur. Your team's structure needs to have clear mechanisms for professionals to spot opportunities or see complexities and lead, meaning they exercise agency to quickly exploit or solve a situation. It's not enough to tell them to "rise to the occasion". The team needs to have clear calls to action and appropriate actions to take. Otherwise, everyone is just encouraged to be confrontational or go rogue.

Self-Correction in leadership is formed by feedback loops, such as working sessions and visualizations that promote professional collaboration and continuous improvement, that ensure agency, collaboration, and improvement for everyone. Resilience and leadership are both promoted through regular activities that **provide** not just an expectation but **a stage for agency** and action. The more that these meetings create opportunities to spot issues or areas where the Right Environment is lacking, the more improvement happens, providing stability for the team and a hedge against anti-collaborative personalities or actions.

Triggers show up here again, this time in response to counteracting anti-collaborative management techniques like hoarding information, centralizing decision making, or increasing bureaucracy. The shared leadership of the team or the company actively triggers a response to keep the company operating effectively. With an active Right Environment, anti-collaborative actions will immediately be treated as a threat to the team's ability to create value and will become a problem to be solved. Self-correction is triggered by the expectation that anti-collaborative actions are unacceptable. Resilience of the system comes from everyone knowing what they are doing and why and valuing the culture to the point that they can coherently educate newcomers of their collaborative ways of working.

Clear Standard and Non-Standard Work is required for collaborative and emergent leadership. Sharing the leadership load requires us to have strong knowledge of our standard work (that work that is known, predictable, and generally free of unknowns) and our non-standard work (work that is complex, very complicated, or has high risks). Further, we have a good idea of actions we take when we are confronted with non-standard work (pair, problem solve, swarm, etc.). Generally, as the risk profile of the work increases, so does the personnel adding to and making decisions.

GIVING THE COLLABORATIVE SYSTEM FORM AND SUBSTANCE

Collaborative leadership must be expressed in tangible, coherent ways. People need to be able to *see it* and *experience it*. The elements in the previous section might seem theoretical because we are not used to them. They have not been an explicit part of our corporate structures. However, if we think about them, they are how every company is *informally* run.

The workarounds that we have always used to get things done in a hostile environment have been guerilla leadership all along. We don't want to be professional despite our bureaucracies; we want our professionalism to be a natural part of our work.

We need collaborative leadership to rid ourselves of the impedance of traditional management and *work together effectively. Leadership and management combine to make this happen by defining work, defining culture, building resilience, and making professional collaboration an expectation.*

Define the Work	Define the Culture	Expect Collaboration	Build Resilence
▸ VSM ▸ Standard Work ▸ Reactions to Complexity	▸ Right Environment ▸ Cultural Roadmap	▸ Agency ▸ Leadership ▸ Acting with Confidence	▸ Working Sessions ▸ Feedback Loops ▸ Distributed Decision Making

Throughout this book, we've examined different kinds of working sessions and visual systems, all aimed at keeping teams and professionals informed so that they can easily distribute work, solve problems, come to alignment, and create value. Every one of these formats, if constantly applied, will help foster, utilize, retain, and distribute information, creates a virtuous cycle of working together, questioning assumptions, reacting positively to change, and building professionalism. Each allows individual professionals to see a need and act in a leadership role when necessary.

Selecting the few visualizations and working sessions in this book has been a difficult task. There are infinite ways to visualize work and to work together. Here, we can look at a few more working sessions specifically aimed at expressing collaborative leadership.

Our goal here is to make sure that healthy leadership can be expressed at the moment it is necessary. This isn't creating a "flat" organization; structure will always exist, and there will always be senior and junior staff. People with different skills will coordinate work, do work, handle administration, and so on. There is no need for everyone to be a generalist or do everything. CFOs, CEOs, project managers, will continue to be part of our working environment.

This means positional power will also always exist. There are roles where certain authorities will be concentrated. Understanding this, but still wanting to maintain the collaborative model, we want the realities of hierarchy to work in concert with the necessary benefits of collaboration. We need to have specific techniques to manage the natural tensions in these two systems.

The Four Horsemen of the Leadpocolypse

Charlie used the A3 to help promote leadership in Randy. Randy used the A3 to promote leadership in his team and in the trades. When we establish a Right Environment in which professionalism and agency are honestly valued and supported, leadership becomes just another natural part of the system. Charlie leveraged the A3 with a specific problem to solve, specific people to collaborate with, and a specific deadline for Randy's work. Randy's work was aspirational (learn to problem solve, learn about curtain wall, learn about dealing respectfully with stakeholders), and it was practical (stop predictable and costly damage from occurring in future floors, solve this before we start work on those floor).

Charlie's goals were to end the costly mistakes (practical) and impart wisdom to a new generation of construction leader (aspirational). Both were leadership; humble hubris tempered the desire to turn it into a "project" allowing this be an opportunity.

Charlie could choose from a wide array of working sessions and tools to facilitate both the practical business needs and the Right Environment needs of professional growth. Let's discuss a few that combined to make this a success. You should make use of these three as quickly as possible.

A3s

Charlie and Randy used a used a Lean A3 to solve a problem. This simple format can do much more. In his book *Managing to Learn*, John Shook creates a dual format where a manager exhibits leadership by coaching a more junior staff person in true problem-solving. Filling out the A3 causes the person to question his assumptions, speak with others with an open mind to find wisdom, and generally discover a reality of work that he did not previously understand.

The A3 format is inherently and beautifully collaborative. It is not only there to problem solve, but also there to *communicate*. With yourself, with management, with the Gemba, and with the problem itself.

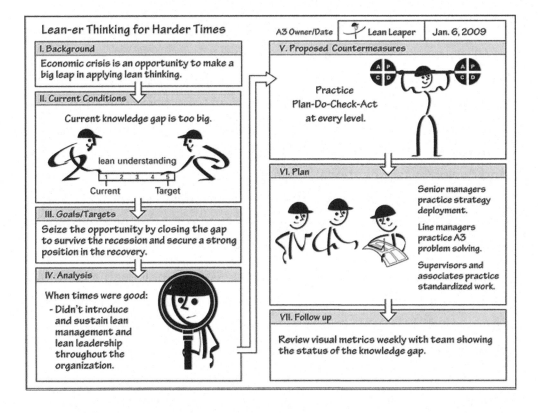

In this typical A3 from the Lean Enterprise Institute, we see how the tool's flow defines the background of a problem, current observations and conditions, what you would like to achieve, analysis and metrics, the proposed experiment(s) to get from your current state to a completed state, and follow up...what are you doing *now* to validate your solution?

This is not a static form to fill in, but a dynamic format that grows with and tracks your collaborative investigation. The collaboration here is key to the success of the A3, something most people unfortunately overlook.

Randy would have simply filled in the form if Charlie didn't show up and ask deeper questions. When Charlie asked deeper questions, Randy learned *how to ask deeper questions*. It wasn't just the curtain wall. It wasn't just learning about that trade. It wasn't just learning about the problem at hand, and it wasn't just learning about A3 thinking. It was *learning the importance of learning*.

That could only be the collaboration of Charlie's experience, Randy's desire to learn, and their shared patience not to take shortcuts.

Leadership in Randy's case was brought about through the A3 itself. The format of the A3 as a visual system triggered Randy to act with confidence by providing him with direction (a format and a problem to solve) and narrative (building out the investigation while expecting that *learning would require pivots*). Culture and professionalism were both underscored by Charlie's leadership in the form of support for Randy as an independent decision maker.

One-on-ones

Charlie met regularly with Randy to go over the A3 and his progress in one-on-one sessions. They were just report outs, intentional conversations about approach, issues, learnings, relationships, and structure. They were coaching, but they were personal. Randy was getting direct and caring attention from senior management.

But one-on-ones don't have to be just one pay grade to another. We find that when leadership is distributed, one-on-ones become valuable for everyone on the project. If we are all to remain informed so we can act with confidence, we are going to also need to look up from our task-lists and see other people. This too, in order to happen as part of our Right Environment, requires a structure.

We worked with a company that made one-on-ones into a regular social and practical expectation. Every week (yes week), every person working at the company would have a one-on-one with someone they worked with, maybe on their team, maybe not.

Collaborative Leadership One-on-Ones:

▸ **Go to coffee:** ...or tea or whatever, but go somewhere together.

▸ **Make an observation:** "I noticed you helped Randy with his A3 and suggested that he showed some of his videos to Susan, I didn't think of that, she helped him see where the other trades could help, that was really cool."

▸ **Make an offer:** "I see you started to work on the project safety manual. I just went through that on my previous project. We can get together, and I can do a brain dump on the roadblocks we hit."

▸ **Make an ask:** "On this project, I've got two stakeholders who seem to be angry all the time. I know you came from the Hell on Wheels project where you were able to get some really angry stakeholders to collaborate; can you give me some advice?"

The structure of these one-on-ones is subtle and beautiful. They happen frequently enough that people expect them *and* always need to pay attention in a way that gives a damn. They need information to share and to request, which means they need to be looking for that as well. This radically boosts their situational awareness, making them more likely to see defects, problems, opportunities, and make better decisions.

This structure drives specific behavior change that the team already wants for their Right Environment. The structure gives them a clear and actionable (required even) way to make it happen.

Bonus: When people who one-on-one regularly get to their quarterly or annual reviews, they have a much clearer idea of who they are, how they relate to others, how they bring value, what they have done, and what they are capable of.

In these one-on-ones, everyone gets to exhibit leadership every week. When management does them, it's not a special meeting you are called in for (power distance) but another opportunity to have a mini-offsite with someone who just happens to be your manager (systemic).

Design Charettes

In Urban Planning you are in the business of constant change. Any project you propose is altering someone's daily routine. Even if the improvement is undeniable, people still suffer from the loss of their status quo, and will wildly differ in opinions on the design for its replacement.

As a young urban planner, I learned early that if you brought someone something that even looked like a solution, they would argue about what was wrong with the solution and strongly resist any attempts to find something the angry resident would like. They would see their fears in your solution and become mired in reactions to their fears. Anything you would say to calm them would only make that worse.

This happens all the time with managers who confuse leadership with top-down action. As urban planners, we saw ourselves as leaders until the power-duo of Elizabeth Plater-Zyberk and Andres Duany[45] launched an idea called the Design Charette. The Charette was a working session where all people impacted by a change would get together and do the conceptual planning and design of that change.

Not respond to preliminary plans, not comment on alternatives, but be *agents of their own change.* In other words, we, as change agents, merely had to identify that change was needed (usually pretty easy to get people to agree to that in principle) and then give them the agency of forming that change themselves.

---

45 DPZ's inspiring body of work can be found at https://www.dpz.com/.

When Randy went to the trades and said, "This is happening, it hurts us all, let's figure out together how to fix it," he was doing a kind of Charette. Together they explored the needs, the root causes, and ultimately created change they all respected and even rejoiced.

In general, a Charette lasts only a day or even a few hours. You can use tools from Design Thinking[46] or Liberating Structures[47] or any number of toolsets, but the goals do not change:

▸ Bring stakeholders together

▸ Have clear shared goals

▸ Refine those shared goals together

▸ Discuss and align around the problem you are trying to solve

▸ Visualize the problem

▸ Visualize the solvable components of your problem

▸ Visualize experiments or solutions

▸ Align around next steps (experiment or solve).

It is imperative that the stakeholders are part of a team that is solving this problem. You are not bringing them a solution. You are allowing everyone gathered to show leadership as necessary. They are using the structure you brought them to lead you, not the other way around.

When we design together, we plan together; when we plan together, we execute together; when we execute together, we all work towards the same, quality product in the same, quality Right Environment.

---

46 Design Thinking is a constantly evolving school of thought, which is rather refreshing in a world of hyper-commoditization, a good overview might be found in Tim Brown's work, but look for specific resources in your industry as well. Brown, T. (2009). *Change by Design: How Design Thinking Creates New Alternatives for Business and Society.* New York: Collins Business.

47 Lipmanowicz H. & McCandless K. (2014). *The surprising power of liberating structures : simple rules to unleash a culture of innovation* (Black and white version). Liberating Structures Press.

PULL LEADERSHIP REQUIRES PULL PLANNING

FungiCorp's leadership failure wasn't the bottleneck; it was allowing their teams to become agency-starved silos. Management specifically created anti-collaborative structures that divorced the needs of the company from the needs of the individual teams. When one team "won", the company, the customers, and everyone else lost (even the individual team members).

Rather than groups freely working with each other, demands from management created isolationist teams who engaged in protectionism and fear.

Management ensured this anti-collaborative behavior by treating the teams like they were all individual service providers serving at the whim of the board and upper management. Teams were assigned independent projects or tasks that excited upper management and the board. They were convinced each team would independently create revenue streams. They gave teams different goals, different paths for individual success, and competing metrics.

It hurts to think of how self-defeating and pervasive this practice is.

Pull Planning would have solved most of these issues. Simply getting the teams together and planning, looking for collaborative opportunities, ensuring goals were coordinated, and making sure bottlenecks weren't being created would have provided stronger services, kept customers, and retained valued team members. Management could still provide direction. Teams would still be strong, focus could be maintained, and relationships would be more resilient.

We used visual systems to help FungiCorp see and repair the damage, but collaborative planning would have stopped their bottleneck before it was even noticeable. They would have built a flexible roadmap that understood the dependencies/constraints/collaborative opportunities.

A Quick Tale of an Evolving Environment

Pull Planning assumes that there is a strategy that the teams are working towards. We assume that there is a shared direction, and the work of the teams are satisfying that direction.

At the beginning of the global Covid lockdowns, we started working with a company we'll call SlashDread, which is comprised of about 15 oblivious teams. **Oblivious teams** are autonomous teams that intentionally ignore each other. They are Agile self-organizing teams that have become self-isolated. They have self-siloed. Similar to FungiCorp, groups produce this by overly focusing on teams while neglecting both individual professionals and value. It is a very common system out of balance.

One of the first fixes for SlashDread came from management who recognized that the teams suffered from constant top-down redirection (Push Planning without information or understanding of why).

That was creating an oblivious culture where people and teams, constantly bewildered by changes in focus, resorted to focusing on the task at hand. No one knew why they were doing something. They just did it and moved on to the next assigned task. They became short order cooks with no menu.

No one could act with confidence.

Management realized that the teams needed to see where assignments were coming from, and why that work was needed. Management then *exhibited leadership* by setting up what they called the **Big Board**. The Big Board's goal was to spur the teams to exhibit leadership through transparency and open conversations about strategy.

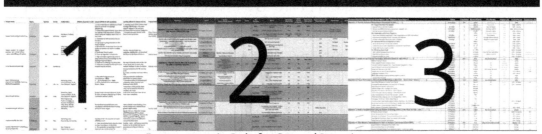

Programmatic Only for Several Iterations

Programmatic Obeya Board   Tactical / Workflow Obeya Board

Spreadsheet and Kanban Views

Management then encountered three problems: language, power distance, and structure.

Language: The original Big Board was a spreadsheet and only a spreadsheet. It had mini-project plans showing priority, goals, KPIs, completion percentages, descriptions of customer need, deadlines, project briefs, and more. This information was all captured in the language of management. When individual developers or team leads looked at the spreadsheet, they saw tons of information they didn't need and couldn't parse. They were staring at a programmatic view of information that could not be used tactically.

Several iterations of this board were created, each becoming more *refined*. Not refined for the teams, but for the needs and logic of management. Each iteration made the Big Board more beautiful to managers and more incomprehensible to the teams. And, perplexingly, the gap between strategy and action *widened* in spite of the tool meant to close the gap.

Power Distance: The cultural history of power distance at SlashDread caused people to see the Big Board as a list of dictates by the COO, not as opportunities to collaborate. It was the most helpful, divisive, inspiring, frightening thing the teams had ever encountered. It was change: welcomed by some, resisted by others.

While the idea was great, the design was designed by management, and the cultural fit didn't exist because *it wasn't designed by the culture*. Due to past Push Planning, iterations of the Big Board were met with skepticism. This was seen as another confusing imposition on a culture that hadn't yet created their Right Environment. The Big Board was nothing more or less than an attempt by management to keep professionals informed and get them involved.

Structure: The design of the Big Board did not foster the desired collaborative professional behavior that management longed for. Looking at the image, we can see why. In the first three, it doesn't matter what the cells in the spreadsheet even say. There is so much information that the eye does not know where to start. The Big Boards were impossible to gain real-time information from. There were no calls to action, no points of conversation.

The teams spasmed, alternating between servitude, indifference, and alienation. They were trying to figure out if the board was punishing them, controlling them, or following a management fad best left ignored. Management tried several ways to describe what the board was for and why, but there was simply no precedent for transparency in the company. The teams felt like the Big Board was being done *to* them and not *with them*. Learned Helplessness isn't a docile malady. The teams here used past professional alienation (proof) to actively resist future change (an hypothesis).

Management's attempt to share leadership was failing. Just like Charlie and Randy, upper management had to find ways to share the ownership of and evolve this board for the good of everyone. Simply put, the company would not survive if people did not have the confidence intended by this board.

Middle management started to grudgingly adopt the Big Board as a middle management make-work program. They would discuss and move things around on the board and then push back against these changes. Mind you, this was during a time where everything in everyone's lives was in flux with Covid lockdowns, suddenly working from home, and global political unrest. This board as a new apparent taskmaster was just one more thing to process. But Covid also gave opportunities for rapid cultural change. As the months proceeded, individual teams were also working on their VSMs and Right Environment exercises. The teams felt underinformed, jerked around, and underappreciated. They wanted more information, but also wanted to just be left alone to do their work. They wanted to see some progress and feel some stability.

Programmatic Obeya Board   Tactical / Workflow Obeya Board

Spreadsheet and Kanban Views

Building a Real Big Board

To make the Big Board useful, it needed to break free of the spreadsheet gulag and become a living set of visualizations in the Obeya. The Big Board also needed to become the Big *Boards*. It wasn't management versus labor...it was *what information does SlashDread need to be successful?* That required a long-term look (the spreadsheet on the left) and the real-time look (the NextGen Kanban on the right).

Bringing in the Teams: Independent of the Big Board, teams were going through some Right Environment Exercises. As they created and thought about their value stream maps, they saw how dependencies, bottlenecks, and redirection were their biggest frustrations...the Big Board suddenly became a major focus. *So that's what it is for!*

Teams began to realize that collaborative planning was the only way to get the stability they craved. Without the information from the Big Board, they would never have insight into upcoming work and the collaborations they would need accommodate.

This changed the conversation from, "who owns the Big Board," to "how can we best work with the information provided," to "what does management need to tell us and what do we need to tell them?"

Notice in the progression from board 1 to 2 to 3, the board became increasingly *programmatic*. It spoke the language of upper management and project management. Team leads and on-the-ground professionals had no idea what to do with all the information. Those boards increasingly *slowed* progress as people tried to make sense of them.

The information on them was crucial to the operations of the company, however. So, in iteration four, we see two things happen. (1) We have a new Tactical Big Board that shows initiatives in flight, waiting to be completed soon, and waiting beyond that. This board shows responsible parties' current action. (2) The Big Board programmatic spreadsheet has been toned down considerably. There is only actionable information on it that can be rapidly understood and acted on.

Version 4 gets closer to a collaborative system. The visual controls display corporate importance. The semi-autonomous teams can quickly understand needed work and anticipate collaborative opportunities. The Big Board is becoming a clear signal not only of upper management leadership, but an enabler of shared leadership throughout the company. Deeper information is linked, allowing quick access, but not visual clutter.

Conversational Kanban

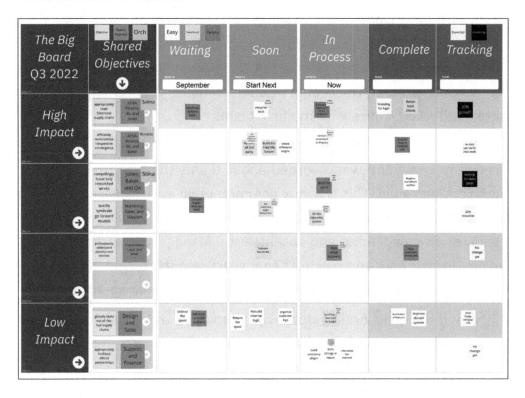

The teams needed to communicate with management in real-time. This could not happen in a spreadsheet or an overly structured visualization.

Having the spreadsheet view for the rarely-changing tracking information was crucial for responsible management. The spreadsheet was made part of their Obeya, always accessible, always convenient for reference.

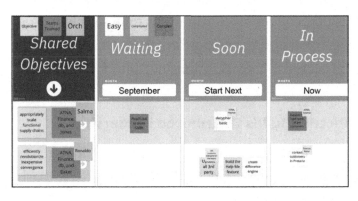

Execution required something more conversational, a visualization that would pass rich state, direction, and narrative information.

The far-left column displayed the Big Board Objectives for the quarter and the teams required to collaborate on that objective. The visualization *starts with the collaboration*, making it clear there is no false "owner" of this shared work. The teams would gather and select what they called an "Orch," short for Orchestra Conductor. This person was a natural manager for the work at hand. They could be subject matter experts, organized, or have good relationships with multiple teams.

The task queues did not exist before. Management didn't think they needed to know and were worried about teams thinking they were being micro-managed. This is a very common ethic in workplaces, allowing teams to "self-organize". Self-organization had become a weird combination of disengagement and absenteeism. Management didn't show up for day-to-day work and reacted negatively when the teams made logical choices that either didn't work or didn't set well with management.

Having the tasks broken down by complexity and collaborative need became incredibly helpful to everyone in the company. The real impact of the work that was requested could be seen and evaluated by all. People began to understand objectives involving complex items better. They began to recognize patterns. This changed how management conceived of and constructed objectives, when they involved other people from the company, and how much lead-time they gave before making an objective active.

The team, which included everyone at the company, began to realize the conversations on this board were more important than simple metrics like how quickly work was done or on-time performance. On-time performance improved because everyone's expectations became more realistic.

How Sharing the Big Picture Builds Distributed Leadership

Good professional work requires information, direction, triggers, and all the other elements of visual management. When the teams at Slash-Dread were in a push system, no matter how benevolent, they were always *waiting for direction*.

And...wait is delay. There is always a cost of delay. If your "strong leaders" are making your professionals wait, they are neither strong nor leaders, they are cost centers.

In almost every business or agency I have worked with, a plague of scared, undertrained managers drives themselves and others crazy by becoming an unnecessary and counter-productive decision and information bottleneck. There is a long-standing demonstrated need to move from this paralysis to professionalism. There are three states to note here that the SlashDread story brings forth:

Existing State: Paralysis and Order Taking: In the past, management expressed leadership by arriving, unannounced, and providing unexpected (re)*direction*. Sometimes this was based on information they didn't share; other times it was just whim. No one knew what was a good or a bad idea, no one could even question what the reasons were. Professionals became order takers. Work happened with no confidence. Planning is push.

Desired State: Professionalism and Leadership: The new system, using the Big Board and other visualizations, would provide a Right Environment where everyone knew what was needed, what was struggling, and how they could help. New demands would arrive in a coherent, professional, and expected manner. Surprises would be at a minimum. Order takers became professionals. Planning is pull.

Reality State: Professional Progress and Learning: SlashDread shows us the leadership of change agents and the frustrations all change agents face. This isn't a take-a-class or read-a-book or give-a-gift and all-is-better situation. SlashDread as a company underwent significant change, requiring significant work on the parts of everyone from CEO to new hire to make this change happen. Leadership was expressed at every level of the company.

The new system, with the Big Board and other visualizations, provided more information to a very busy and growing company. Problems were solved, the company progressed rapidly, people still were interrupted, groups were reorged, collaboration happened, collaborative opportunities were missed. Massive progress acknowledged some massive setbacks. The cultural change was effective, but bumpy.

The teams couldn't just be ordered to have agency. They couldn't be commanded to show leadership. They needed to not only understand the desired system, they needed to know they could steer its future directions. They needed to have the confidence to act.

Over time, they discovered items from the Big Board came from a combination of customer needs, competitive advantage, table stakes, innovation, and backfill.

- ▸ **Customer Needs:** Things the customer specifically has asked for that makes sense to provide.

- ▸ **Competitive Advantage:** Something we do that our competition does not (yet) that can be strengthened, improved, or evolved.

- ▸ **Innovation:** Something that will greatly improve the customer experience that no one has done yet and the customer doesn't know is possible.

- ▸ **Table Stakes:** Functionality customers expect from our product that other competitors provide, and we don't provide or our version is lacking.

- ▸ **Backfill:** Parts of our process, product, or culture that require attention or they will undermine the product.

Finding Lost Opportunities through Collaborative Leadership

A visionary C-level staff person provides the source of corporate direction at many companies. They are short-lived in tenure, mediocre in delivery, and highly compensated. Do not ever be fooled: **If you rely on one visionary to magically direct your organization, you will be disappoint-**

ed. Your hero worship and hope will result in the search for a new CEO and many missed opportunities.

No one person can see the opportunities in customer needs, competitive advantage, innovation, table stakes, and backfill. They certainly won't see the opportunities in combining them. You will get many attempts at one or two of the areas, but not all five, and unfortunately most often you will get none.

At SlashDread, the visionary C-level staff recognized that 300 brains were better than one...

Could the company engage their entire workforce
to bring their professionalism to the table and populate that Big Board?

Could the entire company be leaders?

The key was to get everyone in the company to *pay attention* to the company as a whole, to see beyond their silos.

Everyone needed to be asking, *"What are we building? Who is our customer? Why am I here, in this team, providing this service? How can I help?"*

We had to get the teams to be cohesive and to reach beyond their isolated silo borders.

Isolationism was killing the company; collaboration would save it.

Methodically, as time went on, the engineering, operations, marketing, support, data, and other groups examined their work, saw their collaborative needs, and found where they could do their jobs better by helping others in the company. They maintained their autonomy while gradually and persistently increasing their level of collaboration. They invented and continue to invent new visualizations, new ways of collaborating, and new avenues of shared planning. This is an ongoing, evolving system.

The Big Board became more useful as awareness of how to use strategic information increased. This is exactly what happened with Turner's

Pull Planning exercises. Coney Island's strategic and operational demands (budget, deadline, shipping schedules, logistics) were always there. As the impacts of these demands were made obvious and actionable to the trades daily, the more useful the pull plan became and the easier it became to not only meet schedule, but to maintain a Right Environment for every professional on the project.

With SlashDread, the Big Board was received with the same skepticism as the pull plan, but as leadership made good on their promise to make SlashDread a better place to work by using the Big Board, the collaborative system naturally grew around it, and leadership began to express itself throughout the company.

Building a Collaborative and Flexible Plan

In both shared leadership scenarios, leadership was not expressed through "servant leadership", nor was the company "self-organizing". There were clear business needs for Turner and SlashDread to create an inclusive and collaborative management culture. This wasn't full autonomy. This wasn't anarchy. This wasn't an abdication of responsibility. This was **structured collaboration**.

In both cases, leadership became something that was *expected* from everyone involved: middle management, contractors, and individual professionals. All groups participated in the creation and maintenance of a professional, collaborative system. There was natural resistance to change; management expressed leadership in both cases by insisting that everyone stay engaged and met that insistence by clearly staying engaged themselves.

Everyone was learning, building, and succeeding...and leading...together.

Collaborative leadership requires information. The team needs to know where we are going, where we are, what changes we are facing, and how we are reacting to that change. This information creates collaborative and flexible planning opportunities that greatly increase our chances at successful projects.

Leadership isn't just process or knowing what we will build. Leadership requires *honesty* to see this through. Honesty that we don't know how work will occur, where we will run into difficulties, what other systems might stymie us, and so on. We also require honesty with each other. Honesty that we will find issues, we will change course, we will discover new opportunities professionally.

Whether it is Titanic's twin stories of the radio operator not passing iceberg information to the captain because it was not coded with the right routing information or the captain himself driving the ship too fast to break the crossing record, or if it is the Pearl Harbor story of ignoring radar information because they didn't trust the technology, history is filled with decision makers ignoring crucial information.

We need to build collaborative systems that remove single points of failure, no matter if they are the captain of the ship or the radio operator. The system must have nested loops of collaboration, from those pairing, to the team, to groups of teams, to the entire company. Leadership understands that informed leaders make better decisions, but direction without discussion is negligence. These systems inform, trigger action, and provide checks and balances.

Endgame: A Structure for Collaborative Planning and Leadership

Our truly collaboratively led organization needs a flexible structure. We can't just gather up tools or a manifesto and expect people to start working together. We can't order creativity and problem solving to happen. We must have a collaborative system that allows leadership to naturally emerge from professionals acting with confidence. We cannot buy collaboration, which never comes boxed and ready to use.

We must build a collaborative system that allows leadership to naturally emerge from professionals acting with confidence.

This is a very simple collaboration equation. Collaboratively planning work that does not abide bottlenecks, delays, or poor quality, with current work and objectives fully visualized in an Obeya get every project closer to run as a smoothly as the REDD+ report or the Coney Island Hospital Project.

Every company will go through the bumps of SlashDread and the occasional systemic failures of FungiCorp. But we can build a way to get out of those situations. We can replace the tired call for an "empowered workforce" with a call for real professionalism.

This corporate level system has a deceivingly simple structure that any team with a Right Environment can quickly **adopt and customize** to their own needs:

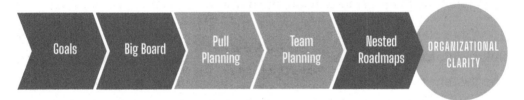

Collaborative Goal Setting

The company needs strategic goals (annual, semi-annual, quarterly, monthly, etc.). These goals can be set by a hidden shadowy cabal, or they can be created by the people who understand the company the best.

Goals are created collaboratively and agreed to by the **company as a whole**. The company plans together creating many options for corporate direction. Work groups refine the options. Then everyone votes, creating an actionable and fully understood short list.

The short list becomes work or projects on the Big Board.

Make it collaborative. Get everyone involved. Use all the brains you can. Agency comes from demonstrated trust.

Make It an Expectation. Every quarter, everyone gets together and aims the company. People will be planning every day they are at work.

Act on Goals Immediately. Plans unacted upon are promises broken.

The Big Wall

SlashDread's Big Board is an example of what a Big Board can do and be. It should be clear that though the Big Board is a spreadsheet, it is neither a visualization nor an Obeya. It, for SlashDread, was a place to start and is being constantly improved. With the information in this book, your Big Board can begin with a more advanced design.

Your Big "Board" would be better served as the **Big Wall**: a wall in your Obeya that holds multiple visualizations of the goals and options selected from the goal setting exercise. This should all be work of corporate significance. The best Big Wall I saw was in the "blue room" at Plant 5 of the GE Appliances company in Louisville, Kentucky. One wall held the strategic direction for their entire French door refrigerator division. Anyone on the line, in middle management, in sales, and so on, could come in and see how the people, the product, and the plans were going. Then they acted on that information.

Big Wall projects almost always involve multiple parts of the company. This wall, like the Obeya for FungiCorp, understands and plans for dependencies from the beginning, ensuring that no one is surprised or left out.

The Big Wall becomes the site of regular weekly meetings that review how work is progressing and honestly deal directly with any shifts in direction that may be occurring or possible. No, this does not mean that if you are General Motors all 150,000 employees meet at the Big Wall every week. It means that you have a larger group of people than you realize that require more strategic information than they are getting. You can give it to them, and everyone can benefit.

Make It Useful

The Big Board is a primary visualization. It shouldn't just be a kanban showing goals. This visualization should include any projects, tasks, teams, people, activities, and metrics. Indeed, the Big Board may be a collection of visualizations.

Make It Flexible and Humane

The Big Board should be considered as definitive direction but should not be considered so binding as to allow bad decisions or to continue down inadvisable paths. The work on the Big Board is a focus, but teams will always have their day-to-day work that must be completed; therefore, the work on the Big Board should take less than 30% of a given team's time.

Pull Planning

Pull Planning is the most disruptive recommendation in this list. Pull Planning immediately improves historically anti-collaborative systems by getting factions that previously didn't communicate to actively plan together. The value of Pull Planning cannot be understated.

It is a regular event, taken on by teams that are going to collaborate over the near future. At Turner, these are usually six-week planning cycles, where we can see just to the end of our certainty. Any upheavals in a six-week plan (weather, power loss, or other surprises) can be dealt with, and even a catastrophic failure (loss of team members, radical funding changes, technology breakdown, pandemic, etc.) can be accounted for.

The teams who are involved in Big Board projects get together and do Pull Planning sessions. These sessions are timed based on the volatility of the work: If the work is highly complex, requires a great deal of inter-team communication, or is in some way risky, Pull Planning sessions could be as often as daily (another huddle). If the work is fairly defined, it could be as much as every six weeks. Weekly or bi-weekly is advisable. Look for opportunities to get cross-team pairs or strike teams to work together closely while doing the shared work.

Make Pull Planning an action and a wall.

Pull Planning should be an activity that people anticipate, both in need and in structure. It will need visualizations that specifically address the work and the difficulties in getting people together to do the work. The Pull Planning exercise should follow the format above initially but use the visualizations to customize it to your needs. The teams must customize the Pull Planning exercises or they will treat them as a chore and not a professional need.

Regular Intervals

The power of predictable planning cannot be understated. Dropping the ball with Pull Planning is like losing control of a two-wheeled suitcase at the airport. The cadence of the planning ensures that the people in the planning cycles stay informed, respected, and relevance. Keep to the six-week cycle; run Pull Planning sessions every two to three weeks. It is okay, or even encouraged, to have "emergency" sessions when something is going to make your Pull Planning board questionable.

Build the Collaboration's Standard work and VSM.

Collaboration is not easy. If your collaboration has importance and weight, get together and do a VSM exercise. It can be a quick one, but make sure there are no assumptions lurking in the cross-team work. We've seen many times where "big teams" take smaller teams or shared resources for granted, do a great job collaborating with the heavy hitters, and then end up running into a delay in localization, graphics, legal, or some other "supporting role". This should make it clear that all collaborators are important—ignore professionals at your peril.

Co-Plan and Co-Work and Co-Improve

If we plan together, we can work together, and we improve together. Look for ways to have shared retrospectives to learn together, not just for how the work went, but for how the Pull Planning went. Make sure you have real feedback loops where people plan, work, learn, improve, and plan again. Plan, Do, Study, Adjust (PDSA) is the loop of feedback and continuous improvement. It must be collaborative. It must be expected.

Structure Time Effectively

When you pull plan, really plan. Schedule time during the meeting. Try to avoid "Rick and Lu will schedule time next week to work on this." Schedule the time, get the tickets on the respective teams' kanban boards, and create the expectation that work will be done and completed. Watch how this works, see what windows of time are appropriate, see what variation there is in the work. Learn to make this professional scheduling standard work, and stop making most of the work for Rick and Lu scheduling their meeting.

Team Planning

Planning together is the main expression of leadership. Teams gather and lead themselves into the future as informed actors and not reactive order-fillers.

Teams should be reviewing their work daily in their huddle and weekly in Retrospectives. If team direction is changed through Pull Planning or a review at the Big Board, the team will need a planning session. These start long as the teams figure out how they plan, after the Obeya has been in operation for a while and the team is more aware, these can be as short as 5 minutes. The planning sessions and huddles are moments to specifically focus on work that is new, novel, or in peril. If work is being discussed at all, there is usually an opportunity for pairing. If it is cross-team work, look for opportunities for cross-team pairs.

Regular cadence: Standard work is a cadence. We are balancing known teamwork with complexity or discovery. If your team does not have standard work, they will manufacture their own complexity, delays, and confusion. We want to plan for the known and make room for the unknown.

Discovery and Calming: They need to understand their standard and non-standard work mix. They need to constantly be taking the new and novel and converting it to the known. That is the process through which improvement and profit are made. Making the known easy and the unknown known is the process of value.

Retrospectives are planning: What you can do requires understanding of what you have done. This is why planning cannot be done by a single product manager. Planning for the future requires the wisdom of what was done in the past. Your team planning must include retrospectives. If the team isn't actively investigating its work, it cannot hope to actively plan it.

Learning and improvement: Through Pull Planning, we learn how to work with others. Through planning our internal teamwork, we learn to work with our team. Through conversations and feedback with the customer we learn to create value. Through trial and error, we learn to solve problems, explore opportunities and calm collaboration. Through continuous improvement we learn to approach all work in a professional way. All of these require the team as a whole to be paying attention and giving a damn. With all this learning, leadership is constantly expressed through agency: professionals understanding that this learning is not overhead; it is the real work of the team. Without it, we have anti-collaborative mediocrity.

Flow and commitment: Almost every team promises or is forced to promise a certain amount of work over a certain amount of time with little or no understanding of their actual capacity. Inevitably, they overpromise and underdeliver, which undermines their professionalism and erodes agency.

What you say **you can do** requires understanding what **you are capable of doing**. Teams need to understand how much work and what types of work they do on a regular basis. They need to understand how much complexity they normally face and how many units of work they regularly complete. Teams should measure real rates of completion through real measures like throughput and cycle time, filtered through the complexity of their work. The more complex the work becomes, the more honest the team needs to be about their completion times.

Nested Roadmaps

The teams need to see their work, which means the work dedicated to their teams and shared with other teams. They need to see **all their work**. This might sound obvious, but if it were done regularly, FungiCorp's situation wouldn't be so painfully familiar.

Each team has a planning horizon where they know their work with varying levels of certainty.

The Big Board gives a macro roadmap, the cross-functional projects will have mezzo roadmaps, the teams will have the micro roadmaps. Each roadmap has an increasing level of granularity and corresponds to the work of that group. The Big Board is interested in a portfolio of projects, the cross-functional work will be interested in a particular project, and the teams will be interested in specific elements of work. Just like in an online map where you can zoom in and zoom out. (Pro tip: this is why your online kanban tools don't work well; they don't allow you to analyze work at different zoom levels.)

As you move through the six-week cycle of the pull plan, your ability to foresee events diminishes. This is why we update the pull plan every two weeks. Each team had their own kanban board, based on their internal roadmap. The pull plan becomes a shared backlog from which multiple teams pull items for their kanban.

	First Two Weeks	Second Two Weeks	Third Two Weeks
Certainty	Very Certain	Somewhat Certain	Getting Hazy
Commitments	Strong Commitments	Planned Commitments	Fungible Commitments
Complexity	Very Good Understanding	Good Understanding	Fair Understanding
Collaboration	Scheduled Times for Collaboration	Some Scheduled Collaboration	Expected Collaboration

The example roadmap on the next page quickly shows the teams required to collaborate on tasks, easily shows the overlap of reliance on specific teams (Jason and Julian). And allows for conversations about the impacts of that reliance. Other teams may take away 20% of their workload from this roadmap; those two may take 60%. This means that the other teams know that when scheduling work or collaborations, you go to the teams with the heaviest workload first.

These roadmaps, alongside your pull plan, will provide all teams and management with much greater transparency into daily needs of individuals and teams, allowing all to make better decisions.

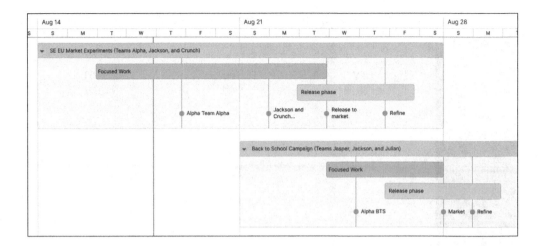

Good Use of Digital Systems

While I prefer tactile Obeya, this is an excellent use for digital tools. They are able to filter shared tasks, build roadmaps that show percentage complete, and can build different types of intelligence like calculating likelihood of making existing deadlines based on current or past performance.

A Must for Shared Obeya Rooms

These roadmaps are a staple in a shared Obeya, the calendar ribbon on Turner projects kept everyone apprised of long-term roadmaps. The pull plans gave short term tactical roadmaps. Around the Obeya, other visualizations provided glimpses into upcoming work for smaller, more focused, teams.

Good Use of Focused Shared Obeya during Times of Intense Collaboration

If this is tactile, with post-it notes or a long roll of paper, notes can be taken, milestones can be moved by crossing one out and drawing it somewhere else. That seems messy, but the mess is a visual record of the difference between your plan and where you have ended up. The messy bits will help you recall and react to learning or change. This not only helps you better plan in the future, but it is also a reminder in conversations with partners or stakeholders when they inevitably ask *why* something happened.

You can physically point to the change, which triggers stronger memories for you, and provide a more satisfying answer.

The Full-On Obeya: The Product and the Focus of a Professional Team

Throughout this book, we have covered all the components for our Obeya. It is the center of our collaboration and the place where our culture and our processes become intertwined. Whether real or virtual, it is one predictable location for all the information the individuals on your teams need to act with confidence. More than simply a dashboard, it is a living part of the progress of your projects. The Obeya is a place where we turn fear and lack of information into agency and action.

We now appreciate that agency, psychological safety, and leadership are all essentially having not only the ability, but the *expectation* to professionally act with confidence. We also understand that professional action requires a Right Environment that is both essentially collaborative and visually managed. The Obeya is the beating heart of any healthy professional team.

Work At Scale Must Be Shared and Understood

Multiple teams, large orgs, medium orgs, digital visualizations, distributed teams, are all the same. They are individuals in teams creating value. The larger the team or the organization, the more important visual management becomes. Why? As your organization grows, the likelihood of one team needing to work with another they are not familiar with also grows.

Leadership's previous definition as Dictatorial Management thrived in the confusion of large organizations. Middle management positions grew and grew, and the information that needed to be exchanged exploded. Each invented role, in essence, was simply doing the work of a few boards. In the search to invent someone to be accountable, we destroyed the ability for people to be responsible.

We want to build practical Obeya for daily use in a Right Environment creating a professional atmosphere filled to the gills with agency. The Big Board is a visual middle manager, but rather than being scared out of its wits at being held accountable for a dozen projects, it is inanimate, providing the right information, the right triggers for action, the right openings for collaboration to the right teams. It has no territory, nothing to provide; it is just information.

The Obeya(s) in your company should be the information exchange that a weekly managers' meeting used to provide, except now it is transparent, always-on, and providing the right information to the right people at the right time. Leadership now truly becomes action and not barking orders. Work becomes collaborations between professionals and not work requests in a ticketing system. Agency becomes the ability to see and solve problems, not merely report them. Psychological safety becomes synonymous with being a professional and not something to yearn for.

Build It Together and They Will Act

We discussed the experience of Amanda and Savanna, who set up an Obeya but then had to intentionally show leadership by getting the rest of the team to own the boards and the room. They show us that *leadership is always expressed by promoting leadership in others*. Leadership is action that causes other action. If our system promotes the idea of one leader, then we will always have limited action in both quantity and quality. If our systems promote leadership by all professionals, we have unlimited potential.

This means that our Obeya needs to promote leadership in others. You can also think of this as simply being *useful*. When something is useful, it means we can use it. We can take its input and create some output.

Your Obeya, then, will always be a social system that is useful to multiple stakeholders. This feels like the more the merrier, but it is actually the more the practical. For Amanda and Savanna, their stakeholders were themselves, the architectural estimation team, their boss, their bosses' boss, the marketing team, the sales team...and so on. For Coney, stakeholders were the individuals working on the project, the teams, the engineering team as a whole, the trades, the owners, the oversight...and so on. For FungiCorp, it was the database team, the other teams, upper management, the board...and so on.

Always defined parties...always *and so on*.

In any collaborative system, work must be visualized, ownership must be shared, and acting with confidence must be a priority. It must truly be useful.

"Build it and they will come" is a romantic notion for loners hoping for redemption. "Build it together and they will act" is a practical foundation for true professional expression and realization.

The Result: Organizational Clarity

With leadership, middle managers, team leads, and individual professionals able to see the relationships between goals, projects, learning, work, and course corrections, people are more likely to act professionally. They make learning known, with confidence that the learning will enhance the impact of everyone in the company. The teams, the groups, and the company can easily change course without it being a surprise and alienating people focusing on specific tasks. They can see the reason for the change, they know what it means, and they can quickly and safely reorient their work.

Without this clarity, changes are made often, yet too late. The changes therefore seem and are capricious. With collaborative visualization, we see the changes as they are made; they are simply logical shifts in work.

CODA: LEADERSHIP IS A VERB

R. Buckminster Fuller said, "I seem to be a verb." Not a resource, not fungible, not a static piece of machinery, but a professional human being evolving as he lived. Experiencing his ideas, the world around him, the needs of all stakeholders, and what was possible.

Deming told us that a bad environment beats a good character every time. In a bad (anti-collaborative) system, a good professional, even if they are ultimately able to act, must fight unnecessary battles to get past sluggish bureaucracy and petty territory battles.

> *I live on Earth at present,*
>
> *And I don't know what I am.*
>
> *I know that I am not a category. I am not a thing—a noun. I seem to be a verb, an evolutionary process. An integral function in the universe.*
>
> —BUCKMINSTER FULLER

In an anti-collaborative environment, where leadership is not a verb, but a position, we in turn are not verbs. Traditional management's centralized control turns us into categories, nouns, and things. We are not evolving; we are not integral even to our companies. In Lean parlance, in traditional companies, people are waste. This is why "leadership" lays people off at the first sign of trouble rather than engaging the entire company to get out of trouble.

Why would we ever allow such obviously self-defeating systems to govern our companies?

For capitalism to survive, leadership must no longer be a title, and must become a verb. It needs to be action that is a call to action. It needs to be a natural process we launch with our Right Environment. It must be part of a Way supported and created collaboratively by all stakeholders. It can and will provide more agency, psychological safety, and professional responsibility. It allows the individuals in your teams to truly provide value.

Acting with confidence is leadership.

Leadership is a verb.

The Enduring Collaboration

LOVING THE AUDACITY OF PRACTICALITY.

How exquisitely human was the wish for permanent happiness, and how thin human imagination became trying to achieve it.

—TONI MORRISON, PARADISE

Love and compassion are necessities, not luxuries. Without them humanity cannot survive.

—DALAI LAMA

I love seeing people working together to make things. To write this book, I had to work with people for decades, in many different capacities from budding neophyte to experienced professional. To discuss everything involved in working together, I found myself discussing the human condition and exploring questions like: *Who are we? Why are we doing these things? How do we become better? How can I really make a difference? Why are people unhappy? Why do they continue to put up with counter-productive abuse?*

Collaboration is the human condition. Describing it has been a monumental challenge. This book was originally over 600 pages long, detailing the sociology, psychology, and operations of collaboration in detail. My collaborators, screeners, and editors were quick to tell me that I didn't have to cover everything, just enough to provide value and get people started. Heh.

That's right. I was that World Bank scientist, trying to write down everything I knew in confusing detail. But, even knowing that, today as I finish these last edits, I know the words *not in this book* and I miss every single one of them.

When talking about how people collaborate, there is so much to cover, so much depth, and so much feeling that this can't be the last book. Rest assured everything in the book can and will be expanded upon.

What this book does do is share a coherent framework for collaboration. How to see collaboration, foster it, share it, and make use of it. And most of all, this is a book about finding your way in a collaborative world. How you participate, how you lead, how you benefit. It's funny, but the personal is the professional. Every chapter is about how to *work* better, but ultimately every chapter is about how to *live* better. Less stressed, more accepting, and more in control of your decisions and actions.

If you see that the Collaboration Equation is open for interpretation, that you can add your own ideas to the lists or run your working sessions in ways tailored to the needs of your teams, then I have done my job. That flexibility is a core strength, the core strength. Any system you build should have the same flexibility.

Through all the phases of my career, from Angry Punk Rocker to Urban Planner to AIDS Activist to Tech Pioneer to Consultant to Author to today, I have only wanted one thing...

I want people to stop wasting time, energy, money, and themselves fighting for no real reason.

In every step of my personal journey, I have worked with and in teams who were abused by anti-collaborative systems, intentional or indifferent.

I have watched teams defeat anti-collaborative systems with unwavering professionalism. They were able to intentionally replace anti-collaboration with collaboration. They built its structure and reaped the benefits. Those teams, those people, have always been my inspiration.

I will end this book with one last story: the honest story of the change agent. It is part of my story. It is part of Tonianne's story. And it is part of the story of many others, though we didn't realize this for a long time.

CHANGE IS NECESSARY, CHANGE IS FRUSTRATING

In 2011, we went to work for a marquee client in the entertainment industry. The group we were going to work with had 80 people in nine teams. Each team answered to a different team manager, a different senior manager, and a different VP. They were strongly encouraged not to talk to each other directly, but to talk only through "official channels". Eighty people working, being "supervised" by over 30 other managers, each with their own agendas and metrics to be judged by.

As you would guess, inter-team communication was terrible, bottlenecks pretty much equaled the number of tasks in their backlog, and morale was abysmal. Management was frustrated with the teams because no work was getting done. The teams were frustrated because the overhead of a simple decision was debilitating. Workarounds were the only way work got done, secret meetings in undisclosed locations before or after working hours with other teams just to get work done.

You might say it was a ClusterWork.

When we asked what the teams wanted, they nearly cried while saying in a deafening unison, "We just want to work together, we want to talk to each other, we want to get work done!"

The VPs told us that they wanted us to fix their staff. We told the VPs they should fire us before we started. They were surprised when we told them that their people were great, that they could fix this in 48 hours, and that productivity and quality would shoot through the roof.

"Then do it!" the VPs cheered.

"I don't think you see what is happening here," I said, "They will reorg without you. *You will all be irrelevant.* You won't stand for that. They will start working together professionally, their system will work. You, however, will only see the impacts on your careers, and you will shut the change down."

They replied, "Well, we tried Agile and it didn't work; we shut it down and no one cared. So, if this is shut down, no one will care."

"No," I said, "Agile is a thing, someone else's thing. They never cared about it. This collaborative system, they are building themselves. They care about it. It's important to them. If it starts, it will work, and it if stops, they will quit."

The VPs couldn't process this. This was a company built on layers of ineffectual middle management and the systematic hoarding of power. When it came to making things better, as Toni Morrison would say, *their imagination was thin.*

They ended the meeting, frustrated with us wasting their valuable time. When the VPs pushed us out of the conference room, the teams already had diagrams and plans of how they would collaborate. From their side, the pent-up demand for professionalism and agency in this bureaucratic gulag was overwhelming.

Over the next two months, productivity shot through the roof, quality improved dramatically, and team definitions became more fluid, but also more relevant.

And people stopped sending reports and stats and work requests to their bosses...they simply weren't relevant. The information was displayed, updated in real time, and the teams made use of it immediately.

The VPs panicked. While they provided tenuous value before, it was clear not that they didn't have a purpose or a function, or even the appearance of one. The teams re-orged naturally without them. Sadly, since the

VPs didn't even consider themselves part of their teams, they refused to participate in the change and, predictably, had no logical functions in the new Right Environment. The VPs had no interest in the actual activities of operations, just in the movement of lines on charts of arbitrary KPIs to give themselves importance. They had every opportunity to be part of a new and healthy system; they opted out because they simply had no training in participation.

The VPs had provided neither management nor leadership for quite some time.

As foreseen, the VPs fired us and reset working back to the way it was before. They never asked the teams if this new way of working could give the VPs better information (it could). They never asked the teams why this new way of working was beneficial (the teams knew). They simply saw the new way of working as an abrupt change (it was) that threatened their job security (it certainly did).

After the shift back to the old way of working, there was an immediate and shocking 20% attrition. One fifth of the staff walked out and found jobs elsewhere. Not because they were disgruntled, but because the company proved to them that they were not valued.

The remainders mumbled, "I knew it was too good to be true," put their heads down, and went back "to work". It is painful to watch people willingly surrender their freedom.

For years, this was the end of the story.

Mediocre corporate management and petty minds killed yet another continuous improvement success story. We would complain about the company, say it was *typical*. And used that jaded mindset to salve our disillusionment as change agents who saw people move towards a better place, only to be tossed back into work hell.

Yes, Virginia, there is a Santa Claus:

But it didn't stay that way.

Today that company works in cross-functional teams, management has an entirely new structure, and the successes we realized are now everyday operations. What we didn't realize was that the experience had changed the people, even the VPs. Enough of them saw the collaboration and the action it created as a benefit. It was clear that the VPs were part of the team, that they needed to be included, and that getting work done was preferrable to stagnation.

They all worked slowly, methodically, and tirelessly to make the company a better place to work. They worked internally to refine, reshape, and improve their Right Environment that included everyone.

We didn't deliver meals, we sowed seeds.

THE AUDACITY OF PRACTICALITY

Every successful team I have ever seen operated *as a team*. Every successful team I have ever seen had *individual professionals* behaving professionally. Every successful team I have ever seen *knew what success looked like*.

We all have a choice; we can make things better or we can make things worse. Sometimes the paths to better look blocked by immovable objects, but there are no immovable objects in the universe. Everything has a lever, everything has a button. There is an irresistible force.

It was painful for Tonianne and me to see those frustrated professionals. They wanted to create value, they wanted to help, but the company's structure was simply too archaic and fear-based to allow it. And they weren't alone.

The fact is most businesses today are in the business of making just enough money to sustain their internal waste and maybe a little bit more. They make terrible decisions, build structures that invite bickering and impedance, and bring in new professionals with great promises that have poorly attempted delivery.

Most businesses, but this is changing.

People are realizing that if business operated perfectly, continuous improvement would be something everyone just did. If business operated perfectly, work would be totally automated (no employees at all). It is the tension between the known and the unknown, the standard and the non-standard, the rote and the emergent, that makes jobs interesting and professionals necessary.

Change is practical. Change is audacious.

THE MODALITY OF HOPE

We do not have to be disheartened that the changes we make lack permanence. Everything on earth does. We can, however, build systems that are more resilient, more collaborative, and more humane. We must, in fact, for these systems are harder to wear away. They are true and enduring impact.

Some businesses, even Turner, have the same problems of every other company, but they are *actively improving*. They fall down, they hurt people, and they find ways to correct. They find opportunities to build confident professionals who can act with confidence. They build the expectation that professionals will be informed, involved, and respected. And those professionals will expect to return the favor.

They will return and amplify that respect with previously untapped attention, creativity, and professionalism.

We humans spent over 2,000 years building structures of information-hoarding and anti-collaboration. We are just beginning to build smarter, more practical, more effective ways of working.

You are now part of that change.

You will be frustrated on your journey to make things better. There has never been a person alive who walked an easy path of continuous improvement.

But we can and must exhibit leadership when it is necessary:

We have the ability, the responsibility, and the right to expect humane and collaborative workplaces.

We have the ability, the responsibility, and the right to expect professional treatment and recognition.

We have the ability, the responsibility, and the right to expect to remain informed and to inform others.

We have the ability, the responsibility, and the right to act with confidence.

We have the ability, the responsibility, and the right to provide a Right Environment for others.

These expectations and actions are how all of us lead, improve, and make the world a better place.

When we deny these abilities, ignore the responsibilities, and abdicate these rights, other less thoughtful people will be there to turn the leadership vacuum to their personal advantage. They will build organizations to serve their needs, deliver shoddy product, and create mediocre or abusive careers. They will ride familiar and time-honored waves of division, dissent, and isolation.

But this ongoing leveraged buy-out of human creativity can no longer be tolerated.

Creating a Right Environment is not easy for humans. We are cursed with things to say and languages that trip up our tongues. We are burdened with the desire to make an impact and ample barriers to the realization of our goals. We want to create with other people, to be our favorite band, only to fall prey to the scathing arguments that happen during the creative process. We want to lead but not always be relied upon. We want to act, but don't want to be wrong. The list goes on and on.

> # COLLABORATION IS THE MOST CRUCIAL THING HUMANS DO.

Collaboration is the most crucial thing humans do; it is also fraught with peril. It is a challenge to build a resilient collaborative system; it is easy to give up in the face of anti-collaborative adversity. *"Fine,"* we say, *"just take it."*

We are always tempted by those who appear with snake oil, ready to solve our problems with a two-day certification, a quick organizational fix, the perfect software, or cheap coaching by those who know jargon but have never solved a problem. The hucksters are legion, they have funding, they appear credible.

Just Build It

From the first chapter of this book, I've shared stories of successful collaborative teams. Some were temporary, some were more long-lived. All these teams **had to do the work** themselves. They had to be professional and humane, building the culture and the process together to ensure quality product delivered in a quality environment. They had to give a damn.

I have also been up front about the challenges of change and being a change agent as well as those of leading and being a leader. People argue, resist, and opt out. Systems fight improvement. But we change agents take on this challenge because we are professionals who improve and people who care. But ultimately, we're not satisfied with silos, mediocrity, and abuse. We want better.

The goal of collaboration is not to just work on things as a group. We should *expect* that when we bring people together to achieve something, everyone involved will benefit from thoughtful, professional, humane action from the team, managers, and even customers. We will not waste our time micromanaging each other or fighting to get our point across. We will not squander the perspective and creativity of our teammates. We will not give in to mediocrity.

> **Individuals work in teams to create value.**

So go. Now. Create...Together.

And thank you.

Jim Benson

On my back porch in the sun
Seattle, WA

August, 2022

I lost my father while writing this book.

This is the first book of mine he can't read.

Everything we do we do together.
Everything he did, he did with my mom.

They had a partnership of frustrations
and joys. I was certainly both.

All your teams will find the same — frustrations
& joys that only work out if you work together.

There is no heaven on this earth, but we alone
have the choice to avoid making it hell.

Thanks, Dad, for doing whatever
you did to teach me that.

And sorry Mom, this is certainly
not the best picture of you.

But I think you agree, this
was the picture to use.

HF OP TYs

HEART-FELT OPERATIONAL THANK YOUs

> *"Don't ever write a non-fiction book about the human condition.*
> *It's not worth it."*
>
> —DAVID BRIN,
> *in a conversation with me over coffee,*
> *Third Place Books, Seattle, sometime (2005?) in my hazy memory.*

I did not listen to David Brin. It hurt. But his final product *The Transparent Society,* despite his discomfort, was a pivotal book for me.

I've written books that I just wrote. You know, I sat down, wrote them, published them, went on with life. This book has taken so long to finish that even that long list of people I thanked at the beginning of the book wasn't enough.

Before Covid, Tonianne and I relied on three companies only: 3M, whoever makes Sharpies, and Alaska Airlines. Other than that, we floated through the global skies, working with companies with the huge suitcase known as "The Weapon of Mass Instruction," filled with Super Sticky Post-Its and Sharpies.

This book would not have been possible if not for a few people and companies, I'm thanking them here because they really were lifesavers.

Tom Ehrenfeld who was and is my editor. Who pulled me back from the brink on multiple occasions where the constant needs of this extremely persnickety manuscript were just too...damn...needy. Thank you, Tom for giving me something to write a Thank You at the end of. This book was like playing in the Highland games in January in northern Iceland wearing only a wet t-shirt and every match involving 33 tie breakers.

Olivier Darbonville who walked out of the digital ocean and proceeded to lay out a beautiful book with unprecedented ease. While there were stressful moments, working with you was a joy.

Shel Israel who gave me the best words of encouragement at the beginning. Nearly nothing of the draft I showed you is left...but our conversations were truly the push that got me to start the last marathon.

iObeya who is a company, they're French, more than a few of the graphics are from their platform. Right now, their tool is literally the only tool on the market I have seen that allows the creation and use of a distributed web-based Obeya. Carol & Anaël, you have been so generous with your time and attention. Modus Cooperandi would have had a much rockier Covid experience if not for you two.

Miro who is also a company, but more Nordic. Many graphics in this use Miro and many of those graphics are real graphics from real REEs or projects.

The Big Board uses Agile Walls' strategy wall format as a base. Bart and Dolf run Agile Walls and the Obeya Association out of their HQ in the Netherlands. They are keen minds in the world of both Obeyas and community. One of those graphics (The Big Board) uses the **Agile Walls** strategy wall format from the keen minds of Bart and Dolf (who also run the Obeya Association).

MODUS PRESS
EXPLORING THE FUTURE
OF WORK

Modus Press got its start with the groundbreaking work Scrumban by Corey Ladas, quickly followed by the award-winning Personal Kanban by Jim Benson and Tonianne DeMaria.

We produce books designed to challenge assumptions, launch new ways of working, and spread learning. We are interested in people working well, together.

Collaboration, continuous improvement, professionalism, and quality are at the heart of how we see all of us working together to create a better working world.

Buy Why Limit WIP

Buy Why Plans Fail

Why Limit WIP

You can't do more work than you can handle. That is obvious, we should limit our work to what we can finish. Focus, finish, and move on.

For people and their teams, this is easier said than done. How can we focus, finish quickly and correctly, learn, and move on?

Why Limit WIP provides several lessons for individuals and teams.

You can't be agile or lean without it.

BY JIM BENSON

Why Plans Fail

We are all *pretty good* at making decisions, but we are surprised when things don't go as expected. We feel like if we have the data, the decision should work without fail. An entire science of Behavioral Economics tells us otherwise.

Why Plans Fail looks specifically at twelve cognitive biases that influence (for good and ill) your decisions and the decisions of those around you.

BY JIM BENSON

Personal Kanban

Personal Kanban is a system to quickly visualize and organize work for individuals or teams. Used around the world for daily work and projects large or small, PK allows you to visualize your work, fight overload by limiting work in progress, and complete with quality.

Build your visual system that lets you see your work, limit your work in progress, and finish with confidence. See why Personal Kanban won a Shingo Research award and has helped hundreds of thousands of people and the companies they work for.

BY JIM BENSON AND TONIANNE DEMARIA

Buy Personal Kanban

Beyond Agile

Agile, Lean, and Kanban are words that alternate between useful and buzz. Beyond Agile takes a practical approach and looks at 12 companies who used both iterative and flow models of work and documents their experiences.

The case studies come from around the world, all reaching success by building systems that address their actual work. What do the people need? What does the work require.

BY MARITZA VAN DEN HEUVEL AND JOANNE HO

Buy Beyond Agile

ScrumBan

Corey Ladas' "ScrumBan" captured the imagination of the software world. Agile methodologies helped software development teams organize and become more efficient. Lean methods like kanban can extend these benefits. This book covers the metrics and day-to-day management techniques that make continuous improvement achievable. Scrumban gives practitioners the background needed to create robust practices combining the best of agile and lean.

BY COREY LADAS

Buy Scrumban

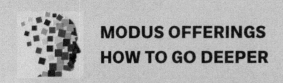

MODUS OFFERINGS
HOW TO GO DEEPER

Would you like to go deeper? Modus has online classes that are both self-paced and instructor-led.

Also, books are available in bulk for companies wanting to improve or for onboarding.

Buy Books for the Teaam

Internal training and onboarding is better with books! Corporate bulk orders for all Modus books and the Platinum Subscription are available from Modus, just scan the chat with us QR code and we will get you set up.

Chat with us

Instructor Led Classes

Bring your team into the 21st Century with fun, engaging, and immediately useful practices like:

▸ collaborative planning
▸ the right environment
▸ prioritization
▸ alignment
▸ meeting facilitation
▸ Personal Kanban
▸ Value Stream Mapping

These classes, with thousands of graduates, are highly customizable to your situation.

Teams from 6 to 18 can learn in person or on line. Contact us through live chat with the QR code or send us an email at **sales@ moduscooperandi.com**

Join The Modus Institute
Platinum Subscription

Get access to every open course, special
subscription-only content, special events,
and access to a global community of
change-makers.

Sign up for our Lean Agile
Visual Management™
Certification and Accreditation

Index

A

A3 *121, 263, 265, 266, 273, 274, 275, 276*

Agile *46, 148, 180, 218, 280, 310, 319, 321*

anti-pattern *86*

Argyris, Christopher *122*

B

Bottleneck *7, 111, 115, 141*

Burger, Gary *123*

C

concierge service *116*

culture *16, 23, 28, 30, 42, 45, 46, 47, 48, 49, 62, 63, 64, 68, 69, 74, 75, 76, 82, 89, 92, 93, 101, 120, 123, 125, 145, 146, 147, 148, 149, 150, 151, 152, 153, 155, 156, 158, 160, 161, 165, 167, 172, 173, 176, 177, 180, 189, 191, 194, 195, 198, 199, 200, 209, 211, 215, 216, 218, 219, 221, 222, 223, 232, 234, 246, 253, 255, 269, 270, 271, 280, 282, 288, 290, 301, 315*

Cynefin *132*

F

feedback *35, 40, 49, 91, 97, 107, 120, 121, 122, 123, 124, 125, 128, 137, 138, 140, 143, 167, 169, 218, 225, 244, 270, 296, 297*

G

Gemba *263, 264, 274*

Goldratt, Eliyahu *112*

H

humble hubris *12, 266, 267, 273*

K

Kaizen *8, 89, 148, 180, 185, 210, 211, 245*

L

Lean *8, 11, 45, 46, 72, 89, 92, 116, 119, 121, 129, 139, 148, 152, 174, 180, 187, 206, 208, 211, 218, 225, 226, 227, 234, 236, 256, 257, 258, 259, 263, 268, 273, 274, 304, 321*

Lean Startup *116, 139*

O

Obeya *7, 8, 34, 36, 37, 41, 42, 44, 45, 50, 65, 66, 67, 91, 103, 104, 105, 107, 116, 117, 122, 128, 130, 131, 138, 142, 146, 158, 184, 185, 189, 191, 192, 193, 194, 195, 196, 198, 200, 202, 204, 206, 208, 210, 212, 213, 215, 216, 218, 219, 228, 233, 235, 237, 242, 244, 248, 249, 255, 257, 258, 259, 260, 261, 262, 263, 268, 283, 285, 292, 293, 297, 300, 301, 302, 303, 319*

P

PDSA *7, 93, 104, 121, 124, 125, 154, 184, 296*

Phoenix Project, the *115, 121*

psychological safety *18, 23, 30, 37, 66, 95, 96, 113, 118, 217, 252, 267, 301, 305*

R

retrospective *89, 244*

Right Environment *6, 7, 8, 15, 16, 30, 42, 48, 62, 63, 64, 65, 66, 67, 68, 69, 71, 72, 73, 74, 75, 89, 93, 107, 123, 143, 145, 146, 147, 148, 149, 150, 151, 152, 153, 155, 163, 171, 173, 177, 180, 182, 184, 185, 188, 189, 191, 194, 195, 196, 199, 213, 215, 216, 217, 218, 221, 241, 242, 244, 246, 255, 268, 269, 270, 272, 273, 275, 276, 278, 282, 283, 287, 290, 292, 301, 302, 304, 311, 312, 314*

S

Shook, John *11, 273*

silos *28, 38, 54, 70, 101, 102, 104, 106, 120, 141, 147, 167, 168, 200, 206, 207, 236, 241, 279, 289, 315*

Snowden, David *132*

System *7, 9, 20, 46, 116, 124, 135, 153, 166, 206, 271*

T

The Goal *88, 112, 121*

V

Value Stream *8, 150, 152, 160, 162, 168, 170, 206, 238, 322*

W

Worst Practice *96, 97, 98, 100*

Z

Zero Sum Game *81*

Made in the USA
Columbia, SC
03 October 2022

68505647R00180